WHAT THE WEST IS GETTING WRONG ABOUT THE MIDDLE EAST

WHAT THE WEST IS GETTING WRONG ABOUT THE MIDDLE EAST

Why Islam is Not the Problem

Ömer Taşpınar

I.B. TAURIS
LONDON • NEW YORK • OXFORD • NEW DELHI • SYDNEY

I.B. TAURIS
Bloomsbury Publishing Plc
50 Bedford Square, London, WC1B 3DP, UK
1385 Broadway, New York, NY 10018, USA

BLOOMSBURY, I.B. TAURIS and the I.B. Tauris logo are trademarks of
Bloomsbury Publishing Plc

First published in Great Britain 2021

Cover design: Adriana Brioso

ISBN: HB: 978-1-7883-1010-9
ePDF: 978-0-7556-0715-0
eBook: 978-0-7556-0716-7

Typeset by Newgen KnowledgeWorks Pvt. Ltd., Chennai, India
Printed and bound in Great Britain

To find out more about our authors and books visit www.bloomsbury.com
and sign up for our newsletters.

Ömer Taşpınar is a professor at the National Defense University in Washington,
DC, and a nonresident senior fellow at the Brookings Institution. He is an
expert on political Islam, political economy, Turkey, American foreign policy, and
the European Union. His previous books are *Kurdish Nationalism and Political
Islam: Kemalist Identity in Transition* and *Winning Turkey: How America, Europe
and Turkey Can Revive a Fading Partnership* (with Philip H. Gordon).

To Gönül

CONTENTS

Preface ix

Acknowledgments xii

Introduction: "Why Don't We Read the Koran?" 1

1 Overstating Islam 15

2 Turkey 57

3 Sunnis versus Shiites 109

4 The Islamic State in Iraq and Syria 147

5 The Western Disconnect 177

6 What Is to Be Done? 217

Notes 237

Bibliography 251

Index 258

PREFACE

The backlash against cosmopolitan elites, globalization, and multiculturalism is a reality of our times. What political scientists call "identity politics" defines this age of poisonous polarization. In Europe, the nativist upswell against a disconnected "establishment" frequently finds its voice in the ballot box with the rise of xenophobic right-wing populism. The same phenomenon, some may say, is already in power in Donald J. Trump's America.

As a naturalized American citizen and a native of Turkey who spent his formative years in France, Libya, and Italy, I can't escape the fact that I am one of those cosmopolitan, multicultural elites. I am worried about the future of liberal democracy in the West and the toxic nature of anti-Muslim hatred. Yet, this book is not about Islamophobia. It is also not an attempt to defend Islam as a great religion. There are already a plethora of books on these subjects.

My primary concern is the alarming collapse of states and weak institutions in the Middle East. The fact that the West is obsessed with identity politics and deeply alarmed about Islam—instead of trying to understand the implications of political and economic collapse in the Middle East—is what led me to write this book. When I first moved to the United States in 1996, Islam was still an exotic religion for most Americans. Unlike Europe, America had no historic or contemporary baggage with Muslims. The events of 9/11, of course, radically changed all that. Fear, alarm, and anxiety about Islam replaced curiosity. Samuel Huntington's clash of civilizations, a gloomy apocalyptic prediction, suddenly became a reality.

If 9/11 shook the world of international politics to its core, the same was true for the impact of the 2008 financial crisis on Western neoliberal capitalism. These two overlapping crises during the first decade of the twenty-first century have mutually reinforced each other. They exacerbated tensions over globalization, identity, inequality, citizenship, and religion. Today, almost twenty years after the collapse of the twin towers and more than a decade since the global financial crisis, the aftershocks of both events are still poisoning global politics. Times of economic hardship hasten the search for scapegoats. The prolonged "Great Recession" of 2008 not only exacerbated economic inequalities in the West but also empowered anti-immigration political parties by unleashing a major backlash against the winners of globalization. It remains to be seen how the coronavirus pandemic of 2020—itself a tragic gift of globalization—will impact identity politics. The first signs, with an impending global recession, are hardly encouraging. The backlash against globalization, multiculturalism, and open borders is likely to gain further momentum in the years to come.

This rising trend of angry nationalism in the West has already made Islam, immigration, and refugees easy targets. Political parties that campaigned against Muslim immigration are now in power in Austria, Italy, Poland, and Hungary, and they define the contours of public debate in Britain, France, and Germany. And we have an American president who not only instituted a Muslim travel ban but also speaks alarmingly of "Middle Easterners" hiding among Latin American refugees at the Mexican border. Not surprisingly, he also makes a point of calling COVID-19 the "Chinese virus."

Unfortunately, the Arab uprisings of 2011 failed to change the image of Islam. Arguably, they made things worse. In Egypt, the Islamist Muslim Brotherhood swept into power, before a military coup removed it. Bloody civil wars in Libya, Yemen, and Syria, coupled with the rise of ISIS, contributed to an already dismal Western perception of Islam. The result has been to reinforce the tendency in the West to look at the Middle East through the distorted lens of religion. From Turkey's transformation under Recep Tayyip Erdoğan to what has been called the Sunni–Shiite sectarian conflict, the Western focus invariably is on Islam, at the expense of almost all other economic and political drivers of conflict.

The fear of Muslim refugees, endless debates about Islam, and its compatibility with democracy, modernity, and secularism are dominating the identity discourse of the West. The perception of Islam as a violent religion that fuels terrorism is part of the same narrative. As I argue in the following pages, these are faulty assumptions based on cultural and religious determinism. Cultural determinists like Huntington often explain global dynamics by overstating religious and civilizational identity at the expense of economic, political, and social factors. And by doing so they often end up contributing to polarization.

I don't have a problem accepting the growing importance of religion in world politics. However, as this book will argue, I refuse to see religion as the "source" of the conflict. Religion is an effective vehicle to mobilize masses—not the root cause of a civilizational clash. Those who seek power tend to use religion, culture, and identity politics to polarize masses for political, financial, and geostrategic ends. Religion, in that sense, is at best the instigator of polarization, not its raison d'être. Therein lies the major difference between culturalism and structuralism based on power politics. While culturalism tends to look at culture, religion, and civilizational identity as the root cause of conflict, the opposing camp of power politics sees primarily political and material motivations behind the pursuit of military, economic, and strategic objectives. While one speaks the language of cultural identity, the other is fluent in the grammar of institutions, governance, and political structures.

These are not merely academic debates. The discord between culturalism and structuralism has serious policy consequences. The wrong diagnosis often leads to wrong prescriptions. The Western obsession with Islam clouds objective analysis and fuels resentment in a Muslim world full of badly governed states with weak institutions and rampant authoritarianism. If unchecked, the current trends of polarized identity politics will not only jeopardize the future of liberalism in the West but also end up fueling more resentment, anger, and radicalization in the Muslim world. In that sense, I hope this book will serve as a modest contribution to shift the debate from religion and identity politics toward the realm of politics and governance.

Washington, DC
April 2020

ACKNOWLEDGMENTS

Writing a book is often a long and arduous journey that can also be lonely. I was very lucky in every step of this project to have the moral and intellectual support of my wife, without whom this book would still be work in progress.

Since my early days as a graduate student, I owe a great deal to Yahya Sadowski, whose peerless teaching style and incisive analysis have been an aspiration. To me, as to many of his students, Yahya is the ideal combination of scholar, mentor, and friend.

In writing this book, I was fortunate in the support received from colleagues at the National War College and the Brookings Institution. My heartfelt thanks go to Adam Oler, Dave Tretler, Cynthia Watson, Maria Longi, and Jim Perriard. Roundtable sessions at Brookings allowed me to receive valuable guidance from fellow think tankers such as Shadi Hamid, Tamarra Coffman Wittes, Kemal Kirisci, Suzanne Maloney, Nathan Sachs, and Jeremy Shapiro. Their feedback helped me shape and test ideas developed in this book.

Perhaps most importantly, I wish to thank Michael O'Hanlon, Philip Gordon, Birol Baskan, and Elif Polat for taking the time to read the manuscript and for their insightful suggestions. I failed to do justice to all of them, but the book is a stronger one thanks to them. And finally, I am very grateful to Sophie Rudland and Tom Stottor from I.B. Tauris for their guidance and encouragement from the beginning to the end of this journey.

INTRODUCTION
"WHY DON'T WE READ THE KORAN?"

This very question colored my first encounter with what Islam came to represent in the West. Only a few months after the 9/11 terrorist attacks, I had started teaching a graduate course titled "Europe and Islam" at a prominent international relations program in Washington, DC. My goal was to focus on Muslim integration problems in countries like France, the UK, and Germany. Freshly minted with a doctoral degree and perhaps a bit overconfident, I strongly believed social and economic problems played a critical role in the radicalization of Muslim youth in Europe. After reading my syllabus and listening to all the different topics I planned to cover, many students in the classroom were surprised by what they considered a glaring omission. "How are we supposed to understand Islamic radicalism without reading the Koran?" one of them asked. I tried to explain the course was on current affairs, not theology. He looked unconvinced.

Almost two decades after 9/11, variations of the same question still haunt me each time I introduce this course to new students. The fallacy that we can decipher the main reasons behind jihadist radicalization or understand "the problem with the Islamic world" by simply reading the Holy Scripture has become symptomatic of our age. We live in a world of identity politics with expectations of shortcuts and easy answers to complex problems. The belief that religion can explain almost everything that is wrong with the Muslim world has proven extremely hard to surmount. And things went from bad to worse with the rise of the Islamic State in Iraq and Syria, jihadist terrorism in Europe, and growing Islamophobia in the West.

Today, in the age of Donald Trump in America and nativist populism across Europe, large majorities see Islam as a source of insecurity and the primary marker of identity and conflict in the Middle East. In almost all regional issues, ranging from Turkey's political transformation under Erdoğan to the Egyptian military coup toppling the Muslim Brotherhood, or from the rise of the Islamic State of Iraq and Syria (ISIS) to the Sunni–Shiite sectarian conflict, the majority of Western analysts look at the Middle East through the prism of Islam. Their verdict is overwhelmingly gloomy. Islam is not compatible with democracy, secularism, modernity, gender equality, and many other progressive values embraced by the West. Islam is also perceived as an autocratic, intolerant, violent, and belligerent religion.

Such sweeping generalizations are seldom seen as superficial assertions based on religious and cultural determinism. Instead, they pass as incisive political diagnosis and find receptive audiences with mounting anxieties after each terrorist attack on their soil. These dynamics exacerbate the obsession with Islam in the West. They also create a vicious cycle of polarization and mutual frustration between Muslims who resent the demonization of their faith and Western audiences who demand higher levels of self-criticism and introspection from the Islamic world.

The Western obsession with Islam is certainly not new. It has deep intellectual roots in the scholarly works of orientalists who have studied the Middle East since Napoleon's army first landed in Egypt in 1798. What we are now facing in the West, however, goes well beyond power politics, imperialism, or intellectual fascination rooted in scholarly inquiry. Our problem with Islam, today, borders on societal paranoia— Samuel Huntington's ominous warning of an impending "Clash of Civilizations" turned into self-fulfilling prophecy.[1] The late Harvard professor was an alarmist believer in the power of religions. A tendency for cultural determinism guided his predictions. Amidst the euphoria of the post–Cold War era, he gloomily argued that the twenty-first century would witness the bloody return of religion with primordial, violent confrontations on a global scale. In a famous book, "The Clash of Civilizations and the Remaking of the World Order" preceded by his influential article in *Foreign Affairs* magazine, he divided the world into civilizational groups and explained that old conflicts based on ideological, political, or economic competitions would be replaced by clashing religious civilizations. Few of his peers wanted to take this gloom and doom seriously. But 9/11 and its aftermath proved him right.

Today, invariably, the Western focus is on Islam. The orientalist cliché depicting Islam not just as a religion but as "a way of life" has been replaced with the view that Islam is the problem. This Western perception fuels not only a civilizational clash but also mounting Islamophobia. It holds religion and religious violence responsible for most of the security problems and almost all political, social, cultural, and economic challenges in Muslim countries. It speaks volumes that even solutions to this predicament such as the call for an "Islamic reformation or enlightenment" are also heavily infused with religious determinism. After all, if Islam is the main problem, why shouldn't it also provide the main solution? At least, this kind of Islamic determinism has the merit of consistency. According to this prescription, to save Islam from itself, all we need is a Muslim Martin Luther who will reform, modernize, and moderate Islam along the lines of the sixteenth-century European clash between Protestantism and the Catholic Church.

The Promised Land beyond Islam

This book is a repudiation of such flawed assumptions and methodology based exclusively on religion. It argues that the Western obsession with Islam and Muslim identity is not only counterproductive but also highly dangerous, particularly in terms of its political implications for policy makers. False diagnosis naturally leads to false prescriptions. The assumption that Islam is the main source of political identity, and therefore the primary cause of all problems, in the Middle East sets in motion misguided strategies in critical areas such as the fight against radicalism or the promotion of democracy. Make no mistake: extremist violence and dysfunctional tyrannical regimes are real problems in the Islamic world. But such political realities need to be analyzed objectively without constantly resorting to lazy cultural and religious determinism.

Overstating religious and civilizational identity at the expense of economic, political, and social factors is the trademark of culturalism. The primary source of differences between the West and the Islamic world should never be reduced to religion. A better balance between culturalism and structuralist approaches, looking at material and institutional dynamics, would help us see the primacy of power politics. Religion is part of the political equation, but more as a driver and instigator rather than the real source of conflicts.

It is therefore critically important to pay more attention to political power, as well as to military, economic, and strategic objectives, each time we hear the primacy of cultural, religious, and civilizational factors invoked.

The stubborn focus on a civilizational clash between Islam and the West, or between Islamic values and democracy, fails to capture the institutional, political, and economic problems in an increasingly complex and diverse Muslim world. Our obsession with Islam creates a major optical illusion that distorts regional realities on the ground— realities that require detailed, contextual analysis. This mirage of Islam, for now, fuels tension, resentment, and increasing polarization between the West and the Middle East. If it goes unchallenged, however, it will exacerbate the already powerful dynamics of Islamophobia and produce another devastating self-fulfilling prophecy: the radicalization of large cohorts of Muslim youth in the Middle East and Europe. Growing numbers of average Muslims are tired of being perceived as potential extremists. A vicious cycle of angry anti-Islamism in the West, leading to anti-Western bias and frustration in Muslim hearts and minds, does not bode well for coexistence and security.

The situation has already reached alarming levels in the last few years. The rise of anti-immigration and xenophobic, right-wing populism in the West consistently fuels suspicion and hatred of the Muslim world. The demonization of Islam and Muslims has now become a critical part of politics in Europe and the United States. Instead of overstating Islam, we urgently need new ways of looking at problems in the Middle East and beyond. This book takes a step in this direction. As someone who is fully aware of this urgency, I seek to offer an alternative to our harmful obsession with Islam. Instead of religion, theology, or culture, this book will focus on institutional problems of governance and the rise of nationalism. My priority will be political, economic, and social challenges rather than religious obstacles blocking security, development, and democracy in the Middle East. I will do so by analyzing three critically important puzzles where the West is wrongly obsessed with Islam: Turkey's transformation under Erdoğan, the Sunni–Shiite sectarian conflict in the Arab world, and the rise of ISIS. I selected these seemingly unrelated cases because the specter of Islam appears to loom large on all of them and this mirage distorts political, social, and economic realities.

By contextualizing each distinct case, we will see that the Western analysis suffers from an overdose of cultural and religious determinism and a dearth of institutional analysis. Problems with Turkey, violent Sunni and Shiite feuds in the Middle East, or ISIS go well beyond Islam, religion, and theology. Yet, the standard approach to Turkey has long suffered from a binary analysis focused on a clash between Islam and secularism. A similar view colors the fact that the current conflict in the Middle East between Sunnis and Shiites is an ancient tribal hatred going back to the seventh century. And ISIS is almost always analyzed as nothing but a jihadist entity, aimed at reviving the Caliphate with apocalyptic barbarity inspired by theology.

Such conventional wisdom focused almost exclusively on Islam is counterproductive. It not only clouds objective analysis and accurate diagnosis but also generates the wrong kind of policy prescriptions. Busy with the supposedly Islamic essence of challenges facing us, we often miss the structural, institutional, and geostrategic factors behind the façade of Sunnis and Shiites confronting each other, Turkey pursuing an autocratic and anti-Western path, or ISIS waging jihad. We also miss the driving power of nationalism: Turkish nationalism in Erdoğan's Turkey, Arab versus Persian nationalism in the context of Sunni–Shiite confrontations, and Sunni nationalism in the context of ISIS, where Baathist officers from Saddam's army have become the striking force of the so-called Caliphate.

All this effort is not meant to argue that Islam plays no role in the Middle East. To be sure, religion is a critically important force in the politics of most Muslim countries. Yet, it is only one factor among many and often not the driving force behind critical developments. Identity politics in the West has blinded most American and European policy makers, analysts, and journalists who now focus almost exclusively on Islam without paying any attention to political, economic, and social drivers of tension and conflict. The problems behind autocracy, radicalism, and underdevelopment in large parts of the Middle East have much more to do with politics and institutional failures than with religion.

My methodology will therefore debunk the myth that it is all about Islam by prioritizing the political, economic, social, and geostrategic dimension of problems. Another, and perhaps more important, aspect of my approach will be to focus on religious nationalism rather than religion as an independent, all-powerful driver. How nationalism interacts with religion to form a highly toxic mix of religious nationalism will provide an important analytical lens for all three cases. The place of religion in Turkish nationalism and the way nationalist states like Iran and Saudi Arabia instrumentalize religion in their Shiite and Sunni sectarian agenda will show us that Islam, alone, can never capture the whole picture. It often needs nationalism for mass mobilization.

The Essentialist Fallacy

The combination of all these factors shows how overstating Islam misses an important part of the picture. In addition to not being an expert on Islamic theology—which is a good reason in and of itself—I will steer clear from a polemical discussion about "the nature of Islam" for another equally important reason: my aversion to essentialism. Essentialism is an academic term. Yet, it is critically important due to its growing relevance and popularity in the Western perception of Islam.[2] According to essentialists, Islam has intrinsic, immutable, and timeless qualities. Islam, in their eyes, is an exceptional religion that resists modernization, secularism, and evolution. All encompassing, Islam thus defines Muslims and answers all their legal, political, social, and cultural questions. In short, without Islam it is impossible to understand the Muslim world. These essentialist ideas have gained widespread intellectual traction in our age defined by the clash of civilizations. The view that Islam is a violent religion or that it is not compatible with democracy follows the same logic and assumptions. Should such assumptions be taken seriously?

The short answer is "no." And I hope my reluctance to deal with these essentialist questions will not be interpreted as an apologetic approach that fully absolves Islam from controversy. It is certainly not my intention to engage in reverse essentialism by arguing that Islam is a religion of peace, tolerance, and justice. Islam, like most religions, is open to interpretation. It can be used to justify peace, tolerance, and coexistence. Or under different conditions, it can be mobilized to wage war. To treat Islam as an exceptional religion that will "always" resist peace, democratization, modernity, and secularism fuels cultural and religious determinism. It is equally pointless to argue that Islam will always promote justice, peace, and equality. Such sweeping generalizations are at the heart of the essentialist fallacy.

My problem with essentialism and Islamic exceptionalism is their simplistic tendency to focus on the sacred text while ignoring the political context. What matters much more than what Islam—and its holy text, the Quran—supposedly postulates is how Muslims construe this divine, revealed message. And the interpretation of religion almost always depends on political, security, economic, and sociocultural conditions. In other words, context shapes the interpretation of the text, not the other way around. And it goes without saying that political Islam is often the product of political conditions.

Attaching excessive importance to theology will generate either highly pessimistic conclusions about the essence of Islam or highly optimistic expectations once the sacred text is interpreted in "enlightened" ways. Realistically speaking, religious doctrine has only limited power to fundamentally shape the complex economic, political, cultural dynamics in any rapidly changing society. More than "reformed" Koranic interpretations, it is political, socioeconomic, and institutional reforms that will bring progressive change to the Middle East. In time, with some luck, better governance in the political, social, and economic environment can also pave the way for a more progressive interpretation of the Muslim faith.

The history of secularization in Western societies followed such a trajectory. More than the compatibility of Christianity with liberalism, democracy, or secularism, it is the progressive evolution of economic, political, and educational conditions that changed the dynamics in Europe. When similar trends of social, economic, and educational progress emerge in the Arab world, there is no reason to expect Islam will eternally resist progressive change. There are already pockets of positive change in the Muslim world—in Tunisia, Indonesia, Malaysia, Bangladesh, and Turkey—where relatively more liberal interpretations of Islam are already visible. Islam is therefore malleable. It is not an immutable force that shapes everything. At the end of the day, Islam will always be what Muslims make of it. And how Muslims interpret their religion will ultimately depend on their diverse social, cultural, political, and economic contexts. Instead of a generalized Islamic monolith, each local and institutional context needs distinct scrutiny.

It's the Political Context, Not the Religious Text

As we will see in the following pages, the Western obsession with an Islamic monolith overshadows two major drivers that shape the contextual diversity of the Middle East: governance and nationalism.

These two separate factors play decisive roles in our case studies. Not surprisingly, both governance and nationalism are primarily about political context and they both gain relevance at the local level rather than at the cosmic scale of religion. Governance may at first sound like a fancy political science term. In reality, it is an easy-to-understand and highly useful concept that comprehensively captures statehood, governmental competence, and what a well-functioning system should look like.[3] The departure point for governance is simple: all states seek to achieve security, capacity, and legitimacy. Only few states, however, manage to attain these three goals simultaneously. When they do, their key to success is "good governance." And the key to good governance— the ability of a state to achieve security, capacity, and legitimacy, without prioritizing one over the other—is to govern with inclusive rather than repressive institutions for the well-being of all citizens.[4]

The concept of governance is of critical importance for this book. In addition to its focus on the political realm, it provides a useful corrective to a common mistake when we think of state power in the Middle East. Most analysts tend to see autocracies in the Arab world as strong states. In reality, the governments that brutally silence their citizens are weak states.[5] They resort to harsh coercive methods and systemic oppression because they feel insecure. They suppress their populations because they lack institutions that can voice, tolerate, integrate, and legitimize systemic dissent. As a result, the security they achieve comes at the expense of accountability, popularity, and legitimacy. Important segments of their citizens feel they are not represented because individual rights and liberties based on the rule of law are simply absent. Such repressive states create a perception of strength that masks their institutional weakness. They are plagued by bad governance and manage to stay in power by either heavily policing their populations or buying their consent—in case of energy-rich autocracies—when they provide economic benefits in return for obedience.

Oil and gas revenues allow some Middle Eastern states to have financial capacity. Such wealth, however, doesn't amount to economic productivity, creativity, or competitiveness. It is also not reflective of good governance. These energy-rich states with no inclusive institutions and no tradition of taxation, representation, or governmental accountability have extractive economic and political systems. Behind the veil of Islamic legitimacy, they are in fact autocracies with weak political foundations. The key questions for good governance are therefore the following: Is the state equipped with transparent, accountable, and inclusive political institutions? Instead of stability with brutal coercion, can the government provide rule of law, economic capacity, political rights, and individual liberties? Can security, economic capacity, and political legitimacy be achieved simultaneously?

These questions can only be answered by developing a solid understanding of institutional dynamics behind governance. My three examples in this book, Turkey, the Sunni–Shiite sectarian conflict, and ISIS, will each illustrate that governance is a key analytical tool. The Middle East has a shortage of good governance and an abundance of states with weak institutions. This is why most states in the region end up resorting to repression. Almost all face security, capacity, and legitimacy challenges. The absence of inclusive and transparent institutions that can combine security with freedom and economic development with political inclusivity is a major characteristic of the Middle East.

In addition to governance, nationalism plays an equally critical role in my analysis. Sweeping generalizations about Muslim culture and political Islam fail to explain why different nation-states, practicing the same religion, have diverging national interests, priorities, and strategies. With competing national security agendas, states in the Middle East pursue often adversarial strategies. Nationalism provides the main corrective to the fallacy of an Islamic monolith. Arab states may speak the same language, share the same religion, and even govern with similar autocratic tendencies. Yet, there is no shortage of nationalist rivalry in the region based on state interests. Even in the heyday of pan-Arab nationalism during the 1960s and 1970s, diverging national security priorities and nationalist agendas among competing states stood in the way of Arab unity and cohesion. Nationalism is key to understanding these regional rivalries.

That different nation-states have competing national interests and strategic objectives should not be surprising. Yet, the tendency to overstate Islam often forgets that not all Muslim states interact with Islam the same way. It also goes without saying that different Muslim nations with different political traditions have also different interpretations of Islam. There are therefore stark differences between Tunisian, Jordanian, and Saudi versions of political Islam. Even pan-Islamist movements such as the Muslim Brotherhood that try hard to put a common face to Islamism have separate agendas driven by their diverse national context. Once again, the local context takes priority over the sacred text. These differences may be lost to American or European audiences focused on a monolithic Islam clashing with the West. But the diversity of Islamist movements in a Muslim world divided by competing nationalisms is not lost on those who pay attention to domestic conditions in each country.

The way nationalism shapes and activates Islam is therefore highly relevant. We will see in the following chapters how nationalism often trumps religion by subordinating Islam and instrumentalizing it based on strategic priorities. For instance, in our rush to label him an Islamist, we seldom recognize the role nationalism plays in Erdoğan's political success. Similar dynamics are at play when we look at Sunni–Shiite sectarian tensions in the Middle East. Our tendency to overstate "ancient Islamic hatreds" going back to the early days of Islam causes us to miss the rivalry between Saudi and Iranian nationalism. Even in the context of ISIS, Sunni nationalism and grievances, combined with the collapse of governance, are behind the façade of jihadist savagery.

Structure of the Book

Governance and nationalism are, of course, two distinct concepts. My focus in this book will be on their interaction and how, combined, they shape dynamics in the selected case studies: Turkey, the Sunni–Shiite sectarian divide, and ISIS. These three case studies are quite diverse. Yet, they have an important common characteristic in the sense that in each of them the Western narrative overlooks governance and nationalism while it strongly overstates Islam. The structure of the book is designed to show this analytical deficiency by proving that the generic prism of religion, theology, and Islamic identity fails to see the primacy of political institutions, governance, and nationalism. As a result, my focus will be on Turkish nationalism and economic governance in the context of Erdoğan, on Arab versus Persian nationalist competition in the context of Sunni–Shiite regional sectarianism, and on Sunni religious nationalism behind ISIS. As we will see, the fact that both the Sunni–Shiite sectarianization and ISIS are largely products of failed, failing, or weak states is also not a coincidence. In all these three cases, we will see Islam taking second seat to nationalism and governance.

This book is divided into six chapters. Before three separate sections on the three cases—Turkey, the Sunni–Shiite sectarian conflict, and ISIS—I begin with a chapter on the larger problem of overstating Islam.

By analyzing the pitfalls of culturalism and religious determinism, this first chapter seeks to answer why we are asking the wrong questions and therefore reaching the wrong conclusions. Whether Islam is compatible with democracy falls in this category of questions that puts the focus on religion instead of politics. The tendency to focus on religion in analyzing the root causes of terrorism is another example. This first chapter, therefore, makes the case for a sharper focus on governance and politics in diagnosing the problem.

The next three chapters are on the case studies and they begin with Turkey. The key theme for this complex and rapidly changing country will not be "Islamization" but the power of nationalist populism in an autocratic domestic context. Most books on Turkey are obsessed with the clash between Islam, democracy, and secularism. The depiction of Ataturk's Western secularism against Turkey's Muslim, Middle Eastern identity dominates this binary cliché. This chapter will transcend this superficial construct by taking a closer look at the historical emergence of Turkish nationalism. We will see that secularism and Islamic identity did not really clash but rather worked harmoniously in the creation of Turkish national identity. In other words, secularism and Islam complemented each other in facilitating the emergence of the most powerful driver in Turkish politics: nationalism.

The problem with the old narrative on Turkey is that it fails to grasp the complexity of crucial drivers such as Kurdish versus Turkish nationalism and the conflict *within* the Islamic bloc and *within* secularist segments of society. This chapter will therefore look at recent developments such as the fratricide between Erdoğan and Fethullah Gulen, the failed military coup in 2016, Turkey's military rapprochement with Russia, and Erdoğan's alliance with ultranationalists and ultrasecularists by going beyond "Islam versus secularism" or "East versus West" as the main Turkish dichotomy and narrative. And I will analyze President Recep Tayyip Erdoğan's rise and rule in terms of his relative success in governance by creating a new middle class. His use of Turkish nationalism infused with religion and his shifting political alliances based on opportunistic calculations will show us that more than an incorrigible Islamist ideologue, he is in fact a populist Machiavellian with no rigid ideological convictions.

The chapter on the Sunni–Shiite conflict will challenge conventional wisdom in a similar pattern. In this section, I analyze the sectarian clash not as a "deeply rooted religious conflict" but rather as Arab versus Persian nationalism. The focus is on sectarianization as a process, rather than sectarian identity that is always ready to explode. And how Tehran and Riyadh are engaged in proxy wars in countries such as Iraq, Syria, Yemen, and Lebanon where institutions and governance structures have either failed or are failing is also a major part of the analysis provided in this chapter. In short, instead of accepting the narrative of ancient religious hatreds fueling sectarian conflict, I will look at how modern Persian and Arab nationalism compete in weak states where governance has collapsed.

Finally, our third case study, the chapter on ISIS, will analyze the reasons behind the emergence of this extremist violent movement. Instead of focusing on jihadist ideology, as most books on the subject do, I will analyze how the collapse of governance in Syria and Iraq combined with Sunni grievances and Sunni nationalism fueled the success of ISIS in establishing itself as a pseudo-state. In other words, we will see how ISIS is the result of the breakdown of state institutions and the marginalization of Sunni populations in Syria and Iraq. The fact that Sunni Baathist generals from Saddam's army—despite their secularist background—became the military backbone of ISIS will help illustrate the role of Arab–Sunni nationalism as a critical driver behind the movement. In a similar vein, the absence of Islamic literacy among foreign fighters, particularly among Muslims from Europe joining ISIS, is also indicative that factors other than radicalized Islamist identity need to be taken into consideration.

After these case studies the fifth chapter will take a deeper look at the Western disconnect with the examined realities on the ground. This chapter will also analyze the policy implications of overstating Islam. Diagnosing Islam as the problem will naturally generate unrealistic, counterproductive, and sometimes dangerous prescriptions. The quixotic urge to reform Islam, the backlash against multiculturalism in Europe and the United States, and the view that the Muslim Brotherhood should be designated a terrorist organization are some examples. This chapter also takes a detailed look at how linking Islam with autocracy or terrorism will only help the radicalization of average Muslims by demonizing their faith.

Finally, the last chapter of the book proposes a path forward by focusing on how the West can help the Middle East surmount its institutional problems of governance. Improving the security, capacity, and legitimacy challenges in the region is a monumental challenge that needs to be approached with a difficult combination of humility and political determination. Prioritizing civil wars fueling sectarian conflict, changing the Western approach to friendly autocracies in the region, and incentivizing inclusive governance with conditional economic and military assistance are some of the ambitious policy recommendations in this final chapter.

At the end of the day, the primary goal of this book is not just to challenge the religious determinism that fuels the clash of civilizations, Islamophobia, and the potential radicalization of Muslim youth. It is also to offer some prescriptions to deal with the political, economic, and social challenges in the Middle East that are the real drivers of radicalization. Promoting moderate or reformist versions of Islam and strengthening interfaith dialogue may be noble objectives, especially compared to coercive, militaristic strategies of regime change in the Middle East. But they will never address the structural challenges in the region related to the absence of good governance.

Changing Islam is an impossible task, especially for the West. Our obsession with Islam will not only eternalize the civilizational clash but also exacerbate the resentment and frustration of millions of Muslims. Empty culturalism, with racist overtones overstating the dangerous nature of Islam, will pave the way to what the West fears the most: ideological radicalization and extremist violence in the Muslim world. As long as the mirage that Islam is the main problem prevails, the United States and Europe will never manage to surmount their dysfunctional disconnect with the Middle East. It is high time for the West to realize that Islam is neither the problem nor the solution. Instead, we need to think harder and without bias about the structural rather than cultural challenges in the Middle East. My hope is that this book will debunk myths that fuel conventional wisdom and offer a modest contribution to studies that pay more attention to institutions, governance, and nationalism.

1 OVERSTATING ISLAM

Consider the following list: the backlash against multiculturalism in Europe; the US travel ban on major Muslim countries; anti-immigration policies targeting Muslims on both sides of the Atlantic; a growing wave of burqa ban in EU countries; the potential designation of the Egyptian Muslim Brotherhood as a terrorist organization by US congress; the failure to understand the driving factors behind jihadist groups such as Al Qaeda and ISIS; and the belief that survival of Western civilization is at stake. None of these are hypothetical scenarios. They are actual challenges and concerns that shape Western policies. And most importantly, they all make alarmist assumptions that overstate Islam.

Overstating Islam is not an academic problem. It is also not confined to the analytical failure of think tanks in Washington, London, Paris, and Berlin. The belief that Islam is a security concern and a political challenge—more than just a religion—is now deeply ingrained as conventional wisdom and accepted as a fact by large majorities in the West. This state of affairs not only fuels Islamophobia in the West but perhaps more alarmingly exacerbates the resentment toward Europe and the United States in the Muslim world. Millions of average Muslims are tired of being seen as potential radicals in the eyes of average Europeans and Americans. We live in a world where relations between the West and the Muslim world are polarized and full of mutual resentment. The stakes involved in misunderstanding the Middle East by overstating Islam are therefore extremely high.

The problem has clearly gained a new sense of urgency with the arrival of the Trump administration to power. The rise of right-wing populist xenophobia in Europe is the mirror image of the same phenomenon across the Atlantic. This disturbing trend is fueled by what has come to be called "identity politics." Identity politics is driven by superficial perceptions of who we are, rather than the deeper intellectual question of what we think. When identity politics dominates, ideology takes second seat to the primordial question of who we are. The fear of Islam is a case in point. It is not surprising that the threat perception is often focused on Islam as a religion, rather than on political Islam as an ideology. President Trump, for instance, famously asserted to CNN that "Islam hates us" as he went on saying, "I deplore the tremendous hatred that defines this religion." Probed whether he meant to say "radical Islam," his answer was: "it's very difficult to separate. It is very hard to define. Because you don't know who is who."[1]

Trump is not alone. Most polls show that growing majorities in Europe and the United States are concerned and fearful about the presence of Islam and Muslims in their vicinity.[2] In the eyes of large masses, the fear Islam instigates is defined by identity rather than ideology. Not surprisingly, such fear contributes to the kind of xenophobia, anti-immigration anxiety, and populist nativism that eventually finds its voice in the ballot box. There appears no end in sight to the electoral victories of racist political parties that specialize in fearmongering. Populist politicians, who used to operate on the fringes, are now defining the political center in Europe and the United States.

Today, in our age of globalization, we may be forgiven for thinking that identity politics has become exceptionally polarizing. In reality, identity politics always existed. Racism, nationalism, and ethnic hatred are not new phenomena. What is different today, however, is the new scale and scope to this problem. We are constantly bombarded by news, images, documentaries, books, movies, and expert opinion about Islam and the threat it poses to Western civilization. The alarmist perception of this faith as a dangerous religion is driven by this new domestic context coupled with the reality of international events that put Islam at the center stage. Jihadist terrorism in the West, wars in the Middle East, and Muslim immigration to Europe are all defining elements of this new context of globalization that fuels unprecedented levels of polarization in identity politics.

Islam and the Roots of Fear

Fallacies and fantasies in the Western perception of the Middle East have deep historical roots. The tendency to overstate the role of Islam as the central driver of all political, social, economic, and security problems in the "Near East" is part of a Western scholarly tradition, going all the way back to the age of imperialism and colonialism.[3] What is different today, however, is that the fascination with Islam goes well beyond "Orientalist" intellectual tradition and scholarship. Because of globalization and the presence of large Muslim minorities in the West, there is now a mounting sense of anxiety about Islam and Muslims.

The Western obsession with Islam is partly understandable. For large majorities in the West the fear of Islam goes hand in hand with the fear of terrorism. Islam turned from an exotic religion into a growing security threat in a relatively recent political context. During most of the Cold War, the West paid hardly any attention to Islam. The focus was on communism and geostrategic rivalry with the Soviet Union. Most analysts understandably see the terrorist attacks of 9/11 as the definitive turning point in the transformation of Islam from religion to security threat for the West. Yet, there were prior pivotal moments, most remarkably in the late 1970s. In fact, anyone who wants to understand the roots of the current "clash of civilizations" between the West and the Islamic world needs to go back forty years in history in order to understand how 1979 turned into a fateful year when seemingly unrelated events in the greater Middle East paved the road for where we are today.

The year started with Ayatollah Khomeini's return to Tehran after fourteen years in exile. The country was in revolutionary turmoil and sensing that his survival was far from certain, the Shah had already left Iran. As he entered the city, five million Iranians lined up the streets of Tehran to greet the homecoming of the Shiite Imam. What was taking place in Iran in 1979 was the closest the Middle East ever came to a paradigm-changing political revolution similar to what happened in Europe in the wake of the French Revolution in 1789. Today, there are different narratives and interpretations of how the Shiite clergy ended up in power. What is not open to debate, however, is the fact that the Shah had alienated almost all segments of Iranian society, ranging from students and the Communist Party to the merchants in the Bazaar; everyone had an axe to grind with the old regime. And of all the social classes involved in massive demonstrations that rocked Iran, it was the best organized and most disciplined one that managed to hijack the revolution. By April 1979 Khomeini declared that he founded the Islamic Republic in the holy city of Qum. About forty years later Iran, the Middle East, and the West are still grappling with the legacy of this critical turning point.

The same year in Saudi Arabia a seismic event was also to have lasting consequences for both the world and the region. November 20, 1979 began as a regular day in the Grand Mosque of Mecca. It was Haj season in the holiest place of worship of the Islamic world. Thousands flocking to the inner sanctum of the mosque were getting ready for the holiest prayer of their lives, unaware that what was soon to unfold would change the Kingdom forever. In a matter of hours, a group of heavily armed fundamentalists gained control of the whole complex. The attackers were not Shiites bent on spreading Iran's Islamic Revolution as Saudi authorities initially claimed. They were hardline members of Saudi Arabia's very own fundamentalist sect, Wahhabism, taking a stand against growing Western influence on the Kingdom.[4]

The event traumatized the Kingdom and proved to be a turning point. The embarrassment for the Kingdom was made even worse by the fact that it took more than two weeks for the regime to regain control of the mosque, only after the intervention of French special forces. Close to a thousand worshippers were killed. The siege of the Grand Mosque was nothing short of an existential threat to the very foundations of the Kingdom built on an alliance between the House of Saud and Wahhabi puritanism. The House of Saud now had a choice: it could either enter a new stage of confrontation with its own puritanical sect by crushing all radical elements within or make peace with them with a strategy of co-optation. The regime decided to pursue the latter, for the sake of peace and stability at home. Soon, Wahhabism was to become the second most important export of the Saudi regime after its oil.

In order to restore its domestic political and religious legitimacy, the Kingdom not only warmly embraced Wahhabism. It also decided to channel the radical energy of its most zealous adherents outside the Kingdom to places like Afghanistan, where the Soviet army that same fateful year, in 1979, embarked on an ill-advised journey. When Soviet tanks rolled into the country in December 1979 they probably had no clue that this quagmire was going to play such a major role in bringing the end of the whole communist system. Soon after the Soviet invasion a jihadist resistance movement financed by Saudi Arabia and the United States emerged. The seeds of Al Qaeda were planted among such Mujahideen groups in Afghanistan. Osama bin Laden, originally from a wealthy family in Saudi Arabia, became a prominent organizer and financier in funneling money, arms, and Muslim fighters into the country.

In short, 1979 turned out to be a fateful year for the future of relations between the Middle East and the West. Turning points like the Islamic Revolution in Iran, the siege of the Grand Mosque in Mecca, and the Soviet invasion of Afghanistan changed the world. These regional developments also paved the road for a new paradigm in relations between the West and Islam much before the terrorist attacks of September 11, 2001. The perception that Islam is an exceptional force, with tremendous political power to shape the fate of individual countries, an entire region, and eventually the whole world emerged that year. Popular journalists such as Thomas Friedman, to this day, argue the world has never been the same after the events set in motion that year.[5]

There is no doubt that 1979 is a turning point. Yet, it is also clear that until 2001 there was still resistance to the idea of an immutable, deeply rooted religious clash between Islam and the West. Samuel Huntington wrote his alarmist essay and subsequent book on the "Clash of Civilizations," shortly after the Soviet Union collapsed and the Cold War came to an end.[6] Events that started in 1979 were well underway by the early 1990s, yet most analysts vehemently disagreed with the notion that the new global conflicts would be fueled by religion.[7] The dominant view was that national, economic, or geostrategic interests, rather than civilizational belonging based on religion, would continue to shape world politics. The neat and oversimplified groupings in Huntington's categorization of civilizations failed to explain the hybrid, multifaceted nature of globalization and presented a monolithic version of complex identities.

And then 9/11 happened. This tragedy turned the clash into a self-fulfilling prophecy with astonishing speed. Jihadist Islam, represented by Al Qaeda, had declared war against the West. The very symbols of American financial and military power were hit with unprecedented lethality. In a few hours, more than three thousand innocent civilians were killed. The perpetrators claimed they acted in the name of Islam, jihad, and revenge. Soon after the dust settled, a Western debate began about what all this meant. The Bush administration quickly launched a global war against terrorism. Unavoidably, in the eyes of millions of traumatized Americans, the problem was Islam and Muslims. The fateful question became: "Why do they hate us?" People rushed to bookstores to buy copies of the Quran—the sacred text of Islam believed to be the very word of God by Muslims—to find answers. An industry of analysts and pundits were more than ready to provide their views.

Something had gone awfully wrong in the Muslim world and Islamic theology and radical fundamentalism were in great part to blame for fueling hatred of the West. The assertion of Islam as the main problem was of course simplistic. Yet, it is also abundantly clear that terrorism compounded the stigmatization of Islam since 9/11. Those who wish to challenge Islamophobia have to recognize this simple reality and think harder about the connections between Islam and extremist violence. Jihadist terrorism is not a Western fantasy nor a perception problem in the eyes of racists. Such politically and religiously motivated acts targeting civilians in Europe and the United States are all too real and still occur with disturbing frequency. The argument that jihadist terrorist attacks have nothing to do with Islam lacks credibility in the eyes of Western majorities. It is critically important to understand this point before engaging in a futile defense of the Muslim faith as a peaceful and tolerant religion.

The Need for Balance and Context

There is, of course, nothing wrong with pious Muslims who want to defend their religion from defamation and demonization. But when terrorist masterminds evoke theology and use the language of religious resistance, there needs to be a less defensive reaction from Muslim communities and more willingness to look at all the causes, including religious ones, of radicalization. In rejecting the essentialist view that Islam is an immutable, timeless, all-powerful force behind everything Muslims think and do, we should not engage in reverse essentialism by arguing that Islam is a force for good. The view that religion has nothing to do with human behavior is simplistic. We need to approach the roots of the Western fear of Islam with an open mind and a flexible methodology. Instead of an exclusive focus on Islamic doctrine, the intersection of politics, sociology, culture, psychology, and foreign policy will certainly prove more fertile ground. Rather than outright rejection of any connection between Islam and violence, we should therefore expand the field of analysis.

The current Western debate about jihadist terrorism, however, goes well beyond a necessary and balanced discussion about the role of religion in fueling extremist violence. There is now an alarming tendency among growing numbers of analysts, politicians, scholars, and citizens to see "radical Islam" as the sole ideological factor behind terrorism.

Perhaps more worrisome is the growing sense that Islam as a religion is also the main obstacle to freedom, prosperity, and modernization in the Middle East. In short, Islam is now to blame for everything that goes wrong, from terrorism to the failure of democratization, secularism, and economic development in the Muslim world. That's where reality meets fantasy.

Given the polarizing nature of this debate, it is important to challenge this fantasy in a rational way, without minimizing the role Islam plays in the politics of Muslim countries. In the following pages, my goal is not to defend Islam or to argue that it is irrelevant. Many books try to absolve Islam of any connection to violence, with the argument that Islam is a religion of peace. This book is not one of them. I believe trying to prove the peaceful nature of Islam is as pointless as the argument that Islam is a violent religion. Such discussions on the "essence" of Islam are counterproductive and generate more heat than light for a simple reason. Islam, like other religions, is open to human evaluation and interpretation. It can be used to legitimize violence if some Muslims are so inclined. It is equally possible that some Muslims will pursue tolerance and peace for religious reasons. Ultimately, what truly matters is not what Islam says but how Muslims decide to believe. What makes theological discussions rich yet inconclusive is the fact that they are subject to linguistic, philosophical, epistemological, and contextual ambiguity.

There is, however, tremendous pressure for a simpler picture of good and evil to emerge in times of identity polarization. Our political context of mass media and mass polarization is not always conducive to a balanced, calm, and poised analysis. Large segments of society are susceptible to identity politics. Populist political parties and politicians that cater to such masses are not in the business of nuanced analysis. They thrive when their target and their message are clear. Those who want to challenge such clarity have to leave the ivory tower of progressive academia and come to terms with the fact that Islam and terrorism have now become part of the same problem.

Consider the following list of facts and events: the rise of Al Qaeda and ISIS with their ability to recruit Muslims from the West; terrorist attacks in Paris, Brussels, London, Madrid, San Bernardino, and Orlando; the Arab Spring turning into a nightmare with civil wars in Syria and Libya; democratic elections leading to Islamist electoral victories in Egypt and Tunisia; the bloody military coup against the Muslim Brotherhood in Egypt; and Turkey's Islamization under Erdoğan. These are all very legitimate reasons for focusing on political Islam. The result is a plethora of books dealing with the subject. Not surprisingly, most of these books see religion as the main problem in the Middle East and make no serious attempt to go beyond Islamist ideology by analyzing political, economic, social, and institutional factors.

Going beyond Islam is not an easy task, particularly when identity politics, religion, culture, and civilization take up all the oxygen in the room. We live in a world where perceptions create their own reality. A highly interconnected world of mass communication adds to the challenge. Thanks to the information technology revolution, knowledge is within instant reach, but facts are increasingly elusive and contested. Objective and balanced analyses are in short supply and there is ample space for manipulation, misrepresentation, and disinformation. This polarized media environment, combined with populist politics, shapes mental images and rapidly constructs "alternative" facts and realities. All these dynamics turn Islam into an easy target.

Another major problem is the scarcity of time and focus. The 24/7 news cycle constantly bombards us with events and opinions. This situation often creates desensitized consumers of information who have shorter and shorter attention spans. We seek instant gratification fed by sound bites and shortcuts. Our intellectual satisfaction often comes in the form of confirmation bias, groupthink, and echo-chambers. In other words, we are happier when we hear what we believe is true. As a result, opposing viewpoints are often dismissed as propaganda or agenda-driven hyperbole. Not surprisingly, all these dynamics generate mutual distrust between diverging and increasingly angry political camps. As a result, in a context where Islam is seen as the main problem, anyone challenging the conventional wisdom risks being labeled a Muslim apologist.

Finally, this polarized political context is compounded by economic and financial dynamics. The "Great Recession" following the global financial crisis of 2008 has exacerbated the economic gap between the rich and the poor. Europe and the United States are still coming to terms with the social and political aftershocks of the worst economic downturn since the Great Depression. Growing income disparity and wage stagnation have widened the gap between the winners and losers of globalization. A major disconnect has emerged between impoverished masses and the financial and political establishment. Without this economic context and grievances, it is simply impossible to analyze the root causes of the dangerous populism that exploits legitimate concerns by stoking fear and nationalism. Xenophobia, racism, anti-immigration policies, and Islamophobia have now become typical ingredients of populist narratives in Europe and the United States.

Populism and identity politics thrive in an information context where there are no longer verifiable facts. The contested information environment, particularly the massive spread of social media, sets the stage for fearmongering and political polarization. Our age of disinformation, bias, and propaganda has an uncanny ability to polarize with anonymous viciousness. All these factors—disinformation, media-driven polarization, angry nativism, xenophobia, economic and social problems, and the elitist disconnect—have greatly contributed to populist electoral victories on both sides of the Atlantic. It is hard to imagine the UK deciding to leave the European Union or the victory of Donald J. Trump in the United States in the absence of such a confluence of diverse factors.

Populist electoral victories become possible in great part thanks to the demonization of political enemies. Group solidarity always requires an "us" versus "them" narrative. The identification of Islam and Muslims as "dangerous enemies" comes in this new political, economic, and social context. Muslims, Islam, radicalism, terrorism, immigration, globalization, recession, unemployment, and economic insecurity are now all part of a political narrative of fear. They come together to form an existential challenge to the national identity, Western civilization, secularism, prosperity, secularism, and freedom. This is the Western context where Islam and Muslims are constantly overstated.[8]

Identity versus Ideology

Identity politics trumps ideology when such a political environment fuels polarization. Unlike during the Cold War, polarization today is more about civilizational, religious belonging rather than ideological competition. This is a critical difference between today and a bipolar global power system based on an existential geostrategic rivalry. It is also worth noting that identity and ideology drive very different types of polarizations. Religion—the major force behind civilizational conflict and cultural divergence—impacts average citizens in a primordial way. Primordial identities such as religion, ethnicity, and clan are *organically* inherited and become part of who you are at childhood. They are absorbed and transmitted in an effortless way compared to political identities and ideological proclivities that are acquired, encountered, or constructed as we get older.

The primordial nature of religious and national identity also makes it more instinctive. Religious and national identities—or sometimes both, in the form of religious nationalism—are easier to mobilize compared to constructed political ideologies that require rationalization, a learning process, and some cognitive skills. Religion and nationalism often generate tribal and nativist loyalties. Such primordial identity is not immutable, however. It can adapt to changing negative or positive contexts, based on threat perceptions in the social, economic, and political environment. It is certainly possible to construct new, overlapping, additional identities that challenge the purity of primordial belonging. Yet, clearly, this becomes a monumental challenge when the environment in not conducive to coexistence. Particularly when faced with existential security threats, primordial identity is not only more easily mobilized but also forms a more natural, organic, and reliable network of solidarity. That communities turn inward for protection when survival is at stake should not come as a surprise. A conflict based on religious identity often creates a potentially more visceral type of polarization. The primordial often trumps the constructed in times of panic and anxiety.

When sociologists and political scientists refer to "ancient tribal hatreds" they often have this image of immutable, timeless, intractable primordial instincts in mind. They blame the primordial identity for fueling the conflict, rather than the context of war for fueling primordialism. All this social psychology over identity politics is relevant for our debate for the following reason: when increasing numbers in the West see Islam as a major security threat, the situation can easily degenerate into primordial, emotional, and existential animosity. How else can one explain the fact that the simple act of speaking in Arabic in an American airplane today can potentially result in being removed by the authorities after being reported as a potential terrorist?[9] This is an alarming situation that needs to be taken very seriously. Anxiety about Islam may have some understandable roots given the fear of terrorism. But when fear turns to hysteria, we can no longer speak of a rational reaction. And the problem gains a systemic dimension when this climate of fear and hysteria finds its voice in the ballot box thanks to exploitation by populist identity entrepreneurs. Islamophobia thrives in this context of primordialism.

The Multiculturalism Debate in Europe

The backlash against multiculturalism in Europe is part of similar dynamics. The extreme right in Europe is motivated by racism. Yet, this ugly side of its political identity hides behind a more legitimate façade that speaks of imminent danger. A climate of fear is instigated: Islam is on the rise, Muslims are invading the West, and they refuse to embrace "our" culture, values, and way of life.[10] What's happening in the fringe of politics soon impacts the center-right and center-left as it gains popular traction. Today most political parties across Europe reject multiculturalism on the grounds that it comes at the expense of integration. Rather than an attempt at more diversity, pluralism, and flexibility in redefining national identity, multiculturalism is presented almost as a national security threat, which paves the way for national disintegration by forming "parallel societies." An excess of tolerance and multiculturalism is now to blame for the failure to integrate Muslims and their potential radicalization.

Multiculturalism, to have a chance, needs to be defined in a way that can reassure both the majority and minorities. The politics of fear, as we will analyze later, sometimes conceptualizes multiculturalism as a slow but steady Islamization of Europe with the legalization of Sharia law parallel to the existing secular legal systems. While the *host* society is anxious to protect its Western identity, political system, and security, Muslim minorities can discern behind this backlash against multiculturalism a thinly veiled racism, bigotry, and Islamophobia. The backlash against multiculturalism has gained ground even in Germany and France—countries where multiculturalism was never practiced. The UK and the Netherlands have at least tried to adopt some level of multiculturalism in attempts to formulate a less rigid understanding of national identity and citizenship.

France has always pursued assimilation as state policy. It sees multiculturalism as a slippery slope toward a multilegal, multiconfessional system, at the expense of equality of all citizens before the law. It also wants to protect its laicism based on a strict separation between state and religion. This is the context in which the headscarf debate turns into a socially and politically polarizing issue in the country. Germany, on the other hand, did not even grant citizenship to immigrants until relatively recently. Even children of second-generation immigrants born in Germany were not accepted as citizens on the grounds that they did not have German blood (jus sanguinis). This ethnic concept of German citizenship with racist undertones remained in place until 2000. Such marginalization finally came to an end when the left/green coalition of Chancellor Gerhard Schroeder revamped the antiquated German citizenship laws despite objections from the Christian Democratic Party and its smaller and more conservative Bavarian branch—the Christian Social Union.

The kind of identity politics, fear, and resentment that fuels the backlash against multiculturalism and Islamophobia in Europe has a mirror image in the Islamic world. Large majorities in the Middle East blame the West for all sorts of domestic problems, ranging from economic underdevelopment to political repression and authoritarianism. The legacy of colonialism and a sense of victimhood fuel conspiracy theories about omnipotent external actors that keep the Arab world in a state of dependency.[11] Iran and Turkey are certainly not immune from this tendency to blame the United States and Europe for domestic failure and dysfunction. The embrace of conspiracy theories is often encouraged from the top, by state authorities and national leaders, who refuse to take responsibility. Sometimes, it is also a more systemic problem, ingrained in the political culture with an education system that fuels resentment against the West. In any case, the result is often the same: growing polarization between the *West* and the *Islamic world.*

Such notions of a monolithic Islam and a singular West can of course be challenged by the fact that the Muslim world is highly diverse and that Islam is open to different interpretations. Similarly, the West is a fragmented and pluralistic entity with clear differences between the progressives and conservatives. Yet, it is also important to recognize that polarization is often driven by mass perceptions rather than objective facts. In a world where factual and objective information is increasingly contested, perceptions based on disinformation, social media, groupthink, and cognitive bias create their own reality. Academic accuracy or analytical objectivity seldom drives mass media and public opinion.

Social media particularly fuels a world of alternative realities where people are now increasingly entitled not only to their own opinion but also to their own facts. "Imagined" and "constructed" realities are therefore undeniable parts of this bitterly polarized context. It is this "Clash of Civilizations" framework that this book will try to deconstruct with one clear objective: to challenge the conventional wisdom that religion is the driver of all problems in the Middle East. This above all requires a clear understanding of how religion came to replace politics and ideology as the main driver of conflicts in the last couple of decades. Our next section will focus on this important source of polarization.

Ideology Out, Religion in

Imagine a much simpler world, where, once upon a time, the main global divisions were primarily ideological and geostrategic. In the Western bloc of this ideological divide, the United States was seen as the leader of the "free world" where capitalism and democracy reigned supreme. The Soviet Union represented the other pole with its socialist economic model and rejection of liberal bourgeois democracy. Ethnoreligious divides mattered little in this bipolar world defined by political ideology and a geostrategic balance of power. Cold Warriors in the Western camp saw the Soviet Union as an "Evil Empire" not because of civilizational differences. Moscow was reviled because it brutally subjugated people under its communist dictatorship and ideology.

Distrust was mutual. True believers in the Communist bloc saw America as an imperialist hegemon that bankrolled fascist dictatorships. In their eyes, the West promoted an exploitative capitalist system that fueled social, economic, and political inequalities. The world came disturbingly close to nuclear oblivion in this global context where each camp ideologically despised the other. Given such perilous dynamics and existential geopolitical stakes, there should be no nostalgia for the bipolar world of the Cold War. Yet, despite the risks involved, from the 1940s to roughly the late 1980s, the essence of global conflict was defined in geopolitical and ideological rather than religious terms. In other words, the polarization, unlike today, was driven by politics rather than religious identity.

As mentioned above, conflicts driven by political ideology are less primordial than the ones instigated by religious identity. Ideologies are modern constructs. Communism certainly was in this category with its roots in the nineteenth-century Marxist challenge to capitalism. And because political and economic ideologies are acquired ways of thinking about the world, they also tend to evolve, adapt, and mutate within changing social, economic, and political contexts. This, after all, is how the ideological clash between capitalism and communism ultimately led to the compromise of social democracy and a welfare state financed by progressive taxation. Capitalism and socialism had to adapt to each other.

Can the same dynamics of adaptation and evolution apply to ideologies inspired by religion? The short answer is a cautious yes because it requires the right political environment. By their own very nature, religious texts tend to be doctrinal. As divinely inspired, sacredly enshrined, and deeply rooted eternal truths, they are much harder to mutate. They also have tremendous mobilization power. Any conflict couched in religious terms is bound to last much longer than ideological rivalries. To be sure, *secular* ideologies such as fascism and communism have been devastatingly brutal and destructive in human history. But civilizational conflicts are by definition all-encompassing. They transcend the nation-state, nationalism, and political ideology by gaining *Godly* and *sacred* dimensions. This is partly why the clash of civilizations has a more intractable, polarizing, and visceral character.

The idea that new conflicts would be of civilizational and religious nature did not emerge without controversy. In the early 1990s, analysts disagreed about what would replace the Cold War's ideological rivalry. Some heralded a "unipolar moment" of American hegemony. America's victory seemed complete with the triumph of capitalism and democracy over Soviet communism. Some, like Francis Fukuyama, saw larger dialectical forces at play. With the end of communism and the collapse of the Soviet Union, Fukuyama argued, there was no longer any realistic alternative or systemic challenge to liberal democracy. "The End of History," with all countries gravitating toward democratic capitalism as the final stage of humanity, seemed like a compelling scenario for the near future at the time.[12] After all, even communist China had adopted capitalism and, sooner or later, Beijing too was likely to embrace democracy and freedom.

Fukuyama's "End of History" is today remembered as the culmination of a naïve sense of Western optimism. The argument that there would be a global convergence toward liberal democracy proved wishful thinking. Instead, another seminal article by Samuel Huntington had much more success in predicting the disturbing dynamics that would define the post–Cold War era. Huntington's "Clash of Civilizations" was an ominous warning about an upcoming world full of primordial conflicts. He argued that far from ending, history would come back with a vengeance. The bloody borders between civilizations, particularly in the case of Islam, would define the new wars of the post–Cold War era. Religion was to become the new driver of global conflict.

Islam's bloody borders had a special place in Huntington's analysis of the looming clash. There was no ambiguity in how Huntington defined Islam and the threat it posed for the West. His conceptualization of Islam did not come with qualifications such as "radical" or "jihadist." As he clearly spelled out:

> The fundamental problem for the West is not Islamic fundamentalism. It is Islam, a different civilization whose people are convinced of the superiority of their culture and are obsessed with the inferiority of their power. The problem for Islam is not the CIA or the U.S. Department of Defense. It is the West, a different civilization whose people are convinced of the universality of their culture and believe that their superior, if declining, power imposes on them the obligation to extend that culture throughout the world. These are the basic ingredients that fuel the conflict between Islam and the West.[13]

This kind of narrative is primarily about simplification of complex, multidimensional issues into a sound bite. In a Huntingtonian world, civilizational identity turns into the most important driver of conflict between nations. Essentialist in nature, such analysis has the distinct advantage of resonating with the primordial instincts of masses. It quickly turns into a narrative of fear based on threat perception. This discourse needs to be taken very seriously because it has serious political implications in a post-9/11 world. Civilizational conflict is no longer an academic viewpoint. It is now at the heart of the Trump administration's worldview. As President Trump asked in one of his foreign policy speeches:

> The fundamental question of our time is whether the West has the will to survive. Do we have the confidence in our values to defend them at any cost? Do we have enough respect for our citizens to protect our borders? Do we have the desire and the courage to preserve our civilization in the face of those who would subvert and destroy it?[14]

Trump is in good company in European politics. The same kind of existential fear colors the politics and language of extreme right populism across the continent. There is indeed a very thin line between Huntington's world of academic analysis and the world of anti-Islamic xenophobia.

The Problem with Cultural Determinism

What is wrong with this approach? The short answer is cultural determinism. Cultural determinists often explain global dynamics by overstating religious and civilizational identity at the expense of economic, political, and social factors. Those who accuse Huntington of cultural determinism, as I do, have no problem accepting the growing importance of religion in world politics. However, we refuse to see religion as the "source" of the conflict. Religion, in our eyes, is an effective vehicle to mobilize the masses—not the driver or the root cause of an upcoming clash. Those who seek power tend to use religion to achieve political, financial, and geostrategic ends. Put simply, we believe religion is the instigator of the conflict, not its raison d'être. Therein lies the major difference between culturalism and power politics. While culturalism tends to look at culture, religion, and civilizational identity as the root cause of conflict, the opposing camp of structuralism and power politics sees primarily political and material motivations behind the pursuit of military, economic, and strategic objectives.

Culturalism and structuralism disagree on more than their analysis of global conflict. There is a fundamental philosophical difference between the two schools based on methodology. This is also why Huntington's cultural determinism has consequences that go beyond the clash between Islam and the West. Culturalism often makes causative assertions about the compatibility of democracy, liberalism, or capitalism with certain religious and cultural traditions. For instance, culturalists clearly believe that Islam is not compatible with enlightenment values that have led to modernization and liberalism. Islam, in their eyes, is not compatible with rationalism, tolerance, democracy, secularism, and gender equality.

When you take cultural determinism and civilizational analysis to its logical conclusion, there emerges a clear sense that differences between Christianity and Islam account for why secularism, liberalism, capitalism, and democracy emerged in Europe and not in the Middle East. In short, cultural determinism is crystal clear in its diagnosis and prescription of the problem. The monumental challenge the West is facing in the Middle East is Islam itself. As a result, what we need is the reformation, modernization, or liberalization of Islam. The rest will follow. Democracy, prosperity, and peace in the Middle East require nothing less than a Muslim version of European enlightenment and reformation. Islam, therefore, has to go through what the West and Christianity went through.

This tendency to see Islam as the main source of all problems in the Middle East is a mirage—a culturalist fallacy, in need of urgent correction with a more balanced approach that includes an analysis of political and socioeconomic dysfunctions in the region. The challenge is not the impossible task of religious reform, but a change in our assumptions and methodology about the central role of religion. We need a more comprehensive approach that will take into consideration multiple factors—economic, political, social, religious, institutional, and geostrategic. In the following pages, I will do so by prioritizing the role of governance and nationalism in my approach to Turkey, the Sunni–Shiite divide, and ISIS. My goal will be to show how the Western obsession with Islam creates a blind spot in analyzing some of the most important current developments in the Middle East.

These cases will illustrate the pitfalls of cultural determinism, inherent in overstating Islam. However, before we start this journey, it is important to remember that no effort at debunking the myth that Islam is the main problem can succeed without taking on the critical issue of jihadist terrorism. After all, it is 9/11 that turned Huntington's gloomy prediction of a bloody clash between Islam and the West into a self-fulfilling prophecy. If the perpetrators of jihadist terrorist attacks claim they act in the name of Islam, why should we not believe them? As Salman Rushdie contends:

If everybody engaged in acts of Islamic terrorism says that they're doing it in the name of Islam, who are we to say they're not? Of course, what they mean by Islam might well not be what most Muslims mean by Islam. But it's still a form of Islam and it's a form of Islam that's become unbelievably powerful in the last 25 and 30 years.[15]

Beyond just terrorism and radicalism, the same kind of cultural and religious determinism often points at Islam as the main reason behind the absence of democracy in the Middle East.

Today, the view that Islam promotes extremist violence coupled with the twin argument that Islam is not compatible with democracy has become the mantra of large masses in the West. These two points are the clearest examples of how religion trumps politics in the parallel universe of culturalism. No challenge to the view that "Islam is the problem" can succeed without addressing the proposition that Islam feeds extremist violence and authoritarianism. This is why before focusing on Turkey, the sectarian divide, and ISIS, we will briefly address in the next two sections the problem of overstating religious doctrine in analyzing terrorism and democracy.

Islam and the Roots of Terror

The question about the root causes of terrorism has generated a highly polarized and inconclusive debate in the West. Generally speaking, two major views have emerged. In one camp, there are those who see ideology, culture, and religion as the main drivers of radicalization. Radical Islam, jihadism, and the clash of civilizations are all integral parts of this camp's narrative. The view that the real clash should be within Islam—between radicals and moderates—represents a more nuanced version of the same argument prioritizing cultural and ideological factors. In the opposing camp, social and economic factors take priority over ideology and religion. Unemployment, poverty, and the absence of upward mobility cause a growing sense of frustration and radicalization.

Those who prioritize ideology and culture reject the argument that socioeconomic deprivation fuels radicalization on the grounds that most terrorists are neither poor nor uneducated. The literature seems to indicate that a majority of terrorists come from middle-class backgrounds. Terrorism, therefore, is seen as primarily an ideological threat with no discernible socioeconomic roots or links to deprivation. The implications of these diverging assumptions for policymaking are clear: while the socioeconomic deprivation camp wants to prioritize development, education, and good governance in the struggle against radicalism, the culture and ideology camp wants to fight terrorism with a single-minded ideological focus on political Islam and jihadism.

So, which argument is right? The path to terrorism defies categorization. There is simply no one-size-fits-all theory of who becomes a terrorist. The key in understanding who joins jihadist groups such as Al Qaeda or ISIS is to go beyond simple socioeconomic factors or pure ideology. In other words, we need to go beyond cultural or socioeconomic determinism. And this requires coming to terms with the fact that radicalization has multiple causes. An ideal breeding ground for recruitment emerges when various social, cultural, economic, political, and psychological factors come together. Dismissing the economic and social roots of radicalization on the grounds that most terrorists have middle-class backgrounds is simplistic and misleading. It is equally wrong, however, to argue that ideology, culture, and religion play no role in the radicalization process.

As we will explore further in the chapter dealing with ISIS, the concept of relative deprivation deserves more attention because it captures both ideological and socioeconomic factors. Unlike absolute deprivation, which primarily deals with abject poverty and lack of education, relative deprivation is about growing expectations and aspirations. What happens when economic and social conditions are in relative improvement and people, especially the youth, develop new ambitions? The answer depends on whether the system can satisfy rising expectations. In case it does not, the results can cause major problems. For instance, growing number of students who gain access to education and develop high aspirations for upward mobility can potentially turn into "frustrated achievers" when they hit obstacles blocking their progress.[16] A widening gap between expectations and opportunities can lead to resentment, anger, and radicalization.

This interplay between socioeconomic factors and ideological, political, and cultural dynamics makes relative deprivation a critically important analytical lens to study radicalization. Relative deprivation thus invites us to examine both cultural and economic factors without focusing exclusively on ideology or development. The place to start is to accept the interconnected nature of political, social, and economic dynamics. In young and rapidly changing societies, when socioeconomic aspirations are on the rise, the challenge for the system is to deliver or at least to maintain the hope that things will get better. The alternative scenario of failure and unfulfilled expectations is likely to generate tension and resentment.

Globalization naturally takes relative deprivation to new levels thanks to the unprecedented level of awareness made possible by easy access to information. Inequality and injustice become disturbingly obvious in an interconnected world. A process of individual and collective resentment can easily follow, as the gap between expectations, opportunities, and accomplishments widens. That such dynamics may drive frustration and radicalization should not be surprising. It is precisely when growing expectations and aspirations hit political, economic, and social walls that we have to pay more attention to the potential for victimhood, humiliation, and ideological radicalization.

Dismissing socioeconomic factors as a potential driver of radicalization can therefore be a faulty approach in the context of the developing world where growing numbers of young people develop hopes and ambitions for upward mobility. The same dynamics apply to young, second- and third-generation Muslim minorities in Europe who have much higher expectations and sensibilities than their parents. Improving educational standards without increasing prospects for employment or providing jobs and economic benefits without creating outlets for political and social participation create a combustible environment where frustrated achievers are increasingly tempted by radicalism.

Education without employment or employment without a sense of political empowerment fuels similar dynamics of humiliation, alienation, and frustration. This is why the growing numbers of educated but unemployed youth are particularly alarming for those who are concerned about the rise of frustrated achievers in the Arab world. Similar factors are at play among Muslim minorities in Europe, where an increasingly better educated but still unemployed youth face additional identity problems such as racism and Islamophobia, which are exacerbating the potential for radicalization.

Finally, relative deprivation is also relevant for those who insist on a civilizational analysis infused with some degree of cultural determinism. Today, the Islamic world collectively shares a sense of frustration and humiliation because it has little to show in terms of its contemporary economic, political, and cultural success. Yet, Islam still has high expectations and aspirations fueled by past accomplishments. Particularly in the Arab Middle East, a sense of nostalgia for the golden age of Islam—during which the Umayyad and Abbasid caliphates far surpassed Europe in science, architecture, and education—generates an inferiority complex. Millions of Arab Muslims share these mixed feelings of pride and shame. The historic achievements of Islamic civilizations compared with the current sense of failure in the Muslim world add a civilizational layer of complexity to relative deprivation.

For Islam, the Christian West is a familiar point of comparison. Geographic proximity and intertwined history create many cultural, religious, and economic points of reference between the Middle East and Europe. Muslim feelings of historic superiority to the West coexist with more recent memories of colonial subjugation and military defeat.

Not surprisingly, this situation creates a sense of victimhood and injustice in much of the Arab world vis-à-vis the West. All these factors significantly compound the level of frustration of a great civilization that seems to have passed its prime but still cherishes nostalgic memories of grandeur. This is why Islam, in certain ways, has attributes of a frustrated achiever as a civilization. The mix of these cultural, religious, economic, and political dynamics leads to frustration among growing cohorts of urbanized, undereducated, and unemployed Muslim youth who are now able to compare their situation with other parts of the world thanks to globalization. In other words, the success of the West has now become highly visible to Muslim masses and the contrast with the dysfunction, chaos, and failure of the Middle East creates a dark image.

All these factors make social and economic dynamics highly relevant in explaining a collective sense of anger and despair in the Arab world. Those who want to focus on development, education, job creation, and political freedom in order to fight the root causes of radicalization and terrorism often make their case based on such arguments. They believe that the middle-class background of terrorists does not change the big picture about radicalism. Terrorism finds acceptance in radicalized societies where social, economic, and political problems are systemic. Poverty and lack of education are part of the problem.

Those who advocate socioeconomic development often make an additional point to counter the image of middle-class terrorists: effective terrorist groups rely on a division of labor between young and uneducated "foot soldiers" and ideologically trained and well-funded elite operatives. While terrorist masterminds and operative leaders tend to come from professional or middle-class backgrounds, the foot soldiers are often poor and uneducated. The implementation of complex terrorist operations requires complex organizational skills. The poorest and least educated foot soldiers would be less effective in complex terrorist operations. Indeed, the more complex an operation is, the greater security risks it entails, and the more likely the participants are to be selected elites that went through a careful screening process.

At the end of the day, no single theory can explain what drives an individual to become a terrorist. We will return to this issue in the context of ISIS in the Middle East and the unexpectedly high numbers of European Muslims who joined the organization. For now, suffice to say that instead of a simplistic approach that overstates Islam, we should appreciate the complexity of the challenge and analyze the problem with all its social, economic, ideological, and psychological dimensions. The challenge is to avoid deterministic causality. An exclusive focus confined to economic development or just Islamist ideology and cultural factors is not likely to produce an accurate diagnosis.

As we will explore later, the best methods will prove to be multidisciplinary and hybrid ones, conscious of the fact that ideology becomes much more important when socioeconomic aspirations are on the rise. Similarly, instead of overarching macro-scale generalizations, researching micro-level, individual paths to radicalization is a much more promising way to address the challenge. The search for meaning, adventure, self-worth, and the zeal that comes with rebellion and conversion to a new ideology and identity are all factors in need of more attention to fully grasp the complexity of what fuels radicalization. A multifaceted analysis of the disturbing journey from radicalization to extremist violence requires an open mind. As we will see next, avoiding sweeping and exclusive generalizations about the religious roots of the problem will also help us to find a more balanced answer to another difficult question: is Islam compatible with democracy?

Islam and Democracy

Questioning the compatibility of any religion with democracy may seem absurd. After all, we seldom ask whether Christianity or Judaism is compatible with a democratic political system. Yet, Islam is different in the eyes of culturalists because of one critical factor: it rejects boundaries between state and religion. Shortly after it emerged, Islam established a state. And it did so in a tribally divided geography, the Arabian Peninsula, where no such centralized authority ever existed. As it turned into a state, Islam provided legal norms—more than just moral guidance—for the communities it assembled under its umbrella. This first Muslim state established by Prophet Muhammad owed its legitimacy to God. All these historical facts stand in sharp contrast to Christianity that remained a stateless religion for centuries and emerged in a geography where a powerful state, the Roman Empire, had already established its authority.

These differences between Islam and Christianity provide the core arguments for orientalism and essentialism. Islam is therefore unique and exceptional because, more than a religion, it is an all-encompassing system of law and governance. Such a conceptualization of Islam, however, conveniently overlooks the fact that Christianity, too, eventually became a state religion. Both Eastern Orthodoxy and Western Catholicism became official religions of powerful states. The Catholic Church even founded its own state with the Papal States in the eighth century. The Holy See exerted tremendous political influence and placed the authority of the Church above the authority of kings and emperors of Europe. The pope became the ultimate conveyor of political legitimacy to kings in medieval Europe and during the long centuries of the Holy Roman Empire.

On the other hand, in time, the Catholic Church and the Papacy slowly lost their power, first to nation-states and later to secularism. The Muslim world, however, did not evolve in the same way. Culturalism maintains that Islam resisted such change and modernization because its political nature became a major impediment for the secularization and democratization in Muslim countries along Western lines. Such assumptions are also behind the argument that democratization in the Muslim world requires an "Islamic Reformation" of sorts. Islam therefore stands above all other drivers—economic, political, social, legal, and institutional—of change. The implication is clear: only a reformed, liberal, progressive Islam would pave the road to modernity, democracy, freedom, and secularism.

There is some consistency to this cultural determinism in the sense that Islam is not only the problem but also the solution. The need for a theological reinterpretation of Islam is therefore top priority. It is also abundantly clear that this camp sees culture and religion as a single unit. There is no daylight between cultural determinism and religious determinism. When there is talk of cultural requirements for democratization, the burden is therefore on Islam. Again, the assumption is very clear: Islam provides the foundation of political and cultural identity for all Muslims. And it also accounts for the weakness of democratic culture in the Islamic world just as it explains other peculiarities of Muslim societies. In the words of the definitive essentialist cliché, Islam is not just a religion but a way of life.

Another aspect of the same narrative that sees Muslim identity as the main impediment to democracy is the belief that everything will be determined by the clash "within" Islam, between radicals and moderates. A victory of the moderates over radicals or the ultimate triumph of the Islamist modernizers against radical fundamentalists will solve all problems and smoothly pave the road to democracy. Not surprisingly, this viewpoint has the strong support of Islamist modernizers who have long argued that "true" Islam is a religion of peace and open to a democratic and egalitarian ethos. The key, in their eyes, is to adopt the "correct" interpretation of Islam.

The common denominator of all these attempts at cultural determinism is the belief that Islam is an exceptional religion.[17] While Christianity makes room for separation of Church and State, such dichotomy is absent in the realm of Islam, a totalitarian faith with a heavy political character. This makes Islam extremely resistant to secularization. After all, the Christian faith refers to the "realm of God" and the "realm of Caesar" with an attempt to separate the two. Such theological references pave the ground for a less political, less militant, and, ultimately, a more "secularizable" Christianity. This is also why culturalists believe liberal democracy and secularism are against the core values of Islam and Muslim societies. The result is a seamless, organic relationship between Islam, Muslim society, and politics. The state is simply an instrument of Islam. Its primary responsibility is to protect the faith of the Muslim community of believers. And Islam's role is to provide legal, moral, and political guidance for the state.

An even more troubling aspect of Islam, in the eyes of culturalists, is its immunity to change. The Quran—the Holy book of Islam—is the unaltered "word of God" and thus leaves no room for dissent or interpretation. It is also the last and final revelation of God. Since there can be no reform, obedience and subservience are the only options. After all, we are told, Islam comes from the Arabic word "submission." Moreover, there is no clergy and no ecclesiastical establishment that can be challenged, the way Protestantism challenged the Catholic Church and clerical establishment. The organizing principle of Islam is the state, not the mosque. This makes state and Islam indivisible. As a result, an uncritical submission to an eternalized status quo—defined by final and perfect nature of the Muslim faith—becomes the essence of the Islamic predicament. Islam, therefore, is destined to govern indefinitely. It will always demand full submission to its principles with no room for compromise, rendering any hope of secularization, democratization, or liberalization the real mirage.

As Yahya Sadowski argued in his excellent critic of Neo-Orientalism,

Like the classical Orientalists before them, the neo-Orientalists portray Islam as a kind of family curse that lives on, crippling the lives of innocent generations after the original sin that created it .... The image that Islamic doctrine presented of the pious believer—fatalistic, prostrate before God, obeying His every whim—served as a trope for discussing not only religious but also political behavior in societies where rulers acted as "the shadow of God upon earth."

Supposedly the great medieval Islamic thinkers, horrified by the periodic rebellions and civil wars that wracked their community, decreed that obedience to any ruler—even an unworthy or despotic one—was a religious duty. "As the great divine Ghazali (d. 1111) declared: 'The tyranny of a sultan for a hundred years causes less damage than one year's tyranny exerted by the subjects against each other.'"[18] In short, orientalism tirelessly argues that Islam explains all there is to explain about the democratic deficit in the Middle East.

Now that we have a clear idea of why the culture club believes Islam is not compatible with democracy, we can turn to the opposite viewpoint. In this camp, we have the primacy of social and economic conditions instead of culture and religion.

Structure versus Culture

I will refer to this view as structuralism because it is focused on underlying institutional mechanism and structures rather than what we see as cultural traits on the surface. Structuralists believe economic and social institutions determine the chances of democratization, not culture, religion, or civilization. In fact, they consider culture "a residual category in which lazy social scientists take refuge when they can't develop a more rigorous theory."[19]

To argue that Islam is not compatible with democracy, in their eyes, falls into this category of intellectual laziness. The simple fact that many Muslim countries, such as Turkey, Indonesia, and Malaysia and more recently Tunisia in the wake of the Arab Spring in 2011, managed to transition to democracy should serve as evidence of the culturalist fallacy. The correlation between economic development, modernization, and democracy plays a critical role in such thinking. With the right economic policies and institutional arrangements democracy would emerge in the Islamic world as it did elsewhere. It remains the case, as political scientist Seymour Martin Lipset, one of the first pioneers of modernization theory, argued fifty years ago, that the more well-to-do a country is, the better will be its prospects for gaining and keeping democracy. Instead of considering religion, reformation, and culture as the main drivers of democratization, structuralism maintains that the real force behind democratic progress was the Industrial Revolution, the emergence of a middle class, and growing prosperity. Economic development, in that sense, is the best predictor of political change.

The Western trajectory toward democratization and universal suffrage seems to confirm this theory. The journey begins with the right to vote confined only to male property owners. The acceptance of universal suffrage is a result of social and economic class struggle. The Industrial Revolution, labor unions fighting for worker rights, and civil rights movements demanding equality for women and minorities are the main protagonists. Culture and religion may have some relevance but little deterministic power in this democratic journey. In fact, it is the other way around: economic and social factors are the real drivers that manage to change cultural norms. Therefore, if Muslim societies want to establish democracies they have to start by changing the underlying social and economic conditions that underpin the political system. Cultural change will follow.

Given such discord between culturalism and structuralism, is there a way to bridge the gap? In their purest forms both groups share the same fallacy: determinism. Culturalism not only overstates Islam but also stubbornly maintains that culture, often defined in great part as religion, is the primary driver of not only conflict but also social, political, and economic change. Orientalism exacerbates the problem by nurturing notions of Western cultural superiority vis-à-vis a static, repressive, regressive, and totalitarian Islam. Structuralism, on the other hand, seems to suffer from the opposite of Western ethnocentricity. It preaches a type of universalism with the belief that the right combination of socioeconomic conditions would generate democratic progress, independently of diverse local political and cultural dynamics. Both have their roots in somewhat outdated nineteenth-century theories of sociology. While culturalism is heavily influenced by Max Weber's view that ascetic Protestantism greatly helped the rise of capitalism, economic determinism is under the intellectual spell of Karl Marx and historical materialism.

A balanced approach to the question of Islam and democracy should start by rejecting both cultural and economic determinism. Democratization is a complex journey with no simple formula for success.

There is no single cultural trajectory or universally accepted economic blueprint. Multiple social, economic, political, and cultural factors have to coalesce in paving the road to democratization. To attach causality to exclusively cultural or economic factors is simplistic and reductionist. As Eva Bellin explains in her insightful essay titled "The Robustness of Authoritarianism in the Middle East": "Cross-regional and cross-temporal comparison indicates that democratization is so complex an outcome that no single variable will ever prove to be universally necessary or sufficient for it. Any notion of a single pre-requisite of democracy should be jettisoned."[20] Similarly, Yahya Sadowski has a tongue-in-cheek list of prerequisites for democratization:

> There are dozens of theories about what factors promote democracy. A country may be more likely to become democratic if it becomes richer, or redistributes its wealth in an egalitarian manner, or specializes in manufacturing consumer durables, or rapidly converts its peasantry into proletarians, or switches to a nuclear family structure, or gets colonized by England or converts en masse to Protestantism.[21]

Bringing Politics and Governance Back in

The most sensible way to bridge the gap between culturalism and structuralism is to focus on the primacy of politics and governance, without minimizing the importance of economic and cultural factors as critical contributors to the political environment. As we will see in the following chapters dealing with Turkey, the Sunni–Shiite divide, and the rise of ISIS, governance provides a key political and institutional approach to democracy that supersedes religion. My approach to governance centers on three concepts: security, capacity, and legitimacy.

Good governance requires institutional and political power for a state to govern within the framework of rule of law, without creating security, capacity, and legitimacy gaps. To govern effectively, the state must provide not only basic security for its citizens. It must also have enough economic capacity to ensure their welfare. Finally, the state must enjoy some level of political legitimacy in the eyes of the people it governs. Each of these concepts, and particularly the first two, security and capacity, are interdependent. In addition to the symbiotic relationship between security, capacity, and legitimacy, there is also some sequential hierarchy between these objectives.

As far as sequencing and prioritization are concerned, the state's most critical function is to protect the life of its citizens. If we were to rank security, capacity, and legitimacy in terms of "vital" priority for citizens, security would always come first. A state that is unable to provide the basic safety and security of its citizens is either a failed or failing state. Security, in that sense, is like oxygen—the sine qua non—for governance. To understand the critical importance of security, we need to remind ourselves of the most basic definition of a state. The most cited Weberian definition of the state is "a human community that claims the legitimate monopoly on the use of physical force within a given territory."[22] As we will discuss shortly, the ability of the state to provide security therefore depends not only on its effectiveness to monopolize the use of coercion but perhaps more importantly to do so, ideally, in a legitimate way.

A state that is unable to secure the monopolization of violence because of civil war, ethnic insurgencies, separatist violent movements, armed militias, or even mafia activities is by definition a weak, failed, or failing state. In failing or failed states there is anarchy and chaos. In such states, humans facing the breakdown of order can no longer rely on state institutions to protect them from chaos, anarchy, and violence. As a result, they turn to primordial instincts and affiliations such as family, clan, tribe, or sect. They do so with the goal to organize some level of protection and solidarity for survival.

Despite the central importance of monopolizing violence, security is not the end of the story. In fact, it is only the beginning as far as a state's ability to provide governance is concerned. Once security is established, the next challenge is capacity. Capacity is primarily about the economic power and capability of the state to provide basic services such as water, electricity, public health, roads, and education. Ideally, in later stages of capacity, such services enable citizens to reach employment opportunities and upward mobility in a productive economy. The ability of a state to provide such capacity depends on its institutional and economic power. Capacity thus constitutes a crucial part of governance. States with no economic capacity to provide basic infrastructure and services for their citizens are by definition weak states that sooner or later also face security problems.

This is why capacity and security are interdependent. The security imperative of good governance in fact requires a certain basic level of fiscal capacity. The reason is simple. Providing security requires economic capacity and a bureaucratic organization. Take the example of law enforcement as the most basic way of protecting the life and property of citizens. A police force that will enforce public order is at the heart of what we call the monopoly of the state to use coercion. Establishing a police force requires fiscal power to recruit, train, and pay the salaries of this security bureaucracy. Unless the country has natural resources owned by the state, the fiscal power of the government primarily comes from one source: taxation of the citizenry. And tax income is significant only if there is economic productivity and capacity in the country. This is why security and capacity are mutually reinforcing in the achievement of effective governance. In short, to establish security, the state needs capacity.

Finally, after security and capacity, there is the third layer of governance: legitimacy. Legitimacy is primarily about political dynamics in the country. Some states achieve order and security at the expense of individual rights and liberties. They often turn into police states. They lack representative, transparent, accountable institutions. If the security they provide is based solely on coercion and the capacity they achieve comes thanks to natural resources, the state may gain some level of legitimacy. But it may never qualify as strong state with good governance because its institutions are not inclusive, and the system is repressive. In that sense, good governance depends on how security and capacity are achieved. A state that resorts to brutal suppression of political dissent is not necessarily a strong state. Achieving security while respecting human rights and individual liberties is a much better predictor of state power.

The nature of the relationship between citizens and governing authority is therefore at the heart of legitimacy. To achieve legitimacy, the state needs to provide security with "legitimate consent," ideally based on a social contract that defines the rules of the game. This agreement need not be based on a Western-style parliamentary democracy. What matters is the presence of inclusive institutions with procedures and mechanisms for power-sharing. Legitimacy, in that sense, requires a rule-based system, inclusion of citizens in decision-making, and the accountability of rulers. At the end of the day, good governance depends on whether a state can combine security and capacity with inclusive and accountable institutions that ensure the legitimacy of the system.

The rule of law is often the most crucial component of good governance.[23] It is also the best assurance the state can offer its citizens for their security, prosperity, and freedom. An independent and impartial justice system, where rulers are not above the law and the state can enforce rules and provide justice in a timely, fair, and judicious manner, provides legitimate governance. This is why accountable and transparent systems based on a social contract between citizens and rulers, where taxation and representation impart legitimacy to the whole enterprise, qualify as strong states with inclusive institutions. In sum, to achieve good governance, a state needs to think of security, capacity, and legitimacy as interdependent and mutually reinforcing layers. The "right" balance between all three depends on whether the state has consensus-based, legitimate, and inclusive institutions that provide security and welfare.[24]

Democracy versus Liberalism

How do states achieve this national consensus that creates legitimacy? For the West, this is where good governance meets democracy. Democracy enables the political representation and participation of citizens in the decision-making process. It is primarily a political and institutional process based on clearly defined procedures, rules, and mechanism. The debate on Islam's compatibility with democracy, however, is not about these political and institutional elements. It is about culture and religious tradition for the culturalists and about economic development and modernization for structuralists.

Bringing the concept of good governance to this polarized debate on democracy has multiple advantages. First, while democracy is a Western invention, good governance is based on the universal criteria of security, capacity, and legitimacy that all states would like to achieve. Second, because governance is primarily about politics and institutional arrangements based on power-sharing, it transcends cultural and economic determinism. Focusing on the primacy of politics is therefore the best way to bridge the gap between the entrenched camps of cultural versus economic determinism.

Once politics and governance are recognized as the primary factors behind democratization, we can focus on procedures and institutions that create political legitimacy. What is the best way to include the voice of citizens in governance? Is there a mechanism to hold decision makers accountable? How is political legitimacy achieved?

The short, yet imperfect, answer to all these questions is a simple one: democratic elections. Free and fair elections, allowing citizens to determine who will govern, play a crucial role in legitimizing political power. Understandably, most states that seek legitimacy see elections as a shortcut to a democratic system. Yet, like most shortcuts, equating democracy with elections is problematic. Although they are crucial, elections alone are hardly sufficient for the *institutional* development and procedural functioning of a democracy. They ensure popular participation and majority-rule. But there is little they can do to guarantee that the elected will not turn their mandate into a "tyranny of the majority." This is where the difference between democracy and liberalism becomes important.

While democracies are often obsessed with elections, liberalism, in the classical European sense of the concept, is about the rules of the game that limit state power. Liberalism does that thanks to constitutional checks and balances and a constitutional system that safeguards individual rights and liberties. An independent judiciary that protects the rule of law is the bedrock of constitutional liberalism. The protection of rights and liberties—such as freedom of speech and assembly—against arbitrary state power becomes possible only when such checks and balances are in place. In liberal systems, the separation of the executive, legislative, and judiciary powers provides the best guaranty against the tyranny of the majority.

A free media and a strong civil society are also critical elements of liberal democracy. The media's ability to function independently from state control and supervision forces governments to become accountable and transparent. All these checks and balances go well beyond an elementary understanding of electoral democracy that crowns victors with unlimited political power. In other words, liberalism is primarily about limiting state power with established norms. It stands against elected dictatorships that will sanctify the ballot box without paying much attention to individual freedoms, minority rights, the rule of law, accountability, and transparency. Bereft of such mechanisms and liberties, electoral democracies can degenerate into populist, illiberal, majoritarian systems where the state, the sovereignty of the nation, or the will of the people is glorified at the expense of individual rights and liberties.

It took centuries for constitutional liberties and the rule of law to emerge in the West.[25] And in the meandering journey toward universal suffrage, constitutional liberalism always preceded electoral democracy. In other words, it was liberalism first, democracy later. Before free and fair elections became the norm, constitutional systems restricted the power of monarchs with clear rules, rights, and freedoms. European political systems evolved very slowly from constitutional and parliamentary liberalism to popular electoral democracy. Elections with the extension of the right to vote to all citizens represented the culmination of a nonlinear path of political, social, economic and cultural evolution.

This bumpy road to democracy often took violent and revolutionary turns with major totalitarian, dictatorial, fascist, populist, and illiberal detours. Wars, industrialization, economic and social modernization, class struggle, civil rights movements, and the quest for gender and racial equality were all parts of the epic journey from constitutional liberalism to electoral democracy. The empowerment of all citizens—not just white and male property owners—with the right to vote was the culmination of this long democratic adventure with many stops along the way. And constitutional liberalism was probably the most important one. When liberalism and electoral democracy finally converged in Western Europe and the United States, the emerging liberal democracies already had one or two centuries of constitutional and parliamentary foundations. It was these political and legal foundations that provided checks and balances within the rule of law against arbitrary state power.

In the non-Western world, however, such sequencing from liberalism to democracy often remains absent. Most new democracies did not go through the same incremental and sequential process that characterizes the emergence of liberal democracies in the West. This perhaps explains why many young democracies, from Turkey to Thailand, from Argentina to Hungary tend to be illiberal political experiments where individual rights and liberties, the rule of law, institutional checks and balances, and separation of power between executive, legislative, and judiciary forces are either absent or at their infancy.

The political system in such a context may still have all the trappings of a democracy: the ballot box functions, elections are held, and the majority is represented in the parliament. But individual rights and liberties, such as freedom of speech and assembly, are not protected. The media is muzzled. The judicial system is neither independent nor impartial. It often protects the state from citizens rather than individuals from an autocratic government. In short, institutional checks and balances are absent, political and economic corruption is rampant, and the rule of law is cosmetic. Elections may still take place. But they are not free and fair because there is no freedom of speech and assembly. And even when the majority wins, minority rights are absent. The will of the people and the sovereignty of the nation are glorified at the expense of individual rights and liberties.

The Arab Deficit in Democratization

Why is this debate on governance, security, capacity, legitimacy, and liberalism important for the question on the compatibility of Islam and democracy? We have so far analyzed the primacy of political institutions and observed the limits of cultural determinism. If religion and culture are not the primary drivers of democratization, we must still find a satisfactory answer explaining the absence of democratic institutions and governance in some parts of the Muslim world. More than the Islamic world at large, which contains many democracies, there seems to be an Arab exception to democratic governance.

Turkey, Bangladesh, Pakistan, India (with its large 200 million Muslim minority), Indonesia, and Malaysia are important electoral democracies of the Muslim world. Almost all have illiberal and sometimes outright autocratic tendencies. Yet, almost all of these countries have also political systems where who governs is determined by democratic elections. This is why despite their illiberalism they still qualify as electoral democracies. And perhaps most importantly, combined, these countries represent around half of the Muslim population in the world. This fact alone should disqualify culturalist arguments about the incompatibility of Islam and democracy.

But our objective is not to prove that Islam and democracy are compatible. Instead, the main contention of this chapter (and the book itself) is that we are overstating Islam in our analysis of democratization. Religion is not the main problem when it comes to prospects for democratization. And it would be a logical fallacy to interpret the presence of democratic systems in certain Muslim countries as evidence that Islam is compatible with democracy. Instead this situation should help us understand the fact that the democratization of these Muslim countries has much more to do with political institutions and governance than with Islam.

On the other hand, the debate on Islam and democracy continues to polarize the world because there seems to be a problem in the Arab core of the Islamic world. The democratic deficit in the Arab world is a fact. But, once again, the question is whether this autocratic blockage in the Arab world is caused by Islam. Before we tackle this question, it is worth remembering that the path to democracy, rule of law, and good governance is always tortuous. Even when the "right" security, capacity, and legitimacy dynamics seemed to be in place during the first half of the twentieth century, the rise of autocratic, fascist, communist, and totalitarian governments in the West has led to two world wars that cost the lives of more than 80 million people.[26] When we complain about the agonizingly slow journey toward democracy in the Arab world, it is therefore useful to remember that Europe's own trajectory from enlightenment to the Industrial Revolution and from liberalism to democracy took several centuries.

It is with such modesty that we should approach the puzzle of the Arab democratic deficit. When the Cold War came to an end, the new wave of political change caused a significant increase in the number of countries with democratic electoral systems. By 1995, the world had 117 countries qualifying as electoral democracies, up from only 74 countries in 1990.[27] The Arab world, on the other hand, had a striking resistance to democratization. When the Arab Spring began in 2011 there were a critical mass of democracies in every major world region except in the Arab Middle East. Lebanon was the only Arab country that qualified as a democracy. Iraq, after the US invasion, was another exception that proved the rule. In short, as Eva Bellin notes, "while the number of countries designated free by Freedom House has doubled in the Americas and in the Asia-Pacific region, increased tenfold in Africa, and risen exponentially in Central and East Europe between 1970 and 2002, there has been no overall improvement in the Middle East and North Africa."[28]

Did the Arab Spring of 2011 change the autocratic blockage in the Middle East? The sad reality about the Arab Spring is that it failed to produce successful transitions to democracy, let alone liberal democracy. With the exception of Tunisia, where there is some room for optimism in terms of inclusive power-sharing arrangements, the rest of the region remains autocratic, illiberal, and, in the case of Syria, Libya, and Yemen, mired in bloody civil wars. The situation in Egypt, the largest Arab country often considered the regional bellwether, is far from promising. A bloody military coup ended the illiberal democratic experiment under the Muslim Brotherhood in 2013, only one year after Islamists came to power by winning the first democratic election in the history of the country.

Why has the Middle East and North Africa failed to democratize at the same rate as the rest of the world? Multiple factors explain the longevity and robustness of authoritarianism in the Arab world. The list is long. The most often cited reasons include the effectiveness of repressive coercive structures against political dissent; the weakness of civil society; the absence of constitutional traditions and institutions protecting individual rights and liberties; the presence of state-controlled, oil and gas-fueled economies; income disparity; high illiteracy rates; patriarchal political cultures strengthened by autocracy, tradition, and religion; and an international world order that puts a very high premium on regional stability. Islam has only limited relevance in this list and it is far being the main problem. It is also clear that there is no single deterministic cause but a combination of political, social, economic, cultural, and strategic factors explaining the survival of autocratic regimes in the Arab world.

Many of the dynamics that fuel authoritarianism in the Middle East are also present in other parts of the world. Political, economic, social, and cultural impediments in Africa, Asia, and Latin America are not that different than the ones in the Arab world. In that sense, the countries in the Middle East are not unique in "their poor endowment with the prerequisites of democracy."[29] Yet, almost half of the countries in sub-Saharan Africa, the vast majority of countries in Latin America, most of East Asia, as well as important states like India, Pakistan, Bangladesh, Vietnam, and Indonesia have transitioned to democracy. An examination of their democratization journey reveals that despite sharing common characteristics with the Middle East, none of these countries suffered from the simultaneous presence of all the obstacles to democratization, which tragically is the case in the Arab world.

In other words, what makes Arab autocracies truly exceptional is not their shared religion but the concurrence of almost all the economic, political, cultural, and strategic factors that favor autocratic stability. From repressive coercive structures and weak civil society to the absence of constitutional traditions, and from state-controlled resource-rich economies to high illiteracy rates and patriarchal political cultures, almost all major obstacles to democratization appear to be simultaneously present in the Middle East.

This unfortunate predicament is compounded by the fact that the region is of crucial geostrategic and economic importance for Western powers and their security interests. For Europe and the United States, the presence of oil, the imperative of counterterrorism cooperation with autocratic regimes, and the delicate balance of the Arab–Israeli conflict are all geostrategic and geo-economic factors to put a premium on regional stability in the Middle East. The Arab revolutions of 2011 did not fundamentally change this picture. It became clear to Western powers that the alternative to autocratic stability in the region is not peaceful transition to liberal democracy but at best the arrival of political Islam to power and at worst civil war, as in the case of Syria, Libya, and Yemen, where jihadist terrorist groups find safe havens and plot attacks targeting Europe and the United States. Tunisia's relative success and stability seem to be an exception that proves the norm.

Under such circumstances why would the West not support the autocratic status quo in the Arab world? The alternatives of political Islam, civil war, and failed states leading to refugee problems and immigrants flocking to the West are not particularly desirable from the European or American point of view. It is within this dual context—international as well as domestic and regional—that the robustness of Arab autocracies needs to be analyzed. Repressive Middle Eastern regimes not only have the coercive capacity and political will to use force in order to maintain autocratic stability. They also have international support in doing so. This lethal combination of domestic and external factors impeding democratization sets the Middle East apart from other parts of the world.

Arab states also appear to have perfected the art of coercion as the most effective part of their autocratic statecraft. Regime survival is top priority for most Arab rulers. Their capacity and will to use coercive measures to crush dissent is a daily reality. The highly efficient secret police and domestic intelligence of these regimes are not bound by the rule of law. As Larry Diamond summarizes in his article titled "Why there no Arab Democracies?":

Although the typical Arab state may not be efficient in everyday ways, its *mukhabarat* (secret-police and intelligence apparatus) is normally amply funded, technically sophisticated, highly penetrating, legally unrestrained, and splendidly poised to benefit from extensive cooperation with peer institutions in the region as well as Western intelligence agencies. More broadly, these states are the world leaders in terms of proportion of GNP spent on security.[30]

The Fiscal Power behind Autocracy

This leads us to the question of fiscal power behind autocracy. Asked in simpler terms, where is the money coming from? The financing of security establishments depends on the overall fiscal capacity of Arab states. In the absence of industrialization, high productivity, and competitive markets, most Middle Eastern states have to resort to internal and external rents to make ends meet. Internal rents often accrue in the form of natural resources, through direct state control over energy revenues. External rents are primarily about foreign and military assistance that the region receives because of its strategic importance. The majority of the Arab states are what political economists call "rentier" states that depend heavily on energy revenues or strategic rents.[31] Such "unearned" income enables fiscal capacity to finance the omnipresent police force.

Oil and gas income has enabled a significant number of Arab states to develop and maintain strong intelligence services and militaries to coerce their populations. Dependence on energy income not only stifles capitalism and entrepreneurial productivity, but perhaps most importantly it also becomes a monumental obstacle for democratization. The reason has to do with the organic link between taxation, representation, and democracy. Simply put, energy-rich countries with no history of industrialization or capitalist development seldom need to tax their citizens. The state already owns natural resources and most of the economic output. National energy companies represent the majority of the economic, productive, and financial capacity in the country. Under such conditions, there is no need or incentive for imposing an effective taxation system on the citizenry.

Historically, the trajectory of democratization in the West shows a strong correlation between taxation and representation. As Samuel Huntington puts it: "The lower the level of taxation, the less reason for publics to demand representation. 'No taxation without representation' was a political demand; 'no representation without taxation' is a political reality."[32] Such dynamics based on politics and political economy has nothing to do with Muslim culture or Islam. The absence of democratization in energy-abundant countries is a global fact. Just look at the political situation in Venezuela where dependence on oil revenues combined with bad governance continues to fuel authoritarianism and political instability. Successful rentier states prefer to co-opt their "subjects" rather than establish organic links with "citizens" that may lead to demands for accountability, transparency, and representation.

Under such circumstances, the civic consciousness expressed in the phrase "I am a tax paying citizen, I have rights and expectations" does not resonate with the political economy of energy-rich states in the Middle East. Moreover, most rentier states are insecure about their economic and political future because they depend on commodity prices in a world where energy prices constantly fluctuate. This perhaps explains also why rentier states are heavily policed and centralized. In the absence of accountability and transparency, they are also corrupt and bereft of any semblance of the rule of law.

Yet, not all Arab countries have abundant oil and gas resources. In the absence of internal rents, this is where "external strategic rents" become highly critical for regime survival. For energy-poor Arab states, foreign aid and security assistance become a substitute for oil income. During the Cold War, external support for Arab regimes came as a result of proxy competition between the United States and the Soviet Union. Today, support for Arab stability comes mainly from Europe and the United States. Many Arab states, such as Egypt, Jordan, and Morocco, are heavily dependent on such external rents to provide the two fundamental elements of governance: security and capacity. Legitimacy, the third element of governance, is often missing in the absence of effective taxation, economic productivity, accountability, and transparency. For many Arab states, dependence on foreign aid and military assistance is like oil. It is unearned income, unrelated to productivity or taxation. It flows into the central coffers of the state and enables the coercive capacity of repressive structures. It also often creates corruption in the hands of bloated public sectors and large bureaucracies.

Finally, another method for autocratic regime survival in the Arab world is cosmetic liberalism or the ability to create a semblance of political space for dissent. Cosmetic liberalism is a common method for regime survival for states that lack natural resources to abundantly finance repressive capacity. Unable to finance generous welfare states like the ones in Gulf monarchies, these states resort to political overtures that create the illusion of political participation. About half of the Arab regimes fall in this category of "liberal autocracy." Repressive political measures in these relatively liberal autocracies are selective. The regime tolerates superficial mechanisms of representation, consultation, and accountability in order to co-opt certain critical segments of society.

Parliaments of cosmetically liberal autocracies have no real power to legislate, supervise, or control their national budget since real political power resides with hereditary kings and presidents. As Daniel Brumberg argues: "Liberalized autocracy has proven far more durable than once imagined. The trademark mixture of guided pluralism, controlled elections, and selective repression in Egypt, Jordan, Morocco, Algeria, and Kuwait is not just a 'survival strategy' adopted by the authoritarian regimes, but rather a *type* of political system whose institutions, rule, and logic defy any linear model of democratization."[33]

Such systems have the additional advantage of being more adaptive to domestic political circumstances as well as external dynamics occasionally pushing for change. There is an ebb and flow between heavy-handed methods of full repression and more moderate policies allowing sham elections creating the illusion of inclusion. Egypt, Jordan, and Morocco are masters at this game of liberalized autocracy where the narrative of "controlled reforms" is highly convenient in order to avoid genuine democratization. The goal becomes to pursue modernization and economic development without democratization.

Finally, in addition to all these domestic political and economic obstacles to democratization, the regional strategic environment that fuels very high defense spending also contributes to Arab autocratic longevity. The delicate regional balance of power between Saudi Arabia and Iran, proxy wars, the security of the Persian Gulf, and sectarianized conflicts are major contributors to regional instability. With the highest military expenditures per capita in the world, these precarious security dynamics come at the expense of social and economic development and democratization. In addition to the intra-Arab and Arab–Persian dimension of regional tensions, the Arab–Israeli conflict further complicates the predicament.

The genuine anger and frustration that the plight of Palestinians generates are often exploited by Arab regimes and their state-controlled media to fuel anti-Israel and anti-American propaganda. Arab regimes are masters of channeling their citizens' attention away from domestic challenges to regional problems such as the Israeli occupation of Palestinian lands and the endless expansion of Jewish settlements in the West Bank. Many analysts and policymakers, especially in the United States, believe that Arab autocracies are not really interested in a peace process that would solve the conflict because such an outcome would deprive these regimes of a very convenient tool to distract their populations.

The Arab–Israeli conflict is important for another reason. It is one of the main factors, together with the presence of oil and the need to maintain strong counterterrorism cooperation, why the West puts a premium on regional security and stability over unpredictable change in the Middle East. The presence of friendly Arab autocracies that no longer pose a militarily challenge to Israel's security is critically important for the United States. Even the European Union which has a more pro-Palestinian approach to the conflict has no appetite for Islamist political parties that will reap the benefits of postauthoritarianism. The stability of autocracies such as Jordan, Egypt, Saudi Arabia, the United Arab Emirates, Morocco, and Algeria is therefore as important for Brussels as it is for Washington. The stake may even be higher for a European Union given geographic proximity and the risk of a massive flow of immigration and political refugees. At the end of the day, the risk of postautocratic instability, the balance of power between Iran and Saudi Arabia, the fragile peace between Israel and its neighbors, the need for predictable oil prices, the imperative of security and antiterrorism cooperation with autocratic Arab states against jihadist networks, and the fear of immigration are all critical factors that explain American and European support of the status quo in the Arab world. There seems to be simply no Western appetite for the risky postautocratic dynamics of democratization.

Conclusion: It's the Institutions, Stupid

What does all this imply? The answer is clear: the argument that Islam and democracy are not compatible overstates the role of religion at the expense of almost all other critical drivers of democratization. The fact that many Muslim countries have experience with democratic politics should put the orientalist argument that Islam is the problem to rest. Religion-centric attempts at explaining democracy are inevitably reductionist. Christianity does not explain why Europe and the United

States are democratic and Judaism does not explain why Israel is a democracy. Yes, religion can certainly play a role in shaping the political culture of countries. But even then, we have to recognize that there are very different interpretations of religion, depending on social, political, economic, and educational backgrounds of citizens. Contextualization is therefore key if we are to avoid the easy trap of sweeping generalizations.

Instead of focusing on Islam with cultural or religious determinism or on economic dynamics with structural determinism, we should therefore avoid determinism altogether and acknowledge that multiple factors play a complex role in transitions to democracy. Democracy primarily requires effective political institutions and a division of labor between state and society. The latter requires a social contract, often in the form of a constitution. More than an agreement on a set of values, democracy is about internalizing a set of rules. Instead of cultural determinism, it is about politics and the primacy of institutions. Good governance (security, capacity, legitimacy), rule of law, constitutional liberalism, and power-sharing mechanisms are much more useful metrics and analytical tools than culture and religion for the study of democracy.[34]

At the end of the day, the contentious debate on Islam and terrorism, just like the equally polarizing one on Islam and democracy, generates more heat than light because of the limits of cultural and civilizational explanations. The primacy of politics, governance, and institutions is the place to start for an objective analysis. Countries that manage to establish the rule of law with institutions that are inclusive rather than extractive have a distinct advantage in terms of providing sustainable security, democracy, and prosperity for their citizens. To be sure, culture and religion can be relevant in the emergence of political institutions. But they are far from being the determinant forces. Their role is within a larger context of multiple social, political, economic, legal, and institutional factors. Most importantly, neither religion nor culture are static, immutable, eternal forces. They evolve as political, economic, and social conditions change.

Ultimately, any attempt to analyze terrorism or democracy in the Middle East needs to go beyond a single-minded focus on Islam, Muslim culture, and Islamic theology. Religion, culture, identity, and especially political culture are part of a much larger set of political and economic problems of the Middle East. But ever since the Clash of Civilizations turned into a self-fulfilling prophecy, the West has been obsessed with Islam at the expense of all other dynamics. This false diagnosis of the predicament creates false assumptions, which in turn guides dangerously counterproductive policies. This is a vicious cycle that exacerbates the polarization between the West and the Middle East. Anti-Muslim sentiment in the West generates anti-Western resentment in the Islamic world, which only exacerbates the Western fear of Muslims. To end this vicious cycle, the West needs to stop seeing Islam as the main problem. Political scientists have a responsibility to explain to larger audiences that the root causes of terrorism, autocracy, and underdevelopment are primarily political and institutional.

Radicalism, violence, and autocracy in the Middle East are products of political dysfunction and failure in the security, capacity, and legitimacy realms. In that sense, governance is the real problem. In the words of Yahya Sadowski: "It is long past time for serious scholars to abandon the quest for the mysterious 'essences' that prevent democratization in the Middle East and turn to the matter-of-fact itemization of the forces that promote or retard this process."[35] In this chapter, we have seen how political institutions, not mysterious cultural essences based on religion or pure economic dynamics, hold the key to good governance. The primacy of politics will become clearer in the next chapters on Turkey, the Sunni–Shiite divide, and the ISIS. As we will see, in each of these three cases, governance, politics, and nationalism are much more important drivers than Islam.

2 TURKEY

Turkey may seem like an odd place to start analyzing Western tendencies to overstate Islam. After all the Turkish Republic is not a "typical" Middle Eastern country. Turkey is not only the oldest democracy in the Islamic world but also the most Westernized country in the Muslim Middle East in terms of its institutional, political, and cultural norms. The founder of the modern Turkish Republic, Mustafa Kemal Atatürk, was a staunch secularist and nationalist who admired the French Revolution and the philosophers of the Enlightenment. As a military hero turned revolutionary modernizer, his legacy has been the top-down Westernization of Turkey. Like most ambitious projects aimed at radical social transformation, the Kemalist cultural revolution of the 1920s and 1930s was hardly democratic. The motto of Atatürk's single-party political regime was "For the people, despite the people." But once the country transitioned to a multiparty system in 1946, electoral competition became a permanent fixture of Turkish politics.

Despite frequent military interventions—in 1960, 1971, 1980, and 1997—and the deeply patriarchal and illiberal nature of the political system, Turks regularly went to the polls. The meddlesome generals made sure it would be civilians, not men in uniform, who run the country. Political power has therefore changed hands more than a dozen times through relatively free and fair elections between 1946 and today. Despite the current trend toward autocratic rule, such regular, peaceful alternation of power makes Turkey a democratic success story compared to most of its Muslim peers. Turkey is also exceptional among Muslim countries thanks to its place in the transatlantic alliance. It is a member of NATO, of the Council of Europe, and has been knocking on the European Union's door for decades in an elusive quest for membership. The country has an export-oriented capitalist economy, vibrant middle class, and a relatively strong civil society. With their glorious imperial past and strong state tradition, Turks are fiercely nationalistic. Yet, at the same time they are highly ambivalent about their place in the world. At the crossroads between Europe and Asia, Turkish identity seems geographically and culturally anchored in civilizational uncertainty.

All these factors differentiate Turkey from conventional dynamics of Middle Eastern authoritarianism and create uniquely "Turkish" problems that defy easy categorization. There is no shortage of complexity and paradox in Turkey's illiberal democracy, civil–military relations, Kurdish conflict, economic dynamics, societal polarization, rivalry "within" its Islamic camp, multifaceted foreign policy, and recent trend toward autocracy. However, such complexity is often overlooked in Western circles where the lazy dichotomy of "Islam versus secularism" dominates all things Turkish. For instance, today, as the strongman of the country, Recep Tayyip Erdoğan, and his Justice and Development Party (AKP) turn increasingly more authoritarian, many equate the notion of this Turkish divergence from Western values and democracy or the fear of "losing Turkey" with the idea of an Islamic revival.

Western media loves to portray Erdoğan as an incurable Islamist who is determined to overhaul the secularist legacy of Atatürk. As we will see, such overstatement of Islam and obsession with secularism often miss the immense role that nationalism plays in Erdoğan's policies in uniting religious conservatives as well as secular progressives. The Islam versus secularism dichotomy also tends to create a simplistic mental map that equates secularism with a liberal democratic Turkish past that actually never existed. This reductionist disconnect makes Turkey a great case for analyzing the Western overstatement of Islam.

The Father State

Most of the challenges facing Turkey require an open-minded and nuanced analysis of the country's illiberal state tradition and political culture, governance challenges, institutional problems, multifaceted identity, and political history. These are all complex issues that go well beyond "Islam and secularism" as the binary polarization in the country. It is my contention that such overstatement of Islam leads to erroneous assumptions and conclusions about Turkish politics. The real problem in Turkey is not Islamization but authoritarianism fueled by an illiberal state tradition supported by both secularists and Islamists.

The state tradition of Turkey is deeply nationalist, patriarchal, and illiberal.[1] Secularists and Islamists are equally nationalist in their approach to the Kurdish question and to relations with the West. Therefore, instead of overstating Islam, or the clash between Islamists and secularists, we should pay more attention to nationalism, illiberalism, and authoritarianism as the main drivers of Turkish politics. Nationalism is a particularly powerful political force because it often unites Turks from different ideological backgrounds and has more explanatory value in describing what is going on in Turkey than religion.

The lens of Islam versus secularism is practically irrelevant in Turkey's growing frustration with the United States and Europe. Today, ultrasecularist circles in Turkish society are even more resentful than Islamists toward the West. What unites the two camps is angry nationalism. The Kurdish question, which remains the most important political challenge in the country, is another example where the meta-narrative of Islam versus secularism explains very little. If anything, the Kurdish problem shows how much Turkish Islamists and Turkish secularists have in common, as they both embrace Turkish nationalism. Analysts, therefore, make a major mistake when they reduce their strategic analysis to a binary "secular pro-Western" Turkey versus an "Islamist anti-Western" one. In fact, not too long ago, the "Islamist AKP" was more pro-EU and pro-American than the "secular" Kemalists. It is increasingly clear that such overstatement of Islam has led many observers to miss the critical role that nationalism continues to play as a major driving factor uniting almost all Turks.

The pitfalls of overstating Islam are not confined to foreign policy. Similar tendencies are at play in domestic politics as most observers fail to see what lies behind Erdoğan's political victories. Erdoğan has not been winning elections after elections since 2002 because conservative masses strongly support his Islamist message. Turkish citizens, like most voters, prioritize bread-and-butter issues over ideology. According to most polls consumer confidence, rising prosperity and purchasing power, and improvements in social and economic services are primary predictors of AKP's electoral success. This is why, more than political Islam, the question of governance—with its security, capacity, and legitimacy dimensions—needs to be studied much more closely in order to correctly analyze the performance of the AKP and the evolution of Turkey under Erdoğan since 2002.

Finally, the fratricide within the Islamic camp between the AKP and the Gülen movement, which culminated with the failed coup of 2016, has nothing to do with the rivalry between Islam and secularism. Instead, it is purely and simply a competition for political power. In short, the beloved "East–West" or "Islam versus secularism" analysis that dominates American and European debates comes at the expense of other powerful systemic drivers such as nationalism, illiberal democracy, and political economy. All these dynamics make Turkey a highly rewarding case to analyze the fallacy of overstating Islam.

At the end of the day, we have to remember that Turkey is an extremely dynamic country where the main "narrative" explaining political developments needs constant revision. Recent developments, ranging from the debilitating intra-Islamic power competition to the political support ultranationalist and anti-Western secularists are giving to Erdoğan, or from Turkey's military incursion in northern Syria to the rapprochement between Ankara and Moscow, all deserve a fresh analysis that goes beyond the stale narrative of Turkey based on Islam, secularism, and civilizational identity.

As we embark on a more accurate perspective, it will be also helpful to correct some misperceptions about both secularism and Islam in Turkey. In many ways, the very reason why Turkey was until recently seen as a success story was because of such misperceptions. Not too long ago, the world admired Turkey as a country where Islam, secularism, and democracy seemed to display a rare, harmonious coexistence. Since the model was portrayed in such terms, the West naturally paid a lot of attention to the balance between Islam, democracy, and secularism. What went wrong with this Turkish model? Has Turkey's slide toward autocracy proved that Islam is not compatible with democracy and secularism? As we explore the answer to these questions, we will see that Turkey's troubling journey from "successful Muslim model" to an "Islamist autocracy" has more to do with an illiberal state tradition, bad governance, and populist nationalism than the clash between Islam versus secularism.

Deciphering Turkish Politics and Identity

There are legitimate reasons behind Western fascination with Turkey's place in the world. A complex civilizational identity or being perceived as a "torn country," using Samuel Huntington's terminology, is nothing new in Turkish history.[2] The difficulty of assigning Turkey to a specific geographical region or to a wider civilization derives from the fact that it had always been a frontier country. A glance at the map shows why Turkey does not fit into any of the clear-cut geographical categories that Western scholars have formulated in order to study a complex world. The country straddles the geographical and cultural borders between Europe and Asia, without really belonging to either.

Geography, on the other hand, only partly explains why most Turks see themselves in a unique category. Historical and political factors play an even stronger role in Turkey's "in between" identity. The Ottoman Empire was historically the intimate enemy of Europe. In religious and military terms, the "Terrible" Turk represented the "other" who played a crucial role in consolidating Europe's own Christian identity. However, as centuries of imperial splendor came to an end and territorial regression began, the Ottoman elite sought salvation in one of the earliest projects of modernization and Westernization. Turkish modernization was pragmatically identified with Europe and the West.

There was no real attempt to distinguish modernization from Westernization. In that sense, Turkey was not Japan. Modernization did not mean adopting just Western technology. Western civilization had to be imported wholesale. Especially in the eyes of the Young Turks, the most ardent supporters of Europeanization during the last Ottoman decades, Western culture, laws, dress, calendar, and alphabet were all seen as elements of a single package. In an ambitious drive to import European civilization, Atatürk's republic abolished the caliphate and disposed of the Arabic alphabet, Islamic education, and the Sufi brotherhoods. It adopted Western legal codes from Germany, Italy, and Switzerland, together with the Latin alphabet and the Western calendar, Western holidays, and Western measuring systems.

The country's official history and language were also reworked. A new education system glorified pre-Islamic Turkish civilizations at the expense of the country's more recent Ottoman past, and many Arabic and Persian words were purged to create an "authentically" Turkish vocabulary. Even the Arabic azan, the Islamic call to prayer, was translated into modern Turkish. The traditional Ottoman headgear, known as a fez, was banned as men were encouraged to wear European-style hats. Similarly, women were discouraged from wearing the Islamic veil. The newly adopted

Western legal codes established gender equality and granted the right to vote to women.

Despite such ambitious reforms, however, Kemalist modernization and Westernization barely infiltrated Turkish society at large. The absence of mass social mobilization behind such reforms was obvious. There was an unmistakable sense of social engineering taking place in Ankara, disconnected from the conservatism in the Anatolian heartland. While the rural and pious masses remained largely unaffected by the cultural engineering taking place in Ankara, it was the military, the government bureaucracy, and the small urban bourgeoisie that adapted most readily to Kemalist Westernization. In short order, the cultural gap between the Kemalist center and the Anatolian periphery had become insurmountable. As Atatürk's Republican People's Party's (CHP) slogan from the 1920s put it, the Turkish government seemed to rule "For the People, Despite the People."[3]

The Peculiarity of Turkish Secularism

Although Kemalist Westernization seemed to go hand in hand with secularist reforms, the Kemalist definition of secularism was highly problematic. Instead of instituting a legal framework where the state would stand in equal distance to all faiths, Turkish secularism did not separate religion and state. Discrimination against non-Muslims gained new and highly paradoxical aspects for a system claiming to institutionalize secularism. Sunni Islam remained the only religion officially recognized by the state and came to be integrated in the governmental bureaucracy of the new republic. In other words, in a remarkable pattern of continuity with the Ottoman state tradition, Turkish secularism saw no problem in accepting Sunni Islam as a de facto "official" religion for the state.

As a result, instead of becoming a constitutional principle based on separation of religion and state, Turkish secularism turned into a social symbol, mimicking a "European" way of life. The sartorial and symbolic aspect of a Western lifestyle passed as secularism. Consumption of alcohol, Western attire, gender issues, the headscarf, and even the preference for classical music and opera over "*alla Turca*" music have become crucial markers of a "secular" way of life associated with civilized, Western norms. As these sartorial, symbolic, and stylistic matters turned into superficial markers of secularism, the concept of secularism lost its fundamental raison d'être: to build a legal wall of separation between the realm of politics and the realm of religion and to ensure that the state would not discriminate based on religion.

Turkish secularism failed to establish a separation between state and Islam for two reasons: historical path dependency combined with political expediency. Kemalist secularism never questioned the deeply rooted Ottoman state tradition of political control of Islam. Atatürk's autocratic and patriarchal approach to politics was in perfect continuity with the imperial norms established during the Ottoman centuries. Such continuity made the emergence of checks against the hegemonic state control of political, cultural, social, and economic dynamics in the country almost impossible. To the contrary, Atatürk's vision of secularism took this Ottoman tradition of state hegemony a step further and maintained an even firmer control over Islam because it considered conservative religiosity as a threat to be contained and neutralized.

Islam, after all, could easily turn into a counterrevolutionary force against Westernization. More fundamentally, the Kemalist revolution saw in Islam the causes of social, cultural, political, and economic stagnation. In that sense, Islam was an impediment to Westernization and modernization. As we will see later, it turns out Kemalism itself had a very strong tendency to overstate Islam in a manner similar to orientalism. Kemalism thus conceptualized secularism as state control of religious affairs, in perfect historic harmony with Ottoman state tradition.

Secularism as Nation-Building

In addition to antimodernism, a perhaps more challenging aspect of Islam was its objection to nationalism. After all, the concept of nation-state was anathema to Islam and its theological ideal to transcend all tribal, ethnic, and sectarian divisions. The Muslim faith seeks the unity of all believers—the ummah—under one state, the caliphate. This made Islam, in the eyes of Kemalism, a major impediment to Turkish nationalism and Turkish nation-building. Secularism and secularization were therefore conceived as an effective way to control, co-opt, and preempt Islam. There was no other way to promote Turkish nationalism without clashing with religion. In the Kemalist context, effective secularism thus required strong political control of Islam. Secularism became part of a heavy-handed social engineering project to build a nation-state. It also served to shape and tame Islam in order to make it "safe for nationalism."

Atatürk was a realist. Having realized that eradicating Islam altogether was not a realistic option, he tried to promote a "civilized" version of it at the service of citizenship and nation-building. Instead of formally separating state and religion, modern Turkey thus monopolized religious functions and incorporated religious personnel into the state bureaucracy. To this day, the government-controlled Directorate of Religious Affairs (DRA) supervises and regulates Islam throughout Turkey. It appoints and pays the salaries of the country's imams and issues standardized sermons at the service of good citizenship and civic duties to be read out in thousands of mosques each Friday. The DRA president is appointed by the Council of Ministers upon the nomination by the president. With hundreds of offices (*muftuluk*) at the province and subprovince levels, this governmental institution is in charge of administrating and supervising all religious institutions and services. The DRA is also entrusted with political authority over the instruction of men of religion. The teachers, textbooks, and curricula of all religious schools are under the supervision of the DRA and the Directorate-General of Religious Education, a branch of the Ministry of Education.

The instrumentalization of religion was particularly apparent in textbooks used in the education of Islam. For instance, as early as in the late 1920s, a certain number of clerics were commissioned to compose new books of religious teaching adapted to the requests of the Kemalist authorities. One of the most prolific authors of that time was Ahmet Hamdi Akseki, president of the DRA. In the numerous pedagogical works that Akseki composed for the education of religion, he prescribed the love of the fatherland, obedience to orders, zealous work, strict compliance with military rules, respect for the Turkish flag, submission to the laws and to the state requirements, sacrifice of one's life for the safety of the nation, and so on.[4]

Other textbooks published during that period aired identical prescriptions: a Muslim truly worthy of that name had to love his country, pay his taxes regularly, respect the laws of the republic, submit to the progressive guidance of the state officials, do his utmost to learn modern techniques, apply scrupulously the principles of good hygiene, consult a doctor in case of illness to avoid being the cause of epidemics, and work energetically for the development of the country.[5] In short, the main responsibility of a Muslim was to become a model citizen.

Educational institutions such as the Schools for Preachers and Chiefs of Prayers (*Imam Hatip okullari*) were also opened with similar objectives.

It is important to note that such instrumentalization of religion in Turkish nation-building is related to the "social engineering" aspect of Kemalism. Out of an Anatolian community that defined itself primarily on religious terms, what had to be produced was a sense of secular Turkish national identity. In fact, Turkish secularism becomes logical only when analyzed in the framework of "nation-building" and "Westernization from above." For instance, in 1928, the government established a committee to reform religious life in accordance with the precepts of reason and science. The committee under the leadership of Mehmed Fuat Köprülü, a prominent historian, declared that "Religious life, like moral and economic life, must be reformed on scientific lines, so that it may be in harmony with other institutions."[6] It recommended that people should not take their shoes off in the mosque, the language of the worship should be in Turkish, and the prayer times should be adjusted to the needs of the work day, and it called for the introduction of Church-style pews and music instead of Koranic recitations.[7]

Secularism as Muslim Nationalism

These reforms were not implemented due to the fear of public reaction. The ideas of the report, however, facilitated the vernacularization of the language of Islam from Arabic to Turkish. For example, in early 1928, the first call to prayer in Turkish language instead of Arabic was aired in Istanbul. In short, it is important to note that in such a critical juncture of Turkish history, secularism represented much more than a constitutional principle separating state and religion. It was perceived as a crucial component of the "imagined" Turkish nation. Once secularism is conceived as Turkish nation-building it naturally gains a very political dimension at the expense of what should be its most important legal dimension: enforcing the state's neutrality toward religion.

Therefore, in addition to maintaining a firm grip over Islam, Turkish secularism made no attempt to create a legal and political framework where the state would be in equal distance to all faiths and religions. To the contrary, by embracing Turkish nation-building and Turkish nationalism as the ultimate objective, the Kemalist republic discriminated non-Muslim citizens of this supposedly secular state. For instance, making a farce of the concept, the rapidly modernizing and Westernizing "secular" Turkey embarked on its nation-building of the 1920s and 1930s by firing all of its non-Muslim (Armenians, Greeks, and Jews) citizens from government jobs.

Ironically, the secular Turkish Republic turned out to be much less tolerant toward its non-Muslim minorities than the "Islamic" Ottoman Empire. Unlike secular Turkey, the Islamic Ottoman Empire employed high-level civil servants and diplomats (even ambassadors) of Jewish, Greek, and Armenian origin. To this day, Turkey does not have a single non-Muslim diplomat, military officer, or high-level civil servant in its state bureaucracy. This situation stands in contrast to many Middle Eastern countries that are supposedly less secular and democratic than Turkey. For instance, the only UN Secretary-General that hailed from the Muslim world was Egyptian diplomat Boutros Boutros Ghali who happened to be a Coptic Christian. This Turkish paradox of secularism that discriminates citizens of non-Muslim background not only proves that Turkish identity is still associated with Islam, but more importantly, for the purpose of our study on the fallacy of the "Islam versus secularism" dichotomy, it also shows that Turkish secularism is in fact not that secular.

Under this warped understanding of secularism, the nationalistic drive of the modern Turkish Republic saw no paradox in its discrimination of non-Muslims. Despite their official acceptance as citizens, Jews, Armenians, and Greeks could never be accepted as loyal members of the nation. Under this supposedly secular model of Turkish governance, non-Muslims were therefore deemed to be insufficiently Turkish because they failed to pass a de facto "religion" barrier. This is the context of the so-called secular system of Turkey where "authentic" Turkishness and loyalty to the state are still associated with being Muslim. As a result, in modern Turkey, nationalism and nation-building remained more than in harmony with Islam. Islam and Muslim faith became a prerequisite for acceptance as Turkish.

All this should give pause to those who insist on using the lens of "secularism versus Islam" as a major dividing line in Turkish politics. Secularism in its Turkish context, it turns out, has no problem with Islam being the quasi-official religion of the country and the primary marker of Turkishness. Turkish secularism has also no problem with the fact that religion and state are not separated. What is left of secular principles in this Turkish context is not surprisingly very shallow. Turkish secularism is reduced to cosmetic "Western" symbols of lifestyle and culture. With a state that controls Islamic affairs and discriminates its non-Muslim citizens, the secularism of the Turkish Republic therefore fails to qualify as truly secular. Instead, it paradoxically promotes a type of Muslim nationalism by considering all Muslims within national borders as Turks and all Turks as Muslim. This pattern of Muslim nationalism is in remarkable continuity with the Ottoman "*Millet*" system that considered only Muslims as first-class citizens.

The paradox of Turkish secularism puts into question the standard narrative of modern Turkish political history, which sees a major rupture between the Ottoman Empire and modern Turkey. This narrative of "secular Turkey turning it back to its Islamic Ottoman past" goes a long way in explaining why "Islam versus secularism" remains to this day such a powerful dichotomy in analyzing Turkish politics. This binary framework misses what both the Islamic Ottoman Empire and the secular Turkish Republic have in common: a patriarchal state tradition that controls religion. It is this very phenomenon that needs to be analyzed in detail to understand the real driving force behind Turkish politics: a state tradition that is highly illiberal and autocratic. In other words, transcending Islam versus secularism as the defining dichotomy of Turkish politics requires a proper understanding of a strong state tradition that established hegemony over both Islam and secularism. This is the topic we are turning next.

Islam under State Control

The Turkish Republic inherited from the Ottoman Empire a long-standing tradition of "raison d'état," which often amounted to state hegemony over religion. In the Ottoman context, such political supremacy over the religious realm was made possible thanks to the incorporation of the Islamic establishment into the administrative apparatus of the empire. In remarkable continuity with Ottoman patterns, secularism in modern Turkey maintained this pattern of firm political and administrative control over the religious establishment. This historical continuity of state-controlled religion in Turkey left no room for a strong clash between secularism and Islam. Instead, what emerged was the integration of state and religion under a powerful bureaucratic framework determined to shape the nation. As we will see, this hegemonic state tradition continues to be a much more powerful driver than religion in fueling autocratic and illiberal dynamics in Turkish politics.

Turkey's hegemonic state tradition has deep roots. Ottomans derived from their Central Asian origins the belief that the state subsisted through the maintenance of a code of laws laid down directly by the ruler. In doing so, the Sultans identified political power with legislative power. This Central Asian and Persian heritage of Turkic states played an important role in the development of an Ottoman tradition of absolutism based on Sultanic fiat, which often went beyond what Islamic laws allowed. Historically, Turkic states managed to effectively control Islam because their state tradition predated the birth of the Islamic faith. In other words, unlike in the Arab world, where Islam's arrival with Prophet Mohammed in the seventh century created a centralized state structure, Turkic tribes from Central Asia already had a tradition of centralized power before converting to Islam at the turn of the millennium. Their conversion to the Muslim faith was not instrumental in establishing the Turkish state tradition.

In the classical institutional structure of the empire, the absolute nature of Ottoman political power took its starkest form to the extent that all civilian, military, and religious officials were at the mercy of the Sultan. The state's ownership of the land and the presence of a centralized system of taxation were additional dimensions of Ottoman absolutism. Such a political and economic framework of centralist absolutism was essentially designed to hinder the development of uncontrollable feudal structures challenging central authority.[8] These Ottoman–Turkish dynamics have prevented the emergence of individual private property rights as well as the rise of alternative sources of political and military power challenging the hegemonic, patrimonial state. Social, political, economic, and religious forces that could potentially turn against the state were deemed dangerous and conducive to debilitating violent conflict.

In the context of Europe, however, competition for power in a decentralized context of authority became historically unavoidable. Feudalistic challenges to central authority, the emergence of legal private property rights, and the conflict between church and state all played a critical role in the emergence of capitalism, constitutionalism, secularism, and liberalism. These dynamics and institutions remained absent in the Ottoman context. As a result, hegemonic rule faced no powerful institutional checks and balances.

Religion, in this centralized Turkish political and economic context, served to legitimize state power in ways pre-Islamic faith systems could not. The new faith came with means of social control and a codified belief system that proved much more appropriate than the mystical and esoteric world of Shamanism for the functioning of patrimonial states.[9] As a result, Turkish states like the Seljuk strongly encouraged conversion to Islam and began to defend its core values. Similar dynamics characterized the Ottoman approach to Islam. Faced, at the time when they were trying to consolidate central authority, with a mix of unorthodox sects, potentially subversive Shiite communities, and unruly nomadic tribes, Ottoman rulers felt the need to establish some form of political control over religion. As Islamic values took their hold over Ottoman society, the *Sharia*—the religious law of Islam—emerged as a sort of "social contract" between the state and its Muslim society. In that sense, an Islamic moral and legal framework came to play an important role in supporting the patriarchal machinery of the state. In other words, devout Sultans began to consider the Ottoman realm not only as a family affair but also as an Islamic establishment that had to be ruled with fairness.

Yet, the founding dynasty remained reluctant to allow Islam the power to determine the political and legal limits of state power. Given the mobilizational power of religion in the wrong hands, even the *ulema*—the guardians of Islamic Law—could become suspect in the eyes of Ottoman rulers.[10] With such a cautious frame of mind, the Ottoman answer to all potential threats coming from nomadic and tribal groups was to establish bureaucratic control over the religious establishment. In that sense, the Ottoman Sultans considered their patrimonial authority over the guardians of Islamic orthodoxy as a natural extension of state supremacy. Since the religious personnel functioned as a bridge between state and society, it was not surprising that they were subject to central surveillance. Moreover, in order to preempt any Islamic objection and to avoid political confrontations with religious functionaries, the *ulema*'s loyalty to the Sultan was of crucial importance.

Yet, behind this seemingly despotic sovereignty over religion, a moral framework provided a protective shield over Ottoman subjects. This moral framework was defined and legitimized by the religious obligations of the state. This religious understanding, in the words of Serif Mardin, amounted to a "tacit social contract" that took its inspiration from the Islamic concept of *hisba*—the concern for a good and just order. Accordingly, an Islamically required "principle of the pursuit of the good" provided certain social, economic, and political safeguards against tyranny and defended the life and well-being of ordinary citizens.[11] The Sultans truly believed that the rightful application of religion generated consent and social harmony and therefore tried to avoid confrontation with the religious class. In that sense, the political center was clearly aware that the legitimacy that underpinned the Ottoman political system owed a great deal to Islam. Religion, under such circumstances, became the key to maintaining political hegemony with societal consent and harmony.[12]

The characteristic features of this mutually beneficial relationship between the *ulema* and the state involved integration and subordination. "High" and "proper" Islam, represented by the *Seyhulislam* (sheik of Islam) at the top of the religious hierarchy, was incorporated into the state apparatus. The livelihood of the *Seyhulislam*, like the rest of the religious class, was granted by the state and the Sultan determined the path he traveled in his career. The *Seyhulislam*, as the supreme religious official and head of the judicial system, sat on the Imperial Council. However, despite his high position within the state hierarchy, like all government officials, he could be easily dismissed during any serious conflict with the Sultan. The case of a *Seyhulislam*, who in 1702 tried to obtain for himself the position of grand vizier and paid with his life for his presumption, clearly illustrates the point.[13] Beyond such effective subordination, integration between state and religion was achieved at the judicial level thanks to a wide network of judicial and administrative positions staffed with district judges (*kadıs*) trained in Islamic law.

Ottoman Secularism and Turkish Islam

State hegemony over Islam under the Ottoman system created "secular" patterns of legislation. Ottoman Sultans often enacted laws outside the realm of Islamic sharia, based on political rather than religious principles. And when Islam and the Ottoman Empire's raison d'état clashed, the latter always prevailed. Such Ottoman raison d'état was in historical continuity with the previously mentioned Central Asian–Turkic precepts of *Yasa*, the origins of which went back to before Genghis Khan. Accordingly, the Sultan could make regulations and enact laws entirely on his own initiative. These laws, independent of Islamic legal codes and known as *Kanun*, were based on political rather than religious principles and were enacted primarily in the spheres of public, administrative, and criminal law as well as state finances.

Given the supremacy of the state over the religious realm, it is not hard to imagine that the Ottoman religious establishment excelled in the intellectual exercise of fitting the *Kanun* within the proper Islamic framework. Most of these laws were later formulated as *Ferman*—sultanic decree. Not surprisingly, *Fermans* always contained a formula stating that the enactment conformed to Islamic law. This allowed the imperial state to claim that Islamic precepts are always respected and integrated in decision-making. It created a sense of unity and harmony between Islam and state, which was expressed in the official motto describing the Ottoman political entity as *"din-ü devlet"*—"religion and state." The message conveyed was that one could not be imagined without the other; the state was conceived as the embodiment of religion and religion as the essence of the state.

In that sense, the Ottoman state had achieved the Koranic ideal of unity of state and religion. This functional integration of political and religious power gained further legitimacy after Sultan Selim (1512–20) captured the caliphate and allowed Ottoman Sultans to wear the spiritual mantle of the successor of Prophet Muhammad. In this framework of unity of state and religion, orthodox Islam had only narrow opportunities to develop into a source of opposition. In the eyes of the Ottoman religious establishment, the legitimacy of the state came from its ability to protect the Islamic realm. Therefore, endangering the state, by definition, meant endangering Islam and made that movement heretical. As a result, in contrast to what was going on in Western Europe, there was no Ottoman equivalent of confrontational relations between state and church. Secularism, as separation between religion and state, is a product of such confrontation in the West. The absence of separation or confrontation between the state and Islam in the Turkish context helps us understand the peculiarity of Turkish secularism, as the state maintained hegemonic control over Islam.

The Kemalist drive for Westernization and nationalism readily grafted itself onto this long-standing tradition of Ottoman hegemony over religion. There was much more continuity than change in the way the secular republic maintained its control over Islam. In fact, Westernization and nationalism increased the stakes in maintaining such control because religiosity was now perceived as a counterrevolutionary force against the nationalistic ideals of the new republic. It is critical to emphasize that what distinguished Kemalist secularism from Ottoman patterns was not the incorporation of religious establishment within the state apparatus but the Turkish Republic's determination to base its legitimacy on nationalism. The sultanate and caliphate had to be abolished because they were prenational Islamic and imperial institutions inhibiting the development of a Turkish national identity, which still had to be invented.

In their attempt to generate a collective sense of Turkish national identity, the founding fathers did not wish to be deprived of the potentially constructive role a "civic" and reformed kind of Islam could play. Since the pious Anatolian masses were likely to react against Ankara's secularist reforms, an instrumentalist approach toward religion, reminiscent of Ottoman patterns, had considerable appeal to pragmatic Kemalists. In that sense, what had to be formulated was a "Turkish Islam" in accordance with a new "Turkish nation." In practice, this meant placing a reformed and nationalized type of official Islam at the service of citizenship building. Not surprisingly, such a plan rendered an effective separation of state and religion all the more difficult. As previously stated, the need to control Islam was compounded by the fact that Kemalist founding fathers saw in Islam the causes of social, cultural, political, and economic decline during Ottoman times.

Similar to Western orientalists, the Kemalists had an essentialist view of Islam. They saw Islam as a regressive force and an all-encompassing way of life. Secularism, as a result, had to be envisioned as a way of life too, instead of a political or legal principle based on the separation of religion and state. What the Kemalists feared most was the exploitation of the Islamic realm by those who wanted to mobilize the rural masses against Westernization and nationalism. This is why the "secularist" Kemalist republic wanted to control Islam even more effectively than the "Islamic" Ottoman Empire. This Kemalist perception of Islam as the binding factor and common denominator of all counterrevolutionary threats to the republic rendered a placid separation of the political and religious realms politically unrealistic. The stakes, therefore, were existential. This was a zero-sum game, with either the state dominating religion or Islam overtaking the state. Separation between Islam and state in this context of continuity between Ottoman Empire and Kemalist republic was not only undesirable but also essentially unachievable.

Turkish Nationalism as the Unifier of Islam and Secularism

Under these circumstances, the monumental challenge facing Atatürk was not to establish a secular state that controlled and co-opted Islam. Such "secular" norms based on raison d'état, as we explained above, were already inherited from the Ottoman state tradition. Missing in this new Kemalist drive for modernity and Westernization, however, was something that needed to be imagined and constructed anew and with urgency: the Turkish nation. While secularism existed in some shape or form in the Ottoman context, the idea of a Turkish nation-state had to be invented. Nationalism rather than secularism set apart Kemalism from Ottoman patterns of governing. Soon after Atatürk declared the abolition of the sultanate and caliphate, the monumental challenge of Turkish nation-building became the republic's top priority.

Nationalism had also proven to be a monumental challenge for the last century of Ottomans. In fact, it caused the end of the empire. Like most dynastic and multinational imperial rulers, the Ottomans were reluctant to fully embrace a nationalism of their own as long as they had a cosmopolitan, multiethnic empire to protect.[14] Ethnic nationalism was an existential threat for Ottoman domains. Yet, it spread like a virus after the French Revolution of 1789 and proved impossible to contain. The *millet* system of the Ottoman domains was based on a confessional rather than ethnic compartmentalization of non-Muslim subjects. This arrangement was essentially a non-assimilative order of cohabitation, which allowed non-Muslims to retain their religious, educational, and judicial autonomy. In that sense, it never encouraged Muslims, Christians, and Jews to share a common Ottoman ethos. And faced with the nationalist contagion, Istanbul's angry imperial instinct was to find a way to hold the empire together rather than promoting ethnic Turkish nationalism. More than Turkish nationalism, it was the same sense of imperial panic that led Ottoman military officers to brutally crush separatist nationalisms.

The sick man of Europe, as the empire was known, suffered an agonizingly long death. Its existence was prolonged thanks to the geostrategic rivalry between Britain and Russia. During the last century of imperial decline, almost all nations under Ottoman rule—Greeks, Serbs, Bulgarians, Albanians, Arabs, and Armenians—embarked on separatist journeys toward national independence. Adopting a nationalistic project of its own would have been counterproductive for the Ottoman ruling elite since it still nurtured delusions of holding the multinational empire together with futile attempts at Ottomanism or pan-Islamism. While the former failed to inspire non-Muslims (Greeks, Bulgarians, and Armenians) who pursued their separatist journeys, the latter foundered on Albanian and Arab nationalism.

Turkish nationalism came to be adopted in this context of Ottoman territorial loss and demographic transformation. It was the last nationalism of the empire. Having emerged as a reaction to imperial disintegration, it had a sense of delayed zeal, vindictiveness, and urgency. It was a product of almost 150 years of decline, military humiliations by Western powers, and apprehension of Western support for Christian ethnic minorities at home. It also came into being in an environment where multiethnic projects of the imperial ruling elite failed to instigate any sense of Ottoman patriotism. One can argue that this nineteenth-century image of the Ottoman Empire, unable to reverse separatist dynamics and fighting for survival, continues to torment the contemporary debate regarding Turkey's national unity. For instance, the current nationalist tendency of Turkish Islamists and secularists to assess the Kurdish problem along conspiratorial lines, with constant references to the Sèvres treaty of 1920, which partitioned what was left of the Ottoman Empire among victors of the First World War, perfectly illustrates this deeply rooted "survivalist" dimension of Turkish nationalism.[15]

During the long reign of Abdul Hamid II (1878–1908), who is considered the last of the powerful Ottoman Sultans and a strong promoter of pan-Islamism, intellectual discussions over concepts of Turkism had already begun. The ones who unambiguously identified with Turkishness mostly came from the mixed communities of border regions. Often sandwiched between Russia and the Ottoman Empire, these Turkish speaking communities constituted an ethnically conscious minority. Armenian and Greek nationalism also played a similar role in raising the ethnic consciousness of Turkish communities in the Balkans and Anatolia. The emergence of nationalism in one community of the empire often triggered a domino effect with reactions in other ethnic communities and helped the consolidation of the image of the "other" as a major point of reference for self-definition. Atatürk's predecessors in the Young Turk movement of the Committee of Union and Progress were ready and willing to adopt a nationalist agenda before the empire totally disintegrated in the wake of the First World War. Yet, it took the end of the empire and the shattering of all hope of multiethnic Ottoman survival for Turkish nationalism to become an official project.

The ethnic and religious composition of the newly established Turkish Republic in 1923 was substantially more homogeneous than the pre-1914 Ottoman population, due to substantial territorial and demographic loss during the First World War. The de-Hellenization of Anatolia, in the wake of the 1919–22 War of Independence and the 1924 population exchange with Greece, was almost complete. The Armenian population of Anatolia was also decimated as a result of deportations and massacres that culminated with the 1915 Genocide. Non-Muslim populations were mostly extinguished (with the exception of Istanbul where a large Greek minority was exempted from the population exchange with Athens) but the newly born state under Mustafa Kemal still had large non-Turkish Muslim communities. Beginning with the mid-nineteenth century Anatolia received a steady flow of Muslim ethnic refugees emanating from the Balkans and the Caucasus. This is why in today's Turkey there are probably more Turkish citizens of Bosnian, Albanian, and Chechen backgrounds than the total populations of Bosnia, Albania, and Chechnya.

The formation of a Turkish nation-state required the assimilation of these non-Turkish Muslims into Turkish identity. It is quite telling that the word *millet* came to be used to conceptualize the Turkish nation— *Türk milleti*. The *millet* concept had the great advantage of appealing to both Islamic religious identity and Turkish national identity. It came to be employed in a manner that suggested a national identity, which incorporated all the Muslim groups of different ethnic backgrounds under a Turkish umbrella. Starting with the War of Independence (1919–22) this expression was used with increasing frequency by Mustafa Kemal who needed to use Muslim identity and the mobilization of Islamic resistance against Christian invaders. Islam and Muslim identity served to mobilize the materially and morally depleted Anatolian communities that were in a state of uninterrupted warfare since the Balkan War of 1912. The fact that Greeks and Armenians, two large Anatolian Christian minorities, were now seen as enemies also facilitated mass mobilization. Especially in Eastern Anatolia, the demobilization of the Ottoman army and the potential return of Armenians was a dreadful scenario that had to be avoided at all costs in the eyes of Turkish and Kurdish Muslim communities that seized Armenian land and wealth.

The Independence War and the struggle of Anatolian soldiers to save their own villages rather than distant Ottoman lands go a long way in explaining the sense of survivalist instinct that to this day colors Turkish nationalism. The War of Independence also crystallized the image of the Greeks and Armenians as familiar enemies in the Turkish nation-building process. They were the enemy within and the object of Turkish nationalist resentment and distrust. And not surprisingly, they were also seen as infidels by pious masses. This made the inclusion of a non-Muslims in a civic Turkish national identity practically almost impossible. This important factor is an additional reason why Turkish secularism failed to become a political principle that stands in equal distance to all faith groups. The proclamation of a militantly secular Turkish Republic did nothing to change the public distrust of all non-Muslim minorities. Discriminatory governmental policies that gave an implicit ethnoreligious dimension to nationalism in Kemalist Turkey remained behind the façade of laicism.

In the newly established secular republic, religion therefore continued to play a thinly disguised role in determining what can be cynically called "the level of Turkishness." Muslim minorities had an easy path to Turkishness since their Muslim identity greatly facilitated their integration and assimilation into the Turkish polity. For non-Muslims, however, even devotion to the Turkish nation and the warm embrace of Turkish nationalism would not be sufficient to pass the test of "authentic Turkishness." As Bernard Lewis argues, "One may speak of Christian Arabs, but a Christian Turk is an absurdity and a contradiction in terms. Even in the secular republic, a non-Muslim may be called a Turkish citizen, but never a 'Turk.'"[16] In that sense, non-Muslim groups (Greeks, Armenians, and Jews) are, even today, called Turk only in respect of citizenship but not nationality.

As a result, Turkish nationalism preserved a religious dimension behind its secular façade. Thanks to its pragmatic nature, Turkish nationalism was flexible and the relationship between ethnicity and Islam underwent opportunist fluctuations. For instance, "Islam and the Caliphate" was the rallying banner during Atatürk's War of Independence. In accordance with the Islamic understanding of religious community (ummet), ethnicity was deemphasized in the formulation of the "National Pact" borders. In the implementation of the population exchange with Greece, religion rather than language and ethnicity became the real criterion.[17] Similarly, in the early 1930s, the request of the Christian Orthodox Gagauz Turks to emigrate from Romania to Turkey was turned down by secular and Kemalist Turkish officials on the grounds that the Gagauz communities were Christian.[18]

The secular Turkish Republic perceived all Muslim ethnic communities as natural members of the Turkish *millet* but discriminated against the non-Muslim minorities. For instance, starting with the early years of the republic, Christians and Jews were excluded from military schools and academies. Not only public sector hiring policies officially began to discriminate against non-Muslims but also certain state organization such as the Turkish Railways and the Anatolian Press Agency laid off their non-Muslim personnel.[19] Moreover, in 1939, soon after the outbreak of the Second World War, the government mobilized all Jewish, Greek, and Armenian males between 18 and 45 years and sent them to special camps in Anatolia.[20]

However, the most systematic governmental discrimination against non-Muslim minorities occurred in the framework of the 1942 Wealth Tax (*Varlik Vergisi*), which targeted those people who allegedly made excessive wartime profits.[21] Although the tax was supposed to be levied without any discrimination, in practice it was almost exclusively used against non-Muslims. Due to the absence of proper standards, non-Muslims had to pay an arbitrary amount that often corresponded to a substantial part of their total wealth. Defaulters—all of them Greeks, Jews, or Armenians—were deported to labor camps in eastern Anatolia. Needless to say, the 1942 Capital Tax law came as a shock to the non-Muslim bourgeoisie of the "secular" republic who painfully experienced the religious discrimination involved in the implementation of economic nationalism.

It is also important to keep in mind that Islam remained the strongest common vocabulary in the social and political life of Anatolia long after the establishment of the secular republic. Like their Ottoman predecessors, the Kemalists exceled at co-opting religion for political ends. Moreover, very few of the founding fathers were atheists opposed to religious solidarity as an additional dimension of Turkish nationalism. What they wanted to achieve was the modernization of Islam, a sort of *Turkish Muslim reformation* rather than the total de-legitimization of Islamic identity. At the same time, it is not very surprising that the cold logic of secularism and positivism had a hard time generating a sense of moral community. Islam came to complement Turkish nationalism in such a context. The association of being Muslim with being Turkish was also at the heart of establishing institutions like DRA that helped Turkish nation-building.

The Kurdish Problem

The Kemalist objective to create a Turkish nation-state faced violent opposition from ethnic Kurds. Unlike other non-Turkish Muslim communities of Anatolia—Albanians, Bosnians, Chechens, Georgians, Circassians, and so on—Kurds were indigenous and demographically the majority in large parts of eastern Anatolia, historically known as Kurdistan. But Kurds had additional reasons to resist assimilation when the republic was established and Turkishness imposed on them. During the Ottoman times, their semi-autonomous principalities had deeply rooted feudal and tribal structures with almost no exposure to centralized authority. In a sense, there was a Kurdish exception to Ottoman centralized political control based on imperial taxation and military conscription. The mountainous geography of Kurdistan, which made centralized control virtually impossible, played an important role in the Ottoman decision to allow considerable autonomy for Kurdish lands. The rival Persian dynasty had a similar administrative arrangement with its own Kurdish tribes.

What kept the imperial center of Istanbul and Kurdish principalities together was a shared religion, Sunni Islam, and a common enemy: Armenian nationalism. Islam and the institution of the caliphate was a crucial religious bond between Ottomans and Kurds. And starting with the 1880s the threat of Armenian nationalism and separatism was a shared threat for both the imperial center of Istanbul and Kurdish tribes concerned about Armenian intentions in Eastern Anatolia. After the Kemalist republic was established in 1923, Kurdish tribes expected the new state to respect the principles established during Ottoman centuries. Yet, they soon discovered that the political context had radically changed.

The country was now under a new and staunchly nationalist management. The regional context had also changed considerably. The common enemy that united Istanbul with the Kurdish tribes—the Armenian threat—was no more. Call it genocide, deportations, pogroms, civil war, or massacres, the Armenian "problem" was tragically "solved." In addition to the new political environment, the religious context was also different. The institution that created an Islamic bond between the

Sultan and Kurdish feudal landlords, the caliphate, was abolished by Atatürk in 1924. With the caliphate and Armenian threat gone and a nationalist government determined to not only assimilate the Kurds but also to establish centralized rule, with direct taxation and conscription, most Kurdish tribes mobilized against Ankara. The era of Kurdish uprisings had begun.

Turkish nationalism unavoidably generated its mirror image as Kurdish dissidents started joining nationalist movements such as *Azadi* (Freedom) in eastern Anatolia. Even some of the assimilated Kurdish members of the Ottoman political and military establishment had a hard time remaining loyal to the new Turkish Republic.[22] It is significant that out of the eighteen anti-Ankara resurrections between 1924 and 1938, seventeen were of Kurdish origin.[23] To this day, Turkish history books explain these Kurdish rebellions of the 1920s as a British conspiracy rather than what they really are: a nationalist reaction to Turkish nation-building and Turkish state formation. The Turkish government had territorial claims over the Mosul province beyond Turkey's newly established borders in 1923. When the first Kurdish uprisings began in 1925, it was assumed that British forces instigated these Kurdish rebellions to convince Ankara that it would have a hard time controlling its own Kurdish territories, let alone claiming new ones in northern Iraq.

The supremacy of the new Turkish nation-state was finally established in Kurdistan only after the military violently crushed all the Kurdish uprisings during the 1920s and 1930s. All references to a land called "Kurdistan" were removed from maps and official documents, and Turkish names gradually replaced the names of Kurdish towns and villages.[24] During the years to follow, the Turkish state embarked upon a program of assimilation whereby the national education system and military service became primary instruments of "Turkification." This bloody chapter of Kurdish insurrections at the infancy of Turkish nation-building left major scars, however. It traumatized the young republic's military leaders and created their suspicion of all things Kurdish, which endures to this day.

The Kurdish issue also reinforced the feeling that the new nation would remain vulnerable to breakup and reinforced the Turkish suspicion of Western intentions. Turks are today very vigilant and suspicious of Western cooperation with Kurds because of memories of the 1920 Treaty of Sèvres when France, Britain, and the United States made plans to carve up the eastern Anatolian remains of the Ottoman Empire by establishing a Kurdish homeland adjacent to an Armenian state. Moreover, it is hard to deny that the Kurdish uprising led by Sheik Said in 1925 influenced the League of Nations' final recommendation for the inclusion of the Mosul province into Iraq, which was then under British mandate. However, there seems to be no evidence of British support for Kurdish nationalist uprisings after the proclamation of the Turkish Republic.

Kurdish nationalism was not something Britain particularly wanted to encourage. After all, Iraq had its fair share of Kurds with 20 percent of the total population. And the territorial integrity of Iraq was a British priority since official commitments were made in this direction.[25] Finally, the fact that Kurdish rebellions within Turkish borders continued long after the resolution of the Mosul question in 1926 supports the view that Kurdish insurrections erupted as a result of domestic dynamics rather than external provocation. Nevertheless, the alleged British role in the Sheik Said uprising continues to historically legitimize the conspiratorial views of many Turks regarding the role of Western actors in fomenting Kurdish nationalism. Today, the sight of American soldiers training Kurdish militia in the fight against the Islamic State in Iraq and Syria (ISIS) is a nightmare for Turkish nationalists who still believe Western powers are determined to harm Turkey's territorial integrity.

All these factors should help us understand why, from the mid-1920s until the end of the Cold War, Ankara denied the very existence of Kurds within its borders. For decades, Turkey sought to assimilate its sizable Kurdish minority, called "Mountain Turks" by authorities. Kurdish ethnicity and cultural rights were brutally suppressed. Any attempt to understand the existential threat Kurdish nationalism posed to Kemalist Turkey should take into consideration the traumatic effect that the Kurdish uprisings had on the nascent nation-state between 1924 and 1938. It is also this fear of separatism, firmly rooted in the still vivid Ottoman memory of imperial disintegration, that led the new republic to follow policies of forced assimilation and heavy-handed suppression of Kurdish dissent.

By the late 1920s it had already become abundantly clear that the Turkish Republic would tolerate no ethnic identity other than a Turkish one for its citizens. However, it is important to note that the Kemalist understanding of Turkish nationalism did not formulate an elaborate ethnic definition of "Turkishness." Instead, Atatürk wanted to define the fundamental elements of the Turkish nation in terms of a "territorial, linguistic and political unity strengthened by a sense of common roots, morals and history."[26] Although Atatürk's reference to common lineage and roots can be interpreted as having ethnic–racial implications, his popular maxim—"Happy is whoever says 'I am Turkish'"—seems to prioritize a personal and political identification with "Turkishness" rather than an ethnic or racial scrutiny of individual citizens. In that sense, "becoming Turkish" and assimilation always remained an option for the Kurds, or any-other non-Turkish Muslim ethnic group. Such civic definition of Turkishness, however, had no room for the inclusion of Jews, Armenians, or Greeks.

On the other hand, whenever the assimilationist and centralist efforts of the Turkish nation-state encountered active armed resistance, the authoritarian nature of the regime gained an ethnic Turkish dimension as well. Particularly during its first twenty years, facing mounting Kurdish armed resistance, Turkish nation-building gained an ethnic character. For instance, the Settlement Law of 1934 used an ethnic map of Turkey and implemented the deportation of dissident Kurdish tribes and sheiks to western and central Anatolia to ensure their assimilation.[27] Such policies of forced assimilation created a vicious cycle of repression and reaction in Kurdish provinces. The counterproductive nature of the Settlement Law became obvious when it also threatened previously loyal Kurdish tribes and contributed to a growing sense of Kurdish ethnic awareness. Ethnic unrest continued until the transition to multiparty politics after 1945. Yet, by that time, most of the Kurdish tribes had also realized that armed resistance against Ankara was futile.

Soon after the end of the Second World War, Turkey's political system, economic policies, and foreign relations underwent fundamental changes. The astute diplomacy of President İsmet İnönü, who replaced Atatürk after his death in 1938, played a major role in keeping Turkey out of the Second World War. However, political and economic discontent within the governing Republican People's Party (CHP) and among Anatolian society at large was clearly on the rise after more than two decades of authoritarian rule. The massive mobilization of the Turkish army during the war had created economic shortages and a major financial crisis. After more than two decades of single-party rule and with the Kemalist legacy institutionally enshrined, Turkish politics seemed ripe for change.

The international climate also played an important role in Turkey's transition to competitive politics. In April 1945, Turkey took part as a founding member of the United Nations in the San Francisco conference where it signed the UN's charter and committed to democratic ideals.

Most importantly, in the emerging Cold War dynamics, the Turkish leadership realized that it could no longer afford neutrality. Soon after the end of the Second World War, Turkey faced Moscow's pressure for border corrections in Eastern Anatolia and for the deployment of a Turco-Russian joint force in the straits. By the time the Truman Plan was declared and Turkey's inclusion in the Marshall Plan came to be accepted, Ankara had already taken steps toward the establishment of a pluralist democracy.

In many ways, the Cold War forced Turkey to enter the age of democracy. The new geostrategic dynamics of a bipolar world dictated Turkey's inclusion in the "West." Sharing borders with a territorially expansionist Soviet Union left no room for neutrality. Before long, Turkey had become NATO's southern bulwark against Moscow, and its credentials as an ally of the West were undisputed. In a Cold War world dominated by nuclear threats and a delicate balance of power, thorny questions concerning Turkey's military interventions, human rights standards, ethnic and religious identity were rarely raised. Turkey's two identity problems—its Muslim identity and the Kurdish question—were hardly relevant in the bipolar configuration of these decades. Ideology now trumped identity and Turkey easily passed the ideological test of "Westerness" by joining NATO and turning its back to Soviet Communism.

Illiberal Democracy under Military Guardianship

During most of the Cold War, Turkish politics witnessed ideological polarization and political instability. Closely associated with the Kemalist ideology, the military remained the most powerful and trusted institution in the country. In many ways, the military bureaucracy identified itself with the deeply rooted state tradition of Turkey. The generals favored a praetorian system and did not hesitate to intervene in politics almost every decade—in 1960, 1971, 1980–83, and 1997. Yet, they also made sure not to stay in power for any prolonged period of time, with the exception of three years after the 1980 coup. There was to be no Turkish equivalent of a military leader like Franco, Salazar, Pinochet, Suharto, Nasser, Assad, or Musharraf. In other words, no Turkish general stayed in power for decades by establishing a dictatorship.

The Turkish General Staff (TGS) never wanted to govern openly and directly because it saw itself above politics, as the protector of the state and the guardian of the Kemalist system. Having played a major role in drafting the 1961 and 1982 constitutions, the top brass believed each intervention had constitutional legitimacy in terms of safeguarding the Turkish Republic. The TGS's role was to make sure that the "realm of the state" would not be harmed by the political and ideological competition in "the realm of politics." Such duty-bound professionalism and reluctance to stay in power differed Turkish military interventions from their Latin American, Middle Eastern, African, Pakistani, East Asian, and Southern European equivalents.

Despite the military's reluctance to exert direct rule, this system of guardianship naturally failed to turn Turkey into a liberal democracy. Individual rights and liberties, effective institutional checks and balances, the independence of the judicial system, and freedom of speech and assembly remained either absent or at their infancy. The system, instead of protecting the citizens from a powerful state, was designed to protect the state from its citizens. Despite its illiberal imperfections, Turkey was still considered an electoral democracy. The will of the people came to be represented in power by competing political parties. Elections regularly took place and governments changed regularly within the realm of politics. In fact, during the 1960s and 1970s the country witnessed considerable instability and ideological polarization thanks to such democratic politics. The bipolar configuration of world affairs and the competition between left-wing and right-wing camps colored Turkish politics as it did in the rest of the democratic world.

In this polarized domestic context, new ideological divides veiled old identity problems. Turkey's Kurdish problem and Muslim identity did not disappear. Instead, Kurdish dissidents and religious conservatives positioned themselves in Turkey's newly emerging ideological landscape. Kurdish discontent found a place within Turkey's burgeoning socialist movement. Political Islam became part of the anticommunist struggle, first within the center-right and later in the 1970s within the more openly Islamist Nationalist Salvation Party. In that sense, right-wing and left-wing ideological dynamics masked Turkey's identity problems during the Cold War. The Kemalist system under military tutelage remained in place. But the political regime and electoral democracy had ample room for competition between the right and left. Populist conservatives established networks of patronage with religious communities and often embraced pro-market, private sector-friendly economic agendas. In the opposite camp, the party founded by Atatürk, the CHP, came to represent the progressive center-left. Identifying with more urban, Kemalist, and educated segments of society, the party maintained strong links with the military and civilian bureaucracy.

Despite their ideological differences, both left and right shared a strong attachment to Turkish nationalism. Tolerant of centrist politics, the generals were particularly vigilant about systemic threats of ethnic and radical ideological nature. The state needed to be protected from Kurdish separatism, communism, and extremist Islamism. The first coup, in 1960, ousted the Democrat Party (DP) that had ruled the country since 1950. During its 10 years in power, the DP won all elections with a conservative and populist message embracing rural masses. As the DP grew more confident and autocratic in power, the military grew increasingly impatient with the cult of personality built around the party leader Adnan Menderes. A pro-market and pro-American populist, Prime Minister Menderes identified himself and his party with the conservative values of Anatolia and the economic interests of the private sector. His agricultural and conservative constituencies opposed state-led industrialization. Although he never challenged Kemalism or the secular system, his brand of conservative populism posed an autocratic threat to the hegemony of military guardianship.

When the generals finally intervened in 1960 against the DP, they had the civilian bureaucracy and the urban intelligentsia on their side. The center-left Kemalist RPP was also supportive of the coup. After being deposed by the military intervention, Adnan Menderes was sentenced to death in 1961 by a military tribunal and executed for "subversion against the constitutional order." By 1962, however, the generals returned to their barracks and electoral democracy resumed under a new constitution. Written by pro-left-wing law professors, the 1962 constitution had progressive characters. It limited the power of the executive, strengthened the legislative body, and created more space for civil society. Adnan Menderes's DP was shut down but a new political party representing the conservative right quickly reemerged under a different name, setting a pattern for what would happen after each military intervention to banned political parties. In addition to establishing the guardianship role of the military in Turkish politics, the most important legacy of the coup was the counterintuitively democratic 1962 Constitution.

Left-Wing and Right-Wing
Polarization under Military Tutelage

Having realized that the 1924 Constitution drafted under Atatürk's single-party regime was conducive to autocratic rule, the military gave its blessing to the 1962 Constitution, which paved the way for more competition, pluralism, and eventually polarization in Turkish politics. Although the conservative right still managed to win most elections, the new electoral system created room for a divided parliament with proportional representation. The 1960s and 1970s also witnessed more robust left-wing movements in Turkey. Thanks to the protection of civil liberties in the 1962 Constitution, student and workers union, progressive civil society groups, left-wing publications, and even small socialist and communist parties became increasingly vocal in Turkish politics.

With pluralism leading to domestic political polarization during the next two decades, the TGS grew increasingly concerned about political instability and the potential rise of a socialist movement. Turkey, after all, shared a border with the Soviet enemy. The next two military interventions, in 1971 and 1980, had therefore strong anti-leftist tendencies. While 1971 was a "soft" coup, with the generals pressuring the prime minister to resign for failing to establish law and order, the coup in 1980 was a full-fledged military affair with lasting political consequences. Highly alarmed about the rise of political violence, anarchy, communism, and, most importantly, Kurdish dissent under a socialist umbrella, the generals banned all political parties, arrested their leaders, and revamped the political system. They stayed in power for three years and drafted the much more repressive 1982 Constitution.

The 1980 coup had long-lasting consequences, some continuing to this day. The most important one has no doubt been the worsening of the Kurdish problem. In the eyes of the Kemalist military establishment nothing was more important than the sacrosanct unity of the Turkish state. The alliance between left-wing groups and Kurdish nationalists was an existential threat that had to be crushed without mercy. Such heavy-handed repression, however, proved highly counterproductive and incited a major backlash in the form of a Kurdish nationalist uprising in eastern Anatolia. Instances of torture and killings in the Diyarbakir military prison between 1980 and 1983 helped plant the seeds of Kurdish ethnic separatism. Shortly after the generals went back to their barracks and electoral politics resumed in 1983, a formerly Maoist Kurdish movement, the PKK (Partiya Karkeran Kurdistan, Kurdish Workers Party), gained stronger regional following and launched a separatist insurgency.

Between 1984 and 1999, during its most intense years, the war against the PKK caused a death toll of 40,000 and cost close to $200 billion in military spending alone.[28] At the height of the insurgency in the mid-1990s almost half of Turkey's large army (around 400,000 troops) were deployed in the Kurdish southeast. As the Cold War was coming to an end, the Kurdish problem that traumatized the early decades of the republic was back with a vengeance. And to this day, the Kurdish problem remains the most intractable challenge facing the Turkish Republic. The consequences of Ankara's ongoing war with PKK have been much more devastating than polarization between Islam versus secularism in the country.

A quick look at Kurdish demographics can help us understand the nature of the challenge for Turkey. Around 15 to 20 million, the Kurds represent about 25 percent of Turkey's population. And of the approximately 35 million Kurds in the Middle East, about half live in Turkey. Despite such demographic weight, it took until the late 1980s for Turkey to officially acknowledge the sheer existence of the "Kurdish reality" in the country. Turkey's illiberal and nationalist state tradition is in great part to blame for this anomaly which to this day stands in the way of a peaceful and democratic solution. Turkey wasted many windows of opportunity on the Kurdish front. One of the most important ones presented itself under the leadership of Turgut Özal, who served as prime minister between 1983 and 1989 and as president from 1989 to 1993. Özal was a reformist on the Kurdish front and pushed for a political solution to the conflict with an open mind. Yet, the military and nationalist circles resisted any kind of compromise.

Despite the deterioration of the security situation in the Kurdish southeast, the 1980s was also a decade of economic liberalization for Turkey under Özal's reformist leadership. A US-educated pragmatic technocrat, Özal believed in market economics and neoliberalism inspired by the World Bank and IMF's "Washington Consensus." His center-right Motherland Party closed the chapter of public sector protectionism and import substitution industrialization. The privatization of state-owned enterprises, deregulation, export-led growth, and the liberalization of the financial and trade regime were all part of the Özal agenda. Turkey's convergence with global trends of Reaganomics and Thatcherism created room for more political and social opening as well. Özal was a strong believer that economic freedom would pave the road for more political freedom. His pro-Western foreign policy was characterized by an unabashed support for the United States in the first Gulf War and Turkey's renewed application to the European Union for full membership in 1987.

Perhaps the most important legacy of the Özal era has been the rise of an entrepreneurial conservative Turkish bourgeoisie. Came to be known as "Anatolian tigers," these export-oriented small and medium companies created their own financial networks and in time challenged the supremacy of the large industrial conglomerates based in Istanbul. This new business community was globally integrated but socially and culturally more insular and pious than the elites in Istanbul and Ankara. It was the same conservative economic groups that would support Recep Tayyip Erdoğan and his AKP by 2002, after the lost decade of the 1990s. In fact, the backing of Anatolian tigers proved crucial in helping the AKP shed its Islamist past and rebrand itself as a pro-market and pro-Western conservative democratic party. But economic and political dynamics turned much worse during the 1990s before they got better under Erdoğan.

The Lost Decade

After the death of Turgut Özal in 1993, Turkey's political instability and the Kurdish predicament gained a chronic dimension. Six different coalition governments ruled the country during the 1990s. The worsening dynamics on the Kurdish front during this lost decade undermined the Turkish economy, which suffered from high inflation, growing budget deficits, public debt, and systemic corruption. As the Kurdish insurgency reached critical dimensions, Ankara's response remained uncompromisingly nationalistic and authoritarian. Without the ideological cover of left-wing versus right-wing politics, Turkey's identity problems—Kurdish nationalism and Islam—were now out in the open. And the military had no willingness to show flexibility for any cultural or political compromise with Kurdish nationalists or Islamist politicians. While the Kurdish problem was clearly the driver of political and security concerns during the 1990s, the military soon realized it also had to deal with the rise of political Islam.

As in the case of Kurdish dissent, the generals were in great part to blame for dynamics on the Islamic front. Their policies during the 1980–83 coup came back to haunt them. By the early 1980s, the generals had seen in Islamism an ideological ally against the radical left and Kurdish nationalism. The peculiar nature of Turkish secularism, based on state supremacy over Islam, made the co-optation of religion against communism feasible. In an attempt to create a united Turkish–Islamic front against communism and Kurdish nationalism, the generals granted pious constituencies new rights. To depoliticize the left-wing student population, the generals expanded the budget of the DRA, increased the number of Islamic high schools throughout the country, and introduced compulsory courses on religion in primary and middle schools. The military also struck a law prohibiting graduates of Islamic high schools from studying subjects other than theology at universities. But by doing so, the military also inadvertently boosted the number of youth sympathetic to political Islam. These young Islamists began to express their views openly when the Cold War and the communist threat came to an end.

Other social and economic factors, such as rapid urbanization, corruption, income disparity, and frustration with center-right and center-left establishment politics, also contributed to the rise of Islamism. By the 1990s, Turkey's normally marginal Islamist political movement, the Welfare Party (WP) led by Necmettin Erbakan, made inroads and created a sense of insecurity among Kemalists. In 1994, at the height of an acute financial crisis and the military struggle against Kurdish separatists, the WP shocked the secularist establishment by winning municipal elections nationwide and capturing Turkey's two largest metropolitan areas, Istanbul and Ankara. The new mayor of Istanbul was the young and charismatic leader of the WP youth movement: Recep Tayyip Erdoğan. A year later, in 1995, another unexpected victory, this time in parliamentary elections, put an Islamist-led coalition in charge of the entire country.

The secularist establishment began to worry that the new coalition government would adopt an overtly Islamic agenda and authoritarian manners. They feared it would suppress the secularist opposition, lift the headscarf ban, and challenge Turkey's alliances with Western states. In fact, the WP and Prime Minister Necmettin Erbakan did nothing of the sort. The WP hardly broke from mainstream Turkish political practices. It did try to plant sympathizers in the WP-controlled ministries, but so had many previous political parties after coming to power. Still, the secularist media rang the alarm, warning of an imminent Islamist revolution. On February 28, 1997, the military—in a concerted effort with civil society organizations and the secularist press—forced Erbakan and his party out of power. The generals exerted political pressure on the system and launched an anti-Islamist social, cultural, and economic campaign. Shortly after this "soft coup" of February 1997, the Constitutional Court, a bastion of Kemalist secularism, shut down the WP on the grounds of alleged antisecular activities. A new government under military guidance was quickly formed and the country once again turned to a semblance of normalcy.

This bloodless coup had major, if unintended, consequences. It paved the way for serious soul-searching among Turkey's Islamists, eventually causing a generational and ideological rift within their movement. The WP's pragmatic young leaders, such as Recep Tayyip Erdoğan and Abdullah Gül, recognized the red lines of Turkish secularism and the need for genuine democratization and liberalism to change them. Erdoğan, as the mayor of Istanbul, learned this lesson the hard way. He had to serve four months in prison in 1999 for allegedly inciting religious hatred when all he did was to recite a poem with Islamic undertones. This heavy-handed secularist backlash orchestrated by the military convinced moderate Islamist politicians of the benefits of liberal democracy. After having participated in democratic politics for over three decades, they had already learned to temper their views in order to gain electoral legitimacy. By the late 1990s, in the aftermath of the soft coup and Kemalist concerns of Islamization, political Islam had no other choice than further moderation and pragmatic accommodation. This became all the more apparent in 2001, when Erdoğan and Gül established a new political party, the AKP. They proudly announced the AKP's ideology adhered to conservative democracy, not political Islam.

Erdoğan was a lucky man. As the lost decade of the 1990s came to a close, the country was ripe for serious change on the security, economic, and political fronts. In 1999, the military campaign against the Kurdish insurgency had a major victory with the arrest of Abdullah Öcalan, the leader of the PKK. There was therefore finally some room for political reforms. By 2001 the economy was in shambles after the worst financial crisis in the history of the republic. Tired of the corrupt and inept old guard running the country, Turkish voters were ready for a new start and a new political party. The IMF came to the rescue of the country with credits and loans contingent on fiscal belt-tightening. This economic crisis was the culmination of the lost decade. It also came shortly after the devastating earthquake of 1999 near Istanbul that caused a death toll of more than 20,000. These developments proved to be the last nails in the coffin of political parties that governed Turkey during the 1990s.

On the foreign policy front, the AKP proved as fortunate as in the domestic context. By the time the party was formed, both the European Union and the United States were ready for good relations with Turkey. In 1997, shortly after the soft coup, the EU had declared that Turkey was no longer part of the enlargement process. But things rapidly changed in 1998 when a center-left German leadership under Chancellor Gerhard Schröder replaced the Christian Democrat Helmut Kohl. This new government played a critical role in reviving Turkey's moribund EU candidacy. By 1999, European leaders declared at the EU's Helsinki Summit that Turkey's eventual membership should not be ruled out as Ankara was put back on track for the enlargement process. This important decision proved critical for Turkey's orientation since EU membership appeared within reach for the first time since the end of the Cold War.

By 2001, shortly after the 9/11 terrorist attacks, Washington also wanted strong relations with Ankara. Turkey's Muslim and Western identity and its place in NATO suddenly gained much higher relevance in a climate where the clash of civilizations turned from a gloomy prediction into self-fulfilling prophecy. All these dynamics on the Western front favored the AKP. With Turkey's EU candidacy back on the agenda, Erdoğan correctly sensed that adopting a pro-Western reformist platform would achieve two crucial objectives: the support of Turkey's business community, liberal intellectuals, and pragmatic middle class, and perhaps more importantly, much-needed political cover against the skeptical military establishment. Europe, after all, had always been the ultimate prize in Atatürk's vision of a truly Westernized Turkey. By distancing itself from political Islam and embracing the West, the AKP was ideologically disarming the generals—at least for a while. Combined with an anticorruption and growth-oriented economic agenda that appealed to lower middle classes, the AKP's political strategy proved highly successful. The party won the first parliamentary elections it entered in 2002, only a year after its formation.

The AKP Era: What Went Right?

Before analyzing Erdoğan's first decade in power and what he did right, it is important to correct a critical misperception in the West. Today, given Erdoğan's dismal image as an Islamist autocrat destroying Turkey's democracy, one can detect a sense of nostalgia for what existed before his hegemony. According to this common narrative, Turkey had a liberal and secular past under Kemalism. As we have seen in our historical overview earlier, the problem with this account of Turkish politics is twofold. First, it is based on the false assumption of a golden age of liberal democracy in Turkish political history. In fact, Turkish politics has always been illiberal and Turkish politicians have always been patriarchal figures functioning in the shadow of an intrusive military. The republic the military protected was based neither on separation of religion and state nor on freedom of religion. Instead, it was inspired by French Jacobin laicism and the anticlerical spirit of "freedom from religion."

The second problem with the current perception of Erdoğan as an Islamist autocrat that destroyed Turkish democracy is that it tends to overlook the achievements of the AKP between 2002 and 2012. It is indeed very hard to deny the success of the AKP during its first decade in power. For a while it looked like Erdoğan would truly transform Turkey into a more liberal and democratic country. Soon after coming to power in 2002, the AKP passed an impressive series of reforms to harmonize Turkey's judicial system, civil–military relations, and human rights practices with European norms. The EU began accession negotiations with Erdoğan's Turkey in 2005, rewarding AKP's democratic reforms and Ankara's constructive approach to Cyprus.

The AKP efforts were not confined to democratization. Following the guidelines from an IMF stabilization program adopted after the 2001 financial meltdown by the previous government, the AKP reaped the economic benefits of belt-tightening and structural reforms. It pursued fiscal discipline, lowered a very high inflation rate to single digits, and prioritized good governance and social services in the areas of health care, housing, and urban infrastructure. Between 2002 and 2008, the Turkish economy grew by an average of 7.5 percent. Lower inflation and lower interest rates helped fuel domestic consumption. Thanks to good relations with the EU and a disciplined privatization program, the Turkish economy began to attract unprecedented amounts of foreign direct investment. The average per capita income nearly tripled, from $2,800 in 2001 to around $8,500 in 2010, exceeding those of some new EU members.[29]

With its ever-expanding grassroots network and thanks to an improved economic climate, the AKP understood that the key to gain even more political support was to target Turkey's large lower middle class. Therefore, in addition to distributing food, subsidizing coal, and improving basic infrastructure in poor urban districts, the AKP governments prioritized upward economic mobility with housing credits for first-time home buyers, increased grants for students, favorable loans to the business community, and new public investment projects helping small and medium companies—the Anatolian tigers. Thanks to higher productivity and production, Turkish manufacture and agriculture also took off. Turkish exports to the Middle East, Africa, Central Asia, and of course Europe—which remained the largest market for Turkish goods—increased fivefold between 2003 and 2010. Turkey's construction sector also boomed during the same years.

Erdoğan's AKP proved equally adept in foreign policy. Thanks to good governance, democratic reforms, and the promotion of minority rights for Kurds and non-Muslims, the AKP's Islamic image faded. At least in the eyes of progressive European political parties, Turkey seemed to embody a rare compatibility between Islamic tradition, secularism, and good governance. Washington also admired and supported Erdoğan's brand of "moderate Islam." Turkey's mediation efforts between Israel and Syria received high praise. Despite its disappointment with Ankara's lack of support for the invasion of Iraq in 2003, the Bush administration still considered Turkey a model for the "freedom agenda" it supported in the Middle East. And as late as in 2012, President Obama named Erdoğan as a friend with whom he established a regular line of communication about developments in the region.[30]

By 2009, after having won two consecutive elections (2002 and 2007), Erdoğan took positive steps toward tackling Turkey's most daunting democratic challenge: the Kurdish question. Secret negotiations with the PKK and the organization's jailed leader Abdullah Öcalan began despite the objections from nationalist circles and the military. These were bold initiatives that no other Turkish political party dared to take in the long history of this ethnic conflict. Civil–military relations were also revamped under Erdoğan. AKP's de facto coalition with a movement led by an influential cleric, Fethullah Gülen, whose followers had gained critical positions within the intelligence, security (police), and judiciary bureaucracy, played a major role in this endeavor.

Although they came from ideologically different Islamic backgrounds, both Erdoğan and Fethullah Gülen shared a common enemy: the ultrasecularist generals. They therefore established a marriage of convenience. Erdoğan and Gülen had legitimate reasons to fear the powerful Turkish military. They both had served short prison sentences—Gülen in the 1970s and Erdoğan in the 1990s—in the wake of military interventions. And both men were suspect in the eyes of the top brass for nurturing hidden Islamist agendas behind their moderate façade. The Kemalists were dismayed by the fact both Erdoğan and Gülen seemed to fool naïve Westerners in search of democratic models in the Islamic world. A nationalist and secularist sense of anger began to build up among Kemalist circles against the United States and the European Union. Some within the military even voiced the need to forge a new alternative strategic orientation for Turkey by building alliances with Russia and China. This "Eurasian" vision of Turkey's future was also a clear reaction to Washington's support for Kurds in post–Saddam Hussein Iraq.

The fact that by the time the AKP came to power Fethullah Gülen already lived in self-imposed exile in the United States did not help to fight the conspiracy theory that he was controlled by the "West." Gülen had become infamous, after the soft coup of 1997, because of a leaked sermon where he encouraged his followers to quietly pursue careers in government "until the time is ripe."[31] By the time he left for Pennsylvania in 1999, he was the most powerful and influential cleric in Turkey. His religious movement was known for having invested in education, interfaith dialogue, the media, and private economic enterprise since the late 1970s. Gülen had established hundreds of schools in Turkey and encouraged his graduates to serve in the government bureaucracy as well as in all the educational, social, media, and economic sectors where his movement was active. His self-imposed exile was a clear indication that he feared prosecution by the military's anti-Islamic campaign. In the eyes of the staunchly secularist army, Erdoğan and Gülen were made from the same Islamic cloth. They tried to appear moderate but shared the same long-term objective: to topple the secular regime founded by Atatürk. And in 1999, the year Gülen left Turkey, Erdoğan began his four-month sentence in prison.

Erdoğan and Gülen openly supported each other between 2002 and 2011. They had a mutually beneficial coalition. The Gülen movement traditionally maintained good relations with centrist parties and kept a safe distance from Islamist politicians. This is why Fethullah Gülen stayed away from the WP's Necmettin Erbakan. When the AKP entered the Turkish political scene as a center-right party that repudiated its Islamist past, the Gülen movement became its natural ally. Erdoğan needed help, particularly educated and pious cadres, in running the state bureaucracy. When he came to power in 2002 after his unexpectedly strong victory, he needed civil servants he could work with and was unprepared to run the whole state apparatus. There was mutual distrust between the secular civilian bureaucracy and AKP. Erdoğan also needed protection from ultrasecularists within the military. After toppling the pro-Islamic WP, the generals remained highly skeptical of the AKP's reformist agenda.

The Gülen movement proved ready to help. Fethullah Gülen had been investing in education and his graduates had acquired midlevel positions within the bureaucracy since the early 1980s. The relationship Fethullah Gülen forged with the AKP was strategic and highly useful for his movement. Gülen needed a powerful governing political party to support his movement's educational, media, and business investments in Turkey and beyond. In return, he was happy to provide the human capital AKP needed to run the bureaucracy with Gülen school graduates and loyalists. In any case, these civil servants were already working in a wide array of governmental institutions ranging from the Ministry of Education to the police department. Now they were to gain upward mobility and much more influence. Moreover, the AKP's brand of "moderate Islam" was in perfect harmony with Gülen's positivist Islamism and the kind of Turkish ethnoreligious "soft power" the Gülen brand represented. By the 2000s, Gülen schools were mushrooming all over the world and had a strong reputation for excellence thanks to dedicated, missionary-like teachers.

In time, the biggest loser from this "coalition of the pious" proved to be the common enemy of Erdoğan and Gülen: the Turkish military. The generals knew that they had to act against this alliance and took a risky step in that direction in April 2007 when the TGS issued a thinly veiled threat to the AKP not to nominate AKP cofounder Abdullah Gül to the presidency. The generals appeared ready to once again take matters into their own hands. The presidency, a symbolic and ceremonial position in Turkey's parliamentary system, was traditionally associated with the secular establishment. Feeling strong in great part thanks to the popularity of his economic and social policies, Erdoğan did not bow to the intimidating tactics of the military. Instead he pushed back, called early elections, and won the July 2007 general elections in a landslide. Soon after this victory, a jubilant Erdoğan and AKP-dominated Turkish parliament nominated Abdullah Gül as president. Shortly after Abdullah Gül's ascendance to the presidency, the military establishment once again challenged Erdoğan, this time by using Kemalist allies in the judiciary branch. The AKP was charged by a staunchly Kemalist prosecutor for promoting an Islamist agenda. The matter came before the Constitutional Court, a bastion of Kemalism, as a case for closure of the AKP on the grounds of anticonstitutional activities. The AKP narrowly survived this potential "judicial coup" in 2008 only by a couple of votes.

Erdoğan had emerged victorious from these two major confrontations—one with the military and the other with the judiciary—with the Kemalist establishment. On the other hand, a day of reckoning between his newly emboldened AKP and the weakened Kemalist political system had now become unavoidable. Shortly after the judicial coup failed, the AKP–Gülen alliance launched a widespread investigation aiming to prosecute activist generals and other alleged coup-plotters within the state bureaucracy. Between 2009 and 2011, the Ergenekon investigation emasculated Turkey's once very powerful military in great part thanks to the leading role of Gülenist prosecutors and informants within the security and judicial establishment.[32] Although some of the evidence against military officers appeared to be fabricated, Erdoğan and Gülen had now the upper hand against the Kemalist establishment.

By 2012 civilian supremacy over the military was firmly established. With the military sidelined, the road seemed wide open for a new liberal and democratic constitution that would consolidate the political reforms in a post-Kemalist Turkey. Erdoğan also appeared increasingly popular in the Middle East. With the Arab Spring in full swing, the AKP came to be seen as source of inspiration at the vanguard of this democratic wave in the Middle East. Very few could have predicted that in a couple of years this sense of hubris in Turkey would turn into gloom and doom.

What Went Wrong?

Today, this so-called "Turkish model" is no more. The country has turned increasingly autocratic, nationalistic, and conspiratorial (against the

West) under the same leader who received so much praise during his first decade in power. Many analysts now speak of Erdoğan as an incorrigible Islamist dictator. Such accusations overstate the role of Islam in Turkey's autocratic turn for an understandable reason. The West once saw in Erdoğan the compatibility of Islam with democracy. It is only logical that the same circles now interpret Turkey's descent into authoritarianism in symmetrical terms: as a clash between Islam and democracy or a conflict between Islam and secularism. In other words, once again the problem is conceptualized around Islam, religion, and secularism.

In reality, the end of the Turkish model has little to do with such views that overstate the role of religion. The real story in Turkey is the rise of nationalist populism, illiberalism, the political clash within the Islamic camp, and the return of the Kurdish conflict. In other words, more than an Islamist dictator determined to bury Atatürk's secular legacy, Erdoğan has turned into an illiberal populist who has the support of ultranationalists and even some of the ultrasecularist pro-Russia Eurasianist circles within the Kemalist establishment. In fact, the most striking development in Turkish politics over the last few years has been the convergence of secular nationalism, represented by the military, and religious nationalism represented by Erdoğan. These twin faces of Turkish nationalism share the same enemies: Western liberal democracy, Kurdish ethnic demands, the Gülen movement, the United States, and the European Union.

In retrospect, events that unfolded in 2013 proved a major turning point in AKP's democratic journey. The brutal suppression of young environmentalist protesters at Istanbul's Gezi Park and subsequent cycles of violence against protesters across the country unveiled the fragile nature of civil liberties in Erdoğan's new Turkey. The crackdown of protests and the suppression of freedom of speech and assembly clearly revealed the absence of rule of law in the country. The same year, the clash between Erdoğan and the Gülen movement turned the political climate from bad to worse. The absence of an independent judiciary became obvious when Erdoğan sacked the Gülenist prosecutors who launched a major corruption investigation against him. There was clear and undeniable corruption within the AKP ranks. It was a well-known fact within AKP circles that Erdoğan himself distributed government contracts and big infrastructure projects to cronies. Yet, Erdoğan managed to project the corruption investigation against him as a coup attempt orchestrated by Fethullah Gülen.

As his alliance with Gülen came to an acrimonious end, Erdoğan forged a new partnership, this time with the ultranationalist and secularist groups in the military that he sidelined only a few years ago. The military was of course more than happy to see the alliance that brought the tutelage system down crumble. The generals were equally happy to see the end of the Kurdish peace process under the weight of authoritarianism at home and the Syrian civil war where the United States was supportive of Kurds aligned with the PKK. By 2015 the dynamics of war were once again dominating the Kurdish question in Turkey. In many ways, Ankara had returned to the old days of illiberalism, authoritarianism, and reactionary nationalism that characterized the lost decade of the 1990s.

It was once again obviously clear that the country lacked a strong civil society, an independent judiciary, and a free media. In other words, institutions that are bedrocks of liberalism were absent. What is left of Turkish democracy was therefore reduced to elections and majority rule. As a result, today's Turkey has turned from a once hopeful model of democratic governance into a textbook example of illiberalism where elections legitimize the tyranny of the majority. Despite mounting political polarization and unrest since the 2013 Gezi Park protests, the AKP remains the most popular political party in the ballot box. With his nationalist coalition, Erdoğan's populism managed to win almost all the local, parliamentary, and presidential elections. The only exception proved to be the 2019 municipal elections when the AKP lost both Ankara and Istanbul. Especially after the transition to a presidential system in 2017, Erdoğan monopolized power and consolidated his hegemony. Populist nationalism, more than political Islam, has become his most powerful weapon in this autocratic centralization process. Given AKP's heavy-handed control of the media and the repression of dissidents, Turkish elections are neither free nor fair. Yet, winning them allows Erdoğan to claim that only the AKP and himself can truly represent the "national will" against dark forces supported by the West who wants to destabilize Turkey and derail its rise as a major world power. His increasingly populist style of politics comes a with a growing dose of conspiratorial Turkish nationalism. Today, despite the electoral defeat at the municipal level in 2019—thanks to opposition parties acting with unprecedented unity—Erdoğan's AKP still comfortably claims to be the most popular political party in the country.

The Clash within the Islamic Bloc

Soon after the corruption investigation in December 2013, Erdoğan declared an open war against all Gülenist groups within Turkish bureaucracy—starting with the judiciary and law enforcement—labeling them a "parallel state" within the state. This growing rift in the AKP–Gülen alliance combined with the end of the Kurdish peace process in 2015 turned into a nightmare for Turkey. Both developments proved extremely detrimental for political stability in the country and they account for the unraveling of the AKP success story that lasted between 2002 and 2012. It is also very telling that neither the AKP–Gülen clash nor the return of the Kurdish conflict fit into the dichotomy of Islam versus secularism. While the Kurdish issue is clearly about a confrontation between Turkish and Kurdish nationalism, Erdoğan's conflict with Gülen is fratricide "within" the Islamic camp and has nothing to do with a clash between Islam and secularism. Instead, it is about a power struggle for supremacy in Turkish politics.

Once their shared enemy—the military—was politically sidelined, the AKP–Gülen alliance rapidly turned into a debilitating competition for power. Erdoğan went after the education network of the Gülen movement and Gülenist prosecutors came after Erdoğan's corrupt network of patronage and crony capitalism. Erdoğan responded to the corruption investigation by launching an all-out war against the Gülen movement. His policies included sacking the prosecutors involved in the corruption investigation, reassigning hundreds of police chiefs, and rewriting laws in ways that would allow government control over the judiciary and corruption probes. After the resignation of four implicated ministers, Erdoğan reshuffled half of his cabinet. In addition to the total number of ninety-six prosecutors and judges that were replaced, the government decided to push through draconian new laws, giving it more control over the judiciary and tightening monitoring of telephones and the Internet. The new legislation also enhanced government control over the High Council of Judges and Prosecutors, which is responsible for judicial functions and the appointments of judges, and thus severely undermined the separation between the executive and judiciary branches. Nothing much was left in the name of rule of law in Turkey as Erdoğan began to call all the shots.

As the corruption probe swirled around his government and his family, Erdoğan also returned to the familiar tactic of blaming his problems on a vast international conspiracy, as part of an orchestrated effort to weaken Turkey. Partly because Gülen lives in the United States and has been critical of Turkey's confrontations with Israel, Erdoğan hinted that corruption allegations were the result of attempts by Israel and the United States to frame his government. By 2013, Turkey's relations with Israel were severely strained due to Turkey's support of Hamas. Erdoğan even threatened to expel the US ambassador on the grounds that he held meetings with opposition figures. The way the AKP handled the corruption investigation clearly exposed Erdoğan's authoritarian leadership and, more importantly, the absence of checks and balances where they were most desperately needed.

The rift between the Gülen movement and AKP took many Western observers who considered Islam as a monolithic bloc by surprise.[33] In reality, political Islam in Turkey always came with multiple faces and the divergence between Fethullah Gülen and other Islamic groups had deep roots. At the ideological level, the predecessors of the AKP had a political tradition close to the Muslim Brotherhood (MB) in the Arab world. The MB is an Islamist movement that wants a governing system in accordance with Islamic legal norms. It seeks to come to power and rejects secularism. Its political and strategic vision looks back with nostalgia at Islam's golden age and prioritizes the universal brotherhood of the "umma" as a supranational community of believers. As such, the MB tradition of political Islam rejects the concept of nationalism and nation-states as a divisive system invented by the West. The predecessor of the AKP, the WP had developed relations with the MB and shared a similar philosophy. Under the leadership of Necmettin Erbakan, the ideological tradition of the WP was known as the "Milli Görüş" movement and followed the precepts of classical political Islam, in the footsteps of Arab Islamist theorists like Sayyid Qutb and Hassan al-Banna in Egypt.

The Gülenists, on the other hand, come from a Sufi Turkish brand of Islam that is not against the nation-state. To the contrary, it embraces Turkish nationalism and shows great respect for the Ottoman–Turkish state tradition. Moreover, the patriotic and nationalist brand of Islam embraced by the Gülen movement has considerable disdain for the Arab world's MB. Unlike political Islamists, the Gülen movement has also no admiration for the Iranian Islamic revolution. The roots of the Gülen movement go back to Said Nursî (1878–1960), a preacher from Eastern Anatolia whose teachings (the Nurcu movement) emphasized the compatibility of Islam with rationalism, science, and positivism.

Nursî's main contribution to Islam was a 6,000-page commentary written during his lifetime on the Koran. This body of work, known as the Risale-i Nur (the Light Collection), advocates the teaching of modern sciences in religious schools and an Islamic age of enlightenment. The Nurcu movement of Said Nursî, in time, has become the most popular brand of Sufism in Turkey. Its patriotic and harmonious approach to Turkish nationalism and positivism also enabled the Gülen movement to develop a less confrontational approach to secularism and Atatürk.

Fethullah Gülen's vision of promoting such an approach to Islam led him to focus on education. The real struggle, according to the Gülenists, had to take place not in the political arena but in the cultural sphere and civil society, by trying to win hearts and minds. This is why the Gülen movement began investing in modern schools that would educate students in line with positive sciences. In time these schools became the main symbol of the Gülen movement, which expanded beyond Turkey, into Central Asia, Africa, the Middle East, Asia, Europe, and the United States. The Gülenists claimed to be above politics. Yet the graduates of Gülen-affiliated schools often entered public service in key government institutions. In the eyes of the army, this amounted to a secret agenda of political infiltration into state institutions and represented an existential threat to the Kemalist-secular foundations of the republic.

It is important to analyze the threat perception of the Turkish military vis-à-vis the Gülen movement. It is eventually this perception that led to a marriage of convenience between the AKP and the Gülenists. In the eyes of generals, the WP's brand of political Islam was a concrete and identifiable phenomenon. The WP, after all, was not a social movement but a political party with a political project. It was controllable because it was out in the open and it clearly promoted an Islamic agenda. The Gülenists, on the other hand, represented a very different kind of threat because of their long-term social, cultural, and educational strategy. Theirs was a generational project. The movement does not deny the presence of sympathizers within the state, but it insists their graduates are not infiltrators but highly motivated individuals who have upward mobility thanks to merit, work ethic, and motivation. Needless to say, such arguments never had credibility in the eyes of the generals who always questioned the end goal of Gülenists.

The raison d'être of the Gülen–AKP alliance was the need for both groups to protect themselves against the military, which considered both groups an existential threat to Kemalism. With support from the

Gülenists, the AKP considerably reduced the role and power of the army. The scope of Gülenist influence over the Turkish judiciary was certainly real, as became clear during the Ergenekon investigation. The investigation targeted a network composed of active duty and retired military personnel, ultranationalist extremists, political activists, and organized crime figures—a conglomeration often referred to as the "deep state"—all united by the desire to bring an end to the rule of the AKP and its ally, Gülen, in order to preserve the Kemalist nature of the republic. According to the Ergenekon trial, the network had hatched a plot to overthrow the government. The net effect of the Ergenekon investigation was the emasculation of the Turkish military.

Wielding its influence in the judiciary and intelligence services, the Gülen movement used its clout during the Ergenekon affair. Yet what started as a legitimate attempt to arrest coup plotters turned into a witch hunt against all enemies of the AKP and the Gülen movement. Instead of targeting only people involved in the conspiracy, Gülenist prosecutors had warrants issued for the arrests of people who appeared hostile to the Gülen community—not only military officers but also journalists, academics, civil society activists, and bureaucrats. There were also disturbing signs of evidence tampering and attempts to frame active duty and retired military officers. The politicization of the Ergenekon investigation earned the Gülen movement international criticism. In time, it also began to undermine relations between the Gülenists and the AKP, with Erdoğan showing signs that he wanted to reach a less confrontational modus vivendi with the military.

Although the AKP and Erdoğan strongly supported the Ergenekon investigation from the outset, once the military was sidelined, the AKP–Gülen rift reemerged. At the broader level, the AKP circles appeared increasingly annoyed and concerned that the executive branch's decision-making power had come to be challenged by the growing influence and presence of the Gülen's community on all levels of the bureaucratic structure, particularly the police, judiciary, and public education system. In many ways the AKP began to see the Gülen network as a "state within a state."

The tension between the two former allies peaked in early 2012, when an Istanbul prosecutor summoned Turkey's top intelligence chief, a high-level confidant of Mr. Erdoğan, to question him about his covert negotiations with Kurdish militants in the framework of the peace process with the PKK. Erdoğan saw the prosecutor's move as a personal attack by the Gülen movement and initiated a purge within the police and the judiciary, demoting suspected members of the movement. The clash escalated when Erdoğan decided to target the educational institutions of the movement by announcing that private prep schools for high school students would be shut down. Many of these schools were a major source of recruitment and revenue for the movement. The Gülen movement then responded by unleashing a corruption investigation against the AKP. In short, once the military was subdued, the alliance between Erdoğan and the followers of Gülen began falling apart.

Yet, the speed with which an embattled Erdoğan rushed to forge an unholy alliance with the Turkish army against the Gülen movement was still astonishing. The clearest evidence of Erdoğan's Machiavellian skills came when his top political advisor suggested that the military was framed by the same Gülenist prosecutors who launched the corruption probe against the AKP. This statement called into question the whole legitimacy of the Ergenekon trial. Almost all of the officers implicated in coup-plotting have quickly been released. Such a development paved the road for a return of the generals as powerful actors in search of retribution. Although another military intervention in Turkey seems far-fetched, the country looked increasingly unstable and polarized. It was no longer possible to rule out a scenario in which the generals would make their presence felt against Erdoğan and the AKP. Yet, no one really predicted the turn the vicious conflict within the Islamic camp would take in July 2016 with the unthinkable: a failed coup against Erdoğan allegedly orchestrated by Gülenist forces within the military.[34]

Erdoğan blamed Gülenist infiltration in the military for this botched affair that cost the lives of 250 people. Fethullah Gülen denied any involvement in the coup and argued Erdoğan is the only one benefiting from all these developments. At the end of the day, the narrative of a Gülenist coup attempt became the official line in Turkey and massive waves of arrests followed. The failed coup of July 2016 exacerbated Turkey's illiberal and autocratic turn and ended up consolidating the anti-Western coalition between AKP and ultranationalists and secularists who always hated Gülen and the United States. The reluctance of the United States to extradite Fethullah Gülen fueled the nationalist conspiracy that Washington was complicit in this coup that was allegedly orchestrated from Pennsylvania. Erdoğan used the coup as an excuse to go after all his opponents with a giant purge of government institutions, civil society organizations, academia, and even the private sector. The Gülen movement, a crucial ally of the AKP for almost all its existence, was now declared a terrorist organization that needed to be annihilated.

In the meantime, Turkey's already strained relations with Washington went from bad to worse. The fact that Washington continued to support Syrian Kurds despite Turkey's warnings created even more anti-American nationalist resentment in Turkey. Shortly after the failed coup in 2016, and again in the summer of 2017, Turkey launched two major military incursions in northern Syria, bringing it close to a potential confrontation with American forces. In the eyes of Turkey, America had partnered with the Syrian wing of the PKK, failed to take serious military action against Damascus, and paid scant attention to Turkey's troubles in absorbing 4 million Syrian refugees. Washington, for its part, believed Turkey supported Al-Qaeda-linked jihadists in Syria and prioritized good relations with Moscow and Tehran in its diplomatic efforts. All these problems on the Turkish–American front were music to the ears of anti-American ultranationalists in Erdoğan's new coalition.

The Kurdish Unraveling and Erdoğan's Turn to Kemalism

If Erdoğan's war with Fethullah Gülen was one of the reasons he had to make peace with the old illiberal order of Turkey, the return of war dynamics with the PKK was the second one. Already by 2015, there was no sign left of the Kurdish peace process in the country. The cumulative effect of the Gezi park unrest and the corruption investigations in 2013 fueled a deep sense of insecurity in the conspiratorial eyes of Erdoğan. He saw external forces behind both events. Feeling increasingly insecure despite his electoral victories, Erdoğan turned even more autocratic and illiberal after assuming the presidency in 2014 with 51.7 percent of the votes. This was the first time the president came to be elected by the people and a big step toward the presidential system Erdoğan so coveted. Rather than staying above politics, as Turkey's parliamentary system and constitution required from the president of the republic, Erdoğan was determined to change Turkey's political system in his favor.

The illiberal dynamics of Turkish politics and Erdoğan's sense of insecurity went from bad to worse when the AKP lost its parliamentary majority in the June 2015 elections despite remaining the party that received most of the votes. The result came as a shock not only to Erdoğan but also to the Turkish nationalist establishment. Erdoğan was denied a parliamentary majority because Turkey's Kurdish political movement managed to win 13.1 percent of the votes and gained eighty seats that would normally go to the AKP. This was a watershed moment for Turkish politics because a Kurdish party had passed the 10 percent requirement for parliamentary representation for the first time. The victory of the Peoples' Democracy Party (HDP) and its charismatic young leader, Selahattin Demirtaş, dismayed the ultranationalist MHP (Nationalist Action Party) and large segments of Turkey's nationalist voters who were concerned about close links between the HDP and the PKK.

With its eighty seats in parliament, the HDP had a larger presence in the legislative body than the MHP. Not surprisingly, this Kurdish victory terrified the MHP leader, Devlet Bahçeli, who declared on the eve of the polls that he would never support any attempts by the anti-AKP opposition parties—the CHP and the HDP—to form a government. MHP's hatred of the Kurds thus blocked any hope of an anti-AKP coalition. Turkish nationalism within the Kemalist CHP also precluded an open alliance with Kurdish nationalists. The result was deadlock in parliament since Erdoğan also vehemently opposed a grand coalition between the AKP and the CHP.

Soon it became clear that the HDP's electoral victory was moving Turkey toward a nationalist realignment. Bahçeli's refusal to form a government with the CHP lay the foundation for a nationalist alliance between the MHP and the AKP. Bahçeli's support to Erdoğan has been conditional on only one demand: to crush Turkey's emboldened Kurdish movement. Erdoğan happily delivered. He had an axe to grind with the HDP for not supporting his presidential agenda despite his overtures to Turkey's Kurds by granting them more cultural rights than any previous Turkish government. Erdoğan had assumed his peace process with the Kurds would generate the critical political support he needed for changing Turkey's political system from a parliamentary regime to a presidential one. Yet, the HDP leader Demirtaş wisely refused to support Erdoğan in the June 2015 elections, on the grounds that the Kurds should not support an autocratic presidential agenda in return for a cosmetic peace process. Erdoğan did not forgive Demirtaş for this "betrayal."

After the AKP lost its parliamentary majority in June 2015, Erdoğan called snap elections in November to undo the stalemate in the parliament.

As the country was heading to polls once again he quickly launched a vicious military campaign in the Kurdish southeast. A growing number of ISIS and PKK terrorist attacks also rocked the country during the summer. Growing signs of distress in the economy and the return of war-like dynamics in the southeast naturally worried Turkish public opinion, accustomed to stability and growth under AKP governments. In November the AKP won easily and regained a strong parliamentary majority. To the dismay of extreme nationalists, the HDP still managed to win 10.76 percent of the votes and gained more parliamentary seats than the MHP. By 2016, the stage was now fully set for a de facto nationalist conservative coalition between the AKP and MHP that turned Turkish politics into a militaristic direction against the Kurds. In July of the same year, the failed coup attempt destroyed the last vestiges of democracy in Turkey. Erdoğan had now everything he needed to purge all his enemies. He started with Gülenists but by November 2016, Selahattin Demirtaş, the HDP leader, was also behind bars.

Turkey's downward spiral kept taking new turns after the failed coup of July 2016. The war against Fethullah Gülen and against Kurdish nationalism, both at home and in Syria, fueled dynamics of proto-fascism as tens of thousands were arrested. Foreign policy was not exempt from Erdoğan's nationalist turn against the West. American military support for Kurds associated with the PKK in Syria gave him the excuse he needed for orbiting toward Moscow.[35] Amidst growing problems with both the EU and Washington and a deteriorating economic and security situation at home, Erdoğan presented himself as the only man strong enough to fight Turkey's growing problems on all fronts. To do that, however, he needed a strong presidential system. Having established a draconian emergency rule after the failed coup of July 2016, Erdoğan's nationalist populism and new alliance with the MHP paid off. In April 2017, he narrowly won a national referendum that changed the Turkish political system from a parliamentary regime to an "imperial" presidency with no checks and balances. By the summer of 2018, Erdoğan was elected president under this new system with close to 52 percent of the votes.

As of this writing, the only consolation for Turkish democracy is that Erdoğan's AKP has lost municipal elections in the summer of 2019 in almost all large cities of Turkey including Istanbul and Ankara. Yet, despite a deteriorating Turkish economy and heavy military incursions into Northern Syria between 2016 and 2020, Erdoğan remains firmly in charge at the presidency and his party still has a supermajority in the parliament. His nationalist coalition with the MHP and the military is as strong as ever. The war against the PKK and Gülen is continuing unabated. And as a clear sign of its frustration with the West, Erdogan's nationalist Turkey has also purchased a Russian missile defense system, despite strong objections from Washington and NATO.

Conclusion

Turkish politics is on the one hand a very straightforward, almost boringly predictable affair, on the other a complex study in paradox. The easy part comes when you focus solely on Erdoğan. It is predictable because Erdoğan has been consolidating power for years. Reading news coming from Turkey is like reading the same story over and over again. It's called "autocracy on the march to dictatorship." Erdoğan is a master performer of time-honored methods from the script book of populist autocrats. He controls the media, silences critics, rewards sycophants, and distributes economic favors to cronies.

The only surprising part of Erdoğan's autocracy is that elections are still held and strongly contested with a high turnout. The municipal election results in 2019 showed that the AKP remains vulnerable on the economic front. The only force that has the power to create problems for Erdoğan is the failure of economic capacity as a critical element of governance. Turkish people, like most electorates, vote more on bread-and-butter issues than ideology. Given such predictability in Erdoğan's autocracy, one has to look beyond the surface of Islam versus secularism to understand what truly drives Turkish politics. An analysis of governance and economic performance combined with a close look at Turkish nationalism proves much more rewarding than overstating Islam.

Erdoğan's populism and constantly shifting Machiavellian coalitions are critical parts of today's Turkish puzzle. Why, for instance, is Erdoğan now increasingly willing to embrace Atatürk's legacy by incorporating nationalism, sovereignty, and independence in his populist discourse? Isn't he an Islamist who wants to destroy the secularist legacy of Kemalism? Unveiling this paradox requires debunking the myth that the main cleavage in Turkish society is one between Islamists versus secularists. As this chapter on Turkey attempted to show, this dichotomy has been problematic for decades. Not only is it superficial and overly simplistic, but more critically, this binary categorization distorts reality by overstating the clash between secularism and Islam in Turkish politics at the expense of the main force driving Turkish politics since the inception of the republic: nationalism.[36]

Anyone who insists on seeing the clash between Islam and secularism as the main problem in Turkey has not been paying attention to the peculiarity of Turkish secularism. As I tried to explain, secularism in Turkey has always been a skin-deep affair based on sartorial symbols. For instance, while the headscarf issue or consumption of alcohol can generate polarization, there is no genuine debate in Turkey about why secularism fails to stop discrimination of non-Muslims by separating religion and state. The deeply rooted state tradition inherited from the Ottoman Empire incorporated Islam within the nationalist norms of the republic, creating a religious nationalism of sorts. As a result, the supposedly secular Turkish Republic remains a Sunni Muslim state where Turkishness is associated with Islam and being Muslim. The foundational codes of the Turkish Republic are therefore not based on secularization. Instead they are based on Muslim and Turkish nation-building and three historic tragedies: the de-Hellenization of Anatolia, the Armenian genocide, and the denial of Kurdish ethnic identity.

In that sense, the overstatement of "Islam versus secularism" fails to capture conservative nationalism as the force majeure that unites the majority of Turks. This marriage of nationalism with conservativism is what gave us the official ideology of the republic: a Turkish–Islamic synthesis of religious nationalism. We should therefore set aside "Islam" versus "secularism" as the primary lens in analyzing Turkish dynamics. What Turkey is facing today is not Islamization, but authoritarianism fueled by an illiberal state tradition supported by both secularists and Islamists. This illiberal state tradition is deeply reactionary and angry with the West. Secularists and Islamists are equally nationalistic in their approach to the Kurdish question whose solution requires liberalism and democracy.

Islam versus secularism will also never help us understand why the AKP and Fethullah Gülen entered into an existential war. This was fratricide and a power struggle within the Islamic camp that had nothing to do with secularism. Similarly, good luck analyzing the most important problem of the country, the Turkish–Kurdish conflict with Islam versus secularism. Here too, the most important driver is not religion but nationalism. Finally, Erdoğan's embrace of Atatürk is also in great harmony and continuity with the authoritarian state tradition of Turkey based on conservative nationalism. The glue that holds this alliance between Kemalism and Erdoğan's pious conservativism is the deeply rooted nationalist desire for full-independence and full-sovereignty against Western imperialists. Seen from this perspective, the alliance between Erdoğan, the ultranationalist MHP, and ultrasecularist military officers is more than an opportunistic coalition: it is the default setting of the Turkish Republic.

3 SUNNIS VERSUS SHIITES

Nothing represents the Western disconnect with the Middle East better than the perception of a region with hopeless, intractable religious conflicts. These people, we are often told, have been fighting each other since time immemorial. It has become almost a cliché to speak of "ancient tribal hatreds" in explaining the Middle East to apprehensive Western audiences. Not only the Israeli–Palestinian conflict but, more importantly, the current Sunni versus Shiite sectarian violence is often cast in such gloomy terms. According to this view, past and present civil wars in Iraq, Syria, Yemen, and Lebanon are mere reenactments of the bloody "struggle within Islam," with roots going back to the early years of the faith.

The argument that a deeply rooted religious conflict is fueling current wars in the Middle East begs a logical question: Are Shiites and Sunnis still fighting the same war? Would they stop fighting if they could suddenly agree on who was the rightful follower of prophet Muhammad? The answer, of course, is a clear "no." Looking at these conflicts through a seventh-century prism is overly simplistic and misleading. As we will see in the next chapter, the same applies to all attempts at analyzing the emergence of the Islamic State in Iraq and Syria (ISIS) by focusing on Islam. In both cases, the Western disconnect suffers from heavy overstatement of religion, sectarian identity, and theology as the main drivers of the conflict. Somehow, very obvious political, economic, and social factors get short shrift.

The main contention of this chapter is that we are once again overstating Islam and theology in analyzing Middle Eastern sectarianism. The view that immutable, ageless religious identities are constantly fueling wars between Sunnis and Shiites in Iraq, Syria, Lebanon, or Yemen is overly simplistic and alarmingly misleading. Such conventional wisdom needs urgent correction. Unless we can diagnose the underlying causes of conflicts correctly, there will be no right prescription. And subscribing to the cliché of intractable conflicts will only continue to generate gloom and doom.

Thankfully, such pessimism is misplaced. The obvious place to start is to put these "ancient" Middle Eastern conflicts in their proper "modern" political context. The civil wars in Lebanon, Iraq, Syria, and Yemen did not emerge in a vacuum. They gained a sectarian dimension for specific reasons. Sectarian conflict in these countries takes place in a context of failed governance—when states can no longer provide security and services. The collapse of state institutions creates a vacuum filled by multiple actors—domestic and external—that manipulate and exploit religious and sectarian identity to their own advantage.

It is not a coincidence that Syria, Iraq, Yemen, and Lebanon are all either weak or failed states. It is often assumed that these states are facing civil wars and chronic political strife because of their deeply rooted sectarianism and religious conflicts. In reality, the reverse is much more plausible: their sectarianized civil conflicts are products of political dysfunction and collapsing governance systems. Somehow the view that sectarian civil wars in Syria, Iraq, Yemen, or Lebanon are caused by modern political failures—not ancient animus—does not find a receptive audience.

Similarly, the geostrategic competition between Iran and Saudi Arabia is seldom analyzed as a nationalist rivalry between two modern states.[1] Given the conventional wisdom of "ancient religious conflicts" the narrative of "modern nationalist struggles" is almost absent in the Western analysis of the Middle East. Such Western reluctance to look at the role of nationalism in the sectarianized conflicts of the Middle East between Sunnis and Shiites is rather strange given the role nationalism played in Europe's own history. Once again, the European and American focus is on the religious, timeless, and intractable nature rather than the relatively new, political and geostrategic character of the competition. In short, while Islam and ancient sectarian hatreds are all the rage in Western circles, the current competition between Persian and Arab nationalism in failed or failing states gets short shrift. As a result, the story of sectarianization and the victory of sectarian agitators in times when survival is at stake is often untold.

The implications of such Western disconnect with reality are twofold. First is a sense of undue pessimism infused with racist undertones. The Middle Eastern conflicts are seen as eternal, preordained, and primordial. Sunnis and Shiites are engaged in these ageless, irrational conflicts because of their religious and sectarian identity. The sectarian divide is almost part of their DNA, an essential element of who they are. This makes them culturally predisposed to sectarian violence. Their fanatical attachment to primordial identities is seen almost as a *biological* predicament.

The second implication of such Western disconnect with reality is the convenience of righteous disengagement. We, in the West, are helpless bystanders. It is their wars and their blood feuds. We are not to blame, we are not responsible, and we certainly cannot fix their incurable ancient hatreds. This approach is shared by both wings of the political spectrum. The American left and right as well as mainstream Western media engage in such self-serving logic. From President Obama, who on several occasions spoke of "ancient sectarian divisions that date back millennia," to one-time presidential candidate Sarah Palin who remarked with folksy wisdom: "Let Allah sort it out!" there are only different shades to this convenient detachment.[2]

As we will see in this chapter, there is an alternative way to analyze the Sunni–Shiite divide by focusing on power politics, nationalism, geostrategic dynamics, and governance. Instead of overstating Islam and ancient hatreds our approach will look at the geostrategic regional rivalry between Iran and Saudi Arabia, as two poles representing Persian versus Arab nationalism. And perhaps more importantly, we will see that the regional states where this rivalry is playing out have major governance problems in terms of security, capacity, and legitimacy.

The nationalist, geostrategic competition between Tehran and Riyadh becomes most destructive in states where governance has either collapsed or is on the verge of collapsing. Political space is open for sectarian manipulation. Empowered substate actors seek external patronage in this context of violence and conflict. Simultaneously, communities turn inward for survival and protection. Weak and failing states have major vulnerabilities on the security, capacity, and legitimacy front. The absence of good governance and effective state institutions leaves a vacuum that is easily exploitable by sectarianism and sectarian actors. This is why, similar to what is going on in Turkey, the real story behind the Sunni–Shiite sectarian divide is seldom only religion and Islamic revival. The interplay between nationalism, power politics, and governance is much fertile ground for both diagnosis and prescription. But the adoption of this method first requires debunking a few myths about ancient tribal hatreds.

Conventional Wisdom: Timeless Conflict, Eternal Animosity

Conventional wisdom often becomes conventional for understandable reasons. It is impossible to deny the reality of sectarianism in Middle Eastern politics or the historical fact that sectarian divergence in Islam has indeed very deep roots going back to the question of succession that emerged soon after Prophet Mohammed died in AD 632. One group within the community argued that the next leader of the Islamic faith should be chosen among the Prophet's close companions, since they were the chosen ones. They would come to be known as the Sunnis (from the term ahl al-sunna wa-l-jama'a), meaning the people of tradition and the consensus of opinion.

The opposing view believed that Prophet Muhammad should be followed by an immediate member of his family. They considered Ali Ibn-u Talib, the prophet's cousin and son-in-law, as his rightful successor and came to be known as the Shiites (from the term shi'at 'Ali, meaning partisans of Ali).[3] In time, this bitter dispute over succession gained some doctrinal and theological significance. For instance, Sunni fundamentalists are particularly critical of Shiite reverence of Ali and their religious practice of worship at shrines dedicated to him and his family. They consider such tendencies as heresy bordering on apostasy. Today, only about 15 percent of Muslims are Shiites. Their status as a minority and the victimhood of Ali and his sons color an important aspect of the faith.

The historic nature of this sectarian schism in Islam needs to be taken seriously. But even then, the problem between Sunnis and Shiites appears to be—at least in its origins—of a political nature rather than theological character. After all, the question of who would replace the prophet was about power and authority, not doctrine. The theological dimension of the divergence had to be "constructed" much later. Politics, in other words, preceded the theological and religious schism. Some may even argue the competition for political power, in fact, caused the doctrinal differences.

Similar dynamics—the primacy of the political over the religious—apply to current sectarian conflicts in the Middle East. Today, a quick contextual and political analysis of sectarianism in the Arab world would show that it has little to do with the ancient schism within Islam. Vali Nasr, who has written an illuminating book on the sectarian question, strikes the right balance when he argues that

> The Sunni-Shi'a is not just a hoary religious dispure, a fossilized set piece from the early years of Islam's unfolding, but a contemporary clash of identities. Theological and historic disagreements fuel it, but so do today's concerns with power, subjugation, freedom, and equality, not to mention regional conflicts and foreign intrigues. It is paradoxically, a very old, very modern conflict.[4]

Most sectarianized conflicts, and particularly the "sectarianization" process, have little to do with religion.[5] The weaponization and mobilization of sectarian identity are always about politics and political power. More than immutable theology, it is the need for survival and protection, all kinds of strategic and tactical calculations, national or subnational interests, and competition for resources that drive most sectarianized conflicts. For instance, the highly flexible and ever-shifting sectarian alliances in Lebanon often reflect the changing domestic political context at home and geostrategic dynamics at the regional level. The idea that there is an intractable, timeless aspect to these conflicts rooted in the history of the first Islamic century therefore defies both logic and political reality on the ground.

Yet, there is a plethora of popular and scholarly analysis that stubbornly refers to unchanging religious nature of these old sectarian hatreds. Islam is itself the main problem and the root cause of political dysfunction according to this pervasive discourse. Therefore, civil wars, weak states, and failing institutions in the Middle East are often seen as products of cultural and religious dysfunction. Overstating Islam becomes conventional wisdom in this context. A closer inspection of social, political, and economic dynamics in the contemporary Arab world rapidly defies such facile generalizations and clearly proves that sectarianism tends to increase when state power declines. Weak, failing, or failed states as in the case of Syria, Iraq, Yemen, and Lebanon clearly show the correlation between governance problems and the rise of sectarianism. It is equally clear that citizens in states where there are no security, capacity, or legitimacy problems have a much better chance of cultivating bonds based on civic and patriotic solidarity. These institutional dynamics are at the heart of the difference between successful nation-building and failed states descending to sectarian chaos.

Nation-building is a long, arduous process during which the political center tries to forge an overarching national identity that transcends and eventually replaces subnational ones. Forging this new identity along civic rather than ethnic lines of equal citizenship is never easy. It requires strong state capacity and inclusive political institutions. When a state has weak institutions, it is unable to secure the well-being of its citizens within the rule of law. This relative absence of good governance can lead to fragmentation within society. Low level of political and social trust in the governing system creates solidarity networks at the group, sect, or family level. When a legitimate social contract between state and society is missing the state can resort to coercion to ensure the obedience and loyalty of citizens. Yet, repression doesn't generate legitimacy based on the rule of law. And in a climate of fear people have no reason to trust each other and have no confidence in the institutions of the government. Instead, they turn inward to their own ethnic, tribal, and communal links for protection.

In strong states where good governance becomes the norm, the system generates civic consciousness based on taxation and representation. Citizens develop a sense of civic loyalty and ownership in their approach to their state. The strength, transparency, accountability, and inclusiveness of the system in time erode tribal loyalties based on clan, sect, or religion. In the Arab world, when individuals turn inward to the communities that will protect them, we therefore need to analyze the weakness of institutions. This also explains why Arab states with weak central authority and governance, such as Lebanon and Yemen, have tribal and sectarian power-sharing arrangements. These subnational and sectarian arrangements rather than the rule of law, equal citizenship, and civic nationalism dominate politics.

In essence, this is the difference between Europe and the Middle East. More than Islam versus Christianity, it is strong states versus weak states that explains the divergence. The cultural differences between the Islamic world and the West thus require a better understanding of political and institutional dynamics. What would have happened if the Arab world had inclusive institutions, good governance, rule of law, productive economies, and citizens who trusted their political systems and each other? The short answer is that the Arab world would be more like Europe in terms of institutional strength, civic consciousness, and good governance. Instead of sectarianism we would be talking about diversity, pluralism, minority rights, or multiculturalism. In short, sectarianism is not a natural state of affairs related to cultural, religious, or historical inclinations. It is a product of institutional and political failure.

If that's the case, why is the thesis of ancient tribal hatreds so persistent and popular in the West? An important reason is the intellectual appeal of pseudo-historic wisdom. Establishing a seamless continuity between the past and today is appealing to our inner historian who wants to demystify complex problems with effortless simplicity. Repetition by respected figures also helps to build conventional wisdom. The argument that religious conflicts in the Middle East have been brewing since the dawn of Islam is constantly reiterated not only by major world leaders but also by the majority of public intellectuals, policy analysts, and media commentators. The goal is to convey in stark terms the hopeless nature of conflicts in the Middle East and to warn against further Western involvement, particularly after the American fiasco in Iraq.

Nader Hashemi and Danny Postel in their book titled "Sectarianization: Mapping the New Politics of the Middle East" provide a wide-ranging compilation from politicians, journalists, and experts who repeatedly make the case of ancient conflicts.[6] Excerpts Hashemi and Postel compiled from all these political and media figures underscore the wide-ranging and standardized nature of this narrative. Senator Ted Cruz, for instance, has suggested that "Sunnis and Shiites have been engaged in a sectarian civil war since 632, it is the height of hubris and ignorance to make American national security contingent on the resolution of a 1,500-year-old religious conflict."[7] Mitch McConnell, the majority leader of the US Senate, has observed that what is taking place in the Arab world today is "a religious conflict that has been going on for a millennium and a half." US Middle East peace envoy (and former Democratic Senator) George Mitchell has also embraced this narrative to explain the turmoil in the Arab world: "First is a Sunni-Shi'a split, which began as a struggle for political power following the death of the Prophet Muhammad. That's going on around the world. It's a huge factor in Iraq now, in Syria and in other countries." *New York Times* columnist Thomas Friedman asserts that the "main issue [in Yemen today] is the 7th century struggle over who is the rightful heir to the Prophet Muhammad—Shiites or Sunnis."

Similarly, comedian and TV host Jon Stewart commented on his very popular Daily Show on the rise and expansion of ISIS with the observation that the last time Sunnis and Shiites coexisted was in AD 950. This is "the only time it has ever happened, over 1000 years ago." The popular TV host and liberal commentator Bill Maher argued that the early modern period was a more accurate reference point for understanding contemporary conflict in the Middle East, in that Muslims were experiencing the equivalent of the Christian wars of religion. "This seems to be like the moment when the Muslims are having their 16th century," he quipped. "The Sunnis and the Shiites are going to have this out and we just have to let them have it out."

The right-wing TV pundit Bill O'Reilly similarly observed that "the Sunni and Shi'a want to kill each other. They want to blow each other up. They want to torture each other. They have fun ... they like this. This is what Allah tells them to do, and that's what they do." And even respectable voices in the academic and policy communities have put forward variations of this thesis. According to Richard Hass, president of the Council on Foreign Relations, a key factor that explains the instability in the Middle East today is that this "is a deeply flawed part of the world that never came to terms with modernity."[8] Given persistent repetition from such a wide range, it should not be surprising that conventional wisdom has popular traction.

It is worth mentioning that the argument of "ancient tribal hatreds" is not confined to the Middle East. Influential author Robert Kaplan popularized the concept when he applied it to the disintegration of Yugoslavia with his bestseller "Balkan Ghosts." It has been widely reported that President Bill Clinton developed major reservations about military intervention after reading Kaplan's book on deeply rooted hatred between Orthodox Serbs, Catholic Croats, and Muslim Bosnians.[9] A whole generation of policymakers and analysts who were jubilant about the West's victory in the Cold War were traumatized by the bloody dissolution of Yugoslavia and the genocidal savagery unfolding in Europe. Ancient hatreds driving intractable and immutable conflicts seemed alive and well.

A couple of decades later, civil war in Syria came to be seen in similar terms under a different American president. A secular, rational, democratic West could never hope to understand the primordial ferocity, sectarian complexity, and religious zeal of the Middle East. Outside intervention would do little good to improve the situation as long as these people were determined to fight. As President Obama said, this was "someone else's civil war."[10] The implication was clear: America had some nation-building to do at home instead of trying to fix ancient sectarian divisions in distant lands dating back millennia. Once the conflict in Iraq or in Syria is defined in such religious terms, it is not surprising that Western public opinion would see disengagement as the most appropriate response. Waiting for these ancient conflicts to burn themselves out appeared as the only viable option. It seemed that indeed only Allah could sort it out.

Disconnect from Contextual Reality

Perceptions create their own reality. But they still need to be challenged, especially when they are in blatant conflict with historical facts. This notion shared by Western analysts that the Balkans and the Middle East are lands where ancient feuds keep resurfacing in the form of ethnoreligious warfare and mass killings is a myth. In fact, both regions have experienced fewer wars throughout history than Western Europe. More than 80 million people were killed in the twentieth century alone in wars that started between Western European nations. Compared to such carnage, places like Iraq, Syria, Iran, Lebanon, or Bosnia-Herzegovina have been relatively peaceful throughout history. Those who complain about ancient hatreds in the Middle East often forget that the rise of a democratic, secular, and prosperous West was not a peaceful and harmonious affair.

Yet, the West seldom engages in similar primordial essentialism in explaining wars between France and Germany. Instead, there is a robust literature on nationalism, imperial competition, power politics, and political economy. The rise of fascism in Europe is often explained within a political and economic context—not with references to Italian or German cultural exceptionalism or immutable historic traits. Applied to Germany, one critic quips, the ancient hatred argument would probably see the roots of Nazi aggression in Gothic Paganism.[11] The argument of an enduring predisposition to violence suffers from lazy contextual analysis, sweeping generalizations, or at worst some form of genetic determinism with racist undertones that should have no place in political science, international relations, or social anthropology. This Western fallacy about historic inclinations for violence in the Middle East does not even pass the commonsense test: if conflict is preordained because of deeply rooted immutable hatreds, why was the Middle East relatively peaceful during most of its long history? If hatred is immutable, what explains long periods of coexistence between Sunnis and Shiites, Muslims and Jews, Arabs and Christians?

History is the battleground of conflicting views about coexistence and confrontation. Those who take the clash of civilizations argument seriously often use the Crusades as historical validation of deeply rooted religious animosity. The mirror opposite of such gloom and doom is a romantic interpretation of Andalusian "Convivencia" in Moorish Spain where Arabs, Christians, and Jews created a "multicultural paradise of cosmopolitan tolerance and coexistence."[12] These historic "grand narratives" of preordained war versus idyllic peace should always be taken with a grain of salt because they often overstate the role of religion without paying much attention to political, social, and economic context. In some ways, they are like theories of human nature without factoring in reasons for change in human behavior. Neither the Crusades nor Convivencia were purely religious affairs proving Christianity's aggression against the Middle East or the peaceful and tolerant nature of the Muslim faith. Only analyzed in their political, social, and economic context will they gain the importance and relevance they deserve as defining moments in the history of Islam and Christianity.

Strong States and Weak States

My main argument about the current Sunni–Shiite conflict in the Middle East is in favor of placing "weak governance" at the heart of the debate. Instead of pontificating about ageless religious and sectarian differences that overstate Islam, we have to pay more attention to changing contexts. Today, the Middle East has a high number of weak states with dysfunctional and repressive institutions.[13] There is almost no simultaneous presence of security, capacity, and legitimacy as elements of good governance. Not surprisingly, the rule of law, which is the real foundation of good governance and the glue that holds security, capacity, and legitimacy together, is missing in almost all Middle Eastern states.

Such weakness at the domestic institutional level is compounded by a geostrategic rivalry between Iran and Saudi Arabia at the regional level. Sectarianized conflicts are taking place in this context, not in a vacuum where they emerge and take shape independently of exacerbating factors. In other words, they are not timeless and eternal. To the contrary, their timing and intensity are indexed to changing conditions. This is why sectarianism comes in waves that correspond to regional dynamics in the Middle East and domestic developments in certain key countries. In other words, there are certain specific conditions that activate sectarianism.

Security collapse is perhaps the most obvious and important. A government unable to establish some form of monopoly over the legitimate use of coercion within its territories—to use Max Weber's definition of the state—is face to face with security collapse. The current sectarian conflicts in the Middle East are not due to a sudden reemergence of religious violence. In Syria, Iraq, Yemen, and Lebanon violent sectarianism did not cause security collapse. It is the other way around: security collapse caused sectarianized violence. It should not come as a surprise that when survival is at stake, people turn to their most trusted social unit—family, sect, tribe, clan, ethnicity, and religion—for security.[14]

The trajectory of Syria and Iraq are cases in point. The violence often starts with political and economic reasons as it did in Syria with young people demanding justice, accountability, dignity, jobs, and freedom. In Iraq, it was the coercive change of an autocratic regime accompanied with the collapse of existing government institutions that led to chaos. In both cases a combination of political, socioeconomic, and geostrategic factors led to violence—not some historic tribal feud. But once security collapsed and violence started, the conflict gained a sectarian dimension. In Lebanon and Yemen, the problems are also structural. In both cases we are dealing with weak states that lack institutional capacity to provide a legitimate sense of security and order. Both states have seen the rise of substate actors and militias providing security for their own members. Both states have no monopoly over the use of force and are unable to gain legitimacy in the eyes of their citizens by providing some sense of political and economic stability.

The sectarian conflicts of Iraq, Syria, Yemen, and Lebanon are therefore taking place in a context of failed, failing, or weak states. Armed nonstate actors at the subnational level have established their own armed militias in defiance of any notion of centralized authority. Security, capacity, and legitimacy at the nation-state level are nonexistent. Local power centers compete with whatever is left from state institutions to establish regional sovereignty. Combined with such state weakness, external intervention or regional proxy wars further exacerbate the whole situation. That tribal or sectarian conflicts have turned most violent in these countries where not only domestic institutional arrangements have collapsed but external geostrategic factors are also in play is not a coincidence. The historic weakness of the state often explains the divisibility—or sometimes total absence—of the nation. A cohesive nation with solid bonds of citizenship is often a product of strong state institutions. Any hope of nation-building in multisectarian, multiethnic, multireligious countries requires the strengthening of state institutions. And establishing security is a crucial first step not only for ending sectarian violence but also for beginning the long process of nation-building.

Yet, how states establish security is perhaps even more important than the final outcome of controlling the population. Arbitrary and abusive coercion without the rule of law is always problematic. Most regimes in the Middle East are brutal and oppressive. Security established under dictatorial regimes is not a healthy indicator of institutional strength or good governance. Such regimes may be good at establishing repressive police states, but they often lack a social contract between state and society that provides legitimacy for the governing center. In that sense, states that provide security and political order at the expense of justice, prosperity, and legitimacy are not strong states. Good governance and especially the rule of law require mutually fair and equal treatment of citizens, reinforcing institutional arrangements between security, legitimacy, justice, and capacity.

None of the states in the Middle East sufficiently meet these criteria. Suffering from varying degrees of institutional weakness and in most cases postcolonial creations, few would qualify as states with strong social, economic, and political foundations. Such weak institutional capacity makes nation-building a daunting challenge. Without centralized taxation, representative institutions, and efficient social and economic services, the relatively young states in the region are often unable to generate a sense of citizenship based on rights, liberties, and responsibilities defined under the rule of law. Instead, their hold over their population depends on division, manipulation, and repression. Such weak states often exploit sectarian, ethnic, and tribal divides and engage in "divide and rule" strategies in pursuit of regime survival.

They resort to such methods because they don't have effective and accountable institutions. Sectarian, ethnic, and religious differences can be surpassed, and a "civic" sense of citizenship can be constructed only when security is combined with socioeconomic upward mobility and trust in political institutions. Upward mobility is a critical contributor for transcending primordial belonging. Even in states plagued with sectarian conflicts, it is not a coincidence that those who are optimistic about coexistence based on civic identity are upwardly mobile, urban, middle-class people.[15]

Identity becomes much more fluid and elastic when survival is not at stake, institutions function properly, and citizens share a certain level of prosperity and educational attainment. It is in university campuses, not in the slums of Baghdad, Damascus, or Beirut, that intermarriage—the clearest sign of civic integration in diverse societies—is more likely to take place. When political and economic dynamics for good governance are in place diversity can easily turn to tolerant coexistence. In weak and failing states, however, diversity often leads to sectarianized polarization. In other words, in strong states religious or ethnic diversity has a strong chance to produce multicultural pluralism. In weak states such diversity has a much better chance of producing sectarianized conflict.

In short, context matters. We need to focus on social, economic, and political conditions when we speak about the root causes of sectarian violence or coexistence. Broad generalizations based on human nature or ancient tribal hatreds have clear analytical limits. The road from sectarian difference to mass murder is neither preordained nor instinctive. There needs to be a political agenda to prepare, instigate, and sustain sectarian violence on a large scale. As we will see in the context of Syria, Iraq, Yemen, and Lebanon, how sectarian identity is mobilized and weaponized under the condition of security collapse is also critically important.

Finally, it is important to recognize the role of external actors that exacerbate sectarianism. In the Middle East, weak states are the theater for geopolitical competition between Saudi Arabia and Iran, both engaged in supporting their proxies. Such assistance from external powers in pursuit of their own strategic and national interests is an important part of the problem. While there are exceptions, Sunni Saudi Arabia usually supports Sunni local actors and Shiite Iran supports Shiite groups. Saudi and Iranian regional competition certainly exacerbates sectarian fault lines, but at the end of the day, it is domestic dysfunction that creates room for interference.

When order breaks down and chaos, fear, and violence reign at home, local actors seek external help and patronage. The military and financial interference of outside actors can turn chronic and structural. This may create the sense that sectarian identities are immutably entrenched when they are in fact products of the chronic and structural weakness of the state. Alternatively, the regional balance of power between competing geostrategic interests can sectarianize domestic conflicts in weak states. This is why both the domestic and regional context needs to be taken into consideration. Having analyzed the basic contours of domestic problems we now shift to external geostrategic dynamics.

Western Disconnect and Nationalism: Iran versus Saudi Arabia

If state weakness is one critical dimension fueling the Sunni–Shiite sectarianism in the Middle East, the second one is the regional rivalry between Saudi Arabia and Iran. The Western disconnect suffers from an understandable obsession with Islam, which on the surface seems to control all political dynamics in these two countries.[16] After all, both countries have regimes that resort to Islam for political legitimacy. As a result, it is easy to think that Islam and a religious competition between the Sunni and Shiite branch define all their domestic and regional strategic calculation. In reality, rational rather than religious and political rather than theological forces are at play in the decision-making of both countries.

True, the two countries are engaged in a strategic rivalry for leadership in the Islamic world and have competing Islamic credentials. This façade of Islamic competition should not lead us to think that the rivalry is religious at its core. Nationalism in the pursuit of regional power and influence is a much more powerful driver of their strategic calculations. Both Iran and Saudi Arabia use and abuse religion, but what motivates their political strategy is realist nationalism more than religious idealism and rational pragmatism more than doctrinal theology. In their decision-making, economic, political, and military dynamics regularly take precedence over religion. In short, more than two Islamic actors driven by sectarian and religious agendas, Iran and Saudi Arabia are two regional superpowers with unique strategic and economic assets in pursuit of their national interests.

In that sense, religious sectarianism (Sunni versus Shiite) is only one dimension of this regional rivalry and it often takes second or even third seat compared to the nationalist (Arab versus Persian), geopolitical, economic (within OPEC), and ideological aspect of the competition. Both countries have competing strategic and political advantages in their pursuit of nationalist agenda. Saudi Arabia's custodianship of Islam's holiest sites and its vast energy resources is a major strategic advantage. Saudi Arabia has a much smaller population than Iran. But Riyadh tends to compensate this disadvantage with the fact that Sunnis and Arabs are a vast majority in the region compared to Shiites and Persians.

Iran, on the other hand, is a more organic state with a much deeper civilizational past than Saudi Arabia. With a population four times larger than Saudi Arabia, Iran has also greater military capacity than Saudi Arabia.[17] On the other hand, Shiites are a minority and the Persians are an even smaller minority in the Middle East. This is why, in order to project power and influence, Tehran had to excel in the art of using proxies by exploiting sectarian divisions in weak states. Iran may not have as deep pockets as Saudi Arabia, but it managed to create deep pockets of influences in critically important countries for its geostrategic interests. Finally, Iran also successfully wears the mantle of resistance in a region where colonialism left deep marks. It considers itself an ideological bulwark against Israel and American hegemony in the Middle East.

It is important to note that despite the Western narrative of an ancient conflict, in fact, there is no immutable, deeply rooted religious animosity between Tehran and Riyadh. In the not too distant past, these two actors formed alliances against common enemies. From the 1950s until the late 1970s Iran and Saudi Arabia were status quo powers that shared similar threat perceptions. Both countries were part of President Nixon's "twin-pillar policy" in the Persian Gulf where they operated as local guardians of US interests against the Soviet Union. Cooperation between Tehran and Riyadh extended to joint military operations in defeating communist elements in North Yemen, Zaire, Somalia, and Oman. Both countries were also highly alarmed by the republican pan-Arabism of Egyptian leader Gamal Abdel Nasser.

Nasser had a clear anti-monarchy message infused with socialism and anti-Americanism that directly challenged the Saudi King and the Shah of Iran. As two status-quo states run by pro-American hereditary monarchies, the Shah's Iran and the Saud dynasty were natural allies against this subversive message coming from Cairo. There was no talk of

Sunni–Shiite hatred or sectarian rivalry in this regional and international context where ideology trumped religious identity. Ironically, the only dispute between the two countries occurred in 1976, not because of sectarian animosity but due to financial and economic interest. The two counties differed on oil prices and production policies.

Even in 1979, when the Saudi–Iranian partnership unraveled in the wake of the Islamic revolution in Tehran, the problem emerged not because of a sudden discovery of sectarian differences but mainly because of a revolution that radically changed the Iranian domestic context. It is quite telling that Saudi Arabia's immediate reaction to the rise of a fellow Islamic regime in Iran was not overwhelmingly negative or alarmist.[18] Yet, things rapidly changed when Khomeini began talking about exporting the revolution and adopted an anti-imperialist and anti-monarchy narrative. Relations quickly unraveled as Saudi Arabia grew increasingly alarmed about its own Shiite population's susceptibility to the revolutionary message coming from Iran.

Do the Math and Act Strategically

Sectarianism is partly a numbers game. Demographically the Shiites are at a clear disadvantage in the Islamic world since they represent only 15–20 percent of all Muslims. Adopting a sectarian message to spread the Islamic revolution of 1979 would have been counterproductive for the Shiite clergy in Iran. Any hope of exporting the revolution had to downplay its Shiite character and emphasize its Islamic essence. This is why the newly empowered Shiite clergy in Iran emphasized the ecumenical nature of the revolution as an Islamic model. This, of course, only worsened the Saudi backlash and threat perception. Riyadh's counterrevolutionary effort emphasized the Shiite nature of Iran's theocratic regime in order to effectively marginalize and isolate it in the wider Sunni world, and perhaps more importantly at home and in the Gulf. The fact that the oil-producing eastern provinces of the Kingdom are home to a Shiite majority exacerbated the sense of Saudi alarm. Similar dynamics were at play in Bahrain where the majority of the population is Shiite.

Under such circumstances, it did not take very long for Riyadh to turn from defense to offense. Spreading Sunni Salafism became an integral part of the Saudi response to Iran's attempt to export its revolution. The sectarian winds were blowing with unprecedented speed in this new regional context. The two former allies were now engaged in a major struggle to win hearts and minds in the Muslim world. Both regimes had theocratic façades where Islam reigned supreme. But the real driver of this seemingly sectarian and religious conflict was political. Iran and Saudi Arabia had competing nationalist and geostrategic agendas. At its core, this was a quest for regional hegemony between two oil-rich states: one Persian the other Arab. Saudi Arabia and Iran have certainly leveraged sectarianism to expand their influence. Yet, sectarian difference was clearly not the root cause of their nationalist competition for geostrategic primacy in the Middle East. While both countries excelled at exploiting sectarian frictions in weak states, the essence of their rivalry has always been about political power and influence in quest of regional supremacy.

In addition to the Islamic revolution in Iran, 1979 was a fateful year for the Middle East and particularly Saudi Arabia for two more reasons: the takeover of the Grand Mosque in Mecca by puritanical Sunni extremists and the Soviet invasion of Afghanistan. As mentioned earlier, the first event pushed the Saudi regime to adopt an even more fundamentalist version of Wahhabism in order to preempt any accusations of departure from Islamic ways. The second development led to Saudi financing of Islamist mujahedeen fighters in Afghanistan under American strategic guidance. Islam and particularly Saudi Arabia's brand of Wahhabi Salafism was now in full action against not only Iran but also Soviet communism. Taken together, all three developments—the Iranian revolution, the siege of the Grand Mosque in Mecca, and the Soviet invasion of Afghanistan—amounted to a turning point for the rising profile of Islam in world politics.

The ground for sectarianism had now become much more fertile and the stage was set for an Iranian–Saudi showdown. Riyadh adopted a more fundamentalist and virulently anti-Shiite Wahhabi identity in this new context. The Iranian versus Saudi nationalist struggle under religious and sectarian garb witnessed three major waves that reflected domestic and regional developments.[19] The first sectarian wave, triggered by the 1979 Islamic revolution, gained a bloody momentum during the Iran–Iraq war when Saudi Arabia and its Gulf allies strongly backed Saddam Hussein. In 1987, when 400 Iranian pilgrims were killed in Mecca during a protest march at the annual Hajj pilgrimage, the Saudi embassy in Tehran was attacked in retaliation. A sense of détente came in the aftermath of the

Iran–Iraq war and the death of Ayatollah Khomeini in 1989. The rise to power of more pragmatic Iranian leaders such as Hashemi Rafsanjani and Mohammad Khatami helped ease tensions during the 1990s.

The second wave of sectarian tension between Tehran and Riyadh came when Saddam Hussein was removed from power by the American invasion of Iraq in 2003. The end of the Baathist regime and the subsequent collapse of order created a vacuum filled by sectarian conflict between Sunni and Shiite nonstate actors. The sectarianized civil war in Iraq unfolded in the context of governance and state collapse. In a context of civil war and chaos, the historically dominant Sunni minority now faced a newly enfranchised Shiite majority. The arrival to power of a nationalist Iranian president, Mahmoud Ahmadinejad, in 2005 made things worse. Already concerned about Shiite demographic majority in Iraq, most Sunni states in the Middle East came to see Tehran as the main beneficiary of the post-Saddam era in Baghdad.

The rise of the Shiites in Iraq combined with the growing regional influence of Iran led King Abdullah of Jordan to memorably warn about an emerging "Shiite crescent" reaching from Iran to Lebanon's Hezbollah.[20] With the war in Yemen, this sense of siege in the Sunni camp has probably turned from a crescent into a "full moon." The presence of Shiite communities in Bahrain, Kuwait, and Saudi Arabia is of course only exacerbating regional Sunni insecurity. It was during this second phase of sectarianism that Al Qaeda in Iraq under the leadership of Al Zarqawi emerged with the clear strategy of targeting Shiite communities and religious symbols in order to foster a sectarian war. This second stage slowly came to an end only when US counterinsurgency efforts with a significant surge in troop numbers helped improve the security situation. Combined with relative progress in intercommunal relations, Iraq appeared to be slowly stabilizing by 2009. The hope of coexistence proved very short, however, as sectarian violence came back as soon as security dynamics deteriorated.

The third wave of sectarianism is the current era in the Middle East. It began as the Arab Spring of 2011, after the promise of democratic revolutions ended up producing political instability and civil wars at the regional level. The Arab Spring had no sectarian dimension. It was the product of a legitimacy crisis in autocratic and corrupt states that suppressed their populations without offering upward mobility or any semblance of social, political, and economic justice. The aftermath of the uprisings exposed the weakness of state institutions. In Libya, Syria, and Yemen, there was full or partial breakdown of domestic order. Nonstate actors and militias emerged and began taking matters into their own hands. The outbreak of violence traumatized and radicalized societies. Survivalist instincts triggered tribalization and sectarianization. It is within this context of civil war and violent conflict that the Sunni and Shiite sectarian identity gained primacy. Coexistence, potentially possible under basic conditions of reasonably good governance, became inconceivable once security collapsed.

Nonstate actors emerged in this context of fractured and collapsing states. Localized and constantly feuding powers tried to replace state functions by providing a modicum of security and economic assistance to traumatized populations. Often, these nonstate actors reflected the sectarian, tribal, ethnic divisions within national borders. Yet, there were also many cases of serious fragmentation within the same sect, as it became evident in Syria, where dozens of rival Sunni militias proved unable to form a united military front against the Alawite regime of Bashar Assad. The collapse of order in Syria and the weakness of the state in Iraq became drivers of sectarianism and a magnet for external manipulation. In this third wave of sectarianism, the Syrian civil war replaced Iraq as the center of gravity for the regional power struggle between Iran and Saudi Arabia. The Islamic State, as we will analyze in detail in the next chapter, also emerged in this context.

It would be an important mistake to see the sectarianized conflicts in the Middle East exclusively as products of Saudi and Iranian manipulation. There is no determinism and certainly no single causal explanation as to why sectarianized conflicts emerge. The role of external support for domestic actors engaged in fighting is certainly important and it is abundantly clear that Iran and Saudi engage in such proxy battles. Yet, such external interference becomes possible only under certain domestic conditions of "exploitability" in places like Iraq, Syria, Yemen, and Lebanon. In that sense, as we will see next, if Iran and Saudi Arabia are external actors that can manipulate and compete "from above," they are able to do so mainly thanks to cooperation "from below."[21] The symbiotic nature of these domestic and external factors is critically important to analyze for an accurate understanding of how sectarianized conflicts emerge. In short, the *ripeness* of domestic context needs to be taken into consideration as much as external dynamics of manipulation.

Sectarianized Conflicts in Iraq, Syria, Yemen, and Lebanon

As a general rule, sectarianism gains fertile territory when state power recedes. The breakdown of order and security in failed states leaves citizens with no option other than turning to their own tribal, regional, sectarian, or ethnic communities for physical protection and economic subsistence. This is why in two of our cases, Lebanon and Yemen, where the state has never been fully successful in establishing central authority, people traditionally relied on their tribal and sectarian identity for their well-being.

Compared to Lebanon and Yemen, Syria and Iraq are more coercive states where dictatorial regimes have established police states. In the absence of rule of law, neither Iraq nor Syria had good governance. What they had, however, was the ability to monopolize the use of force. This gave their rulers and the ruling elite some strength, even if they did not enjoy much political legitimacy.

Behind this strong façade, however, both states shared a critical weakness: the rulers were from the sectarian minority. Sunnis in Syria are the demographic majority, but the ruler is an Alawite, closer to the Shiite branch. And the Shiites in Iraq are the demographic majority, but Saddam Hussein was Sunni. Being from the minority sect for the ruling clan in Baghdad and Damascus created a legitimacy problem. Both regimes tried to deal with this challenge by adopting Arab nationalism as official ideology. There was, therefore, no overt embrace of sectarianism despite the sectarian and politically repressive nature of the regime. This legitimacy gap at the top, between the ruler and governed, meant that both Iraq and Syria were much weaker than they appeared on the surface.

Iraq: Epicenter of Sectarianized Conflict

Any analysis of sectarianism in Iraq should start with the Baathist era. Of the four countries we are analyzing only Iraq has a Shiite majority. Iraq is also the birthplace of Shiite Islam with the holy sites of Najaf and Karbala. Due to the secular characteristics of the Baathist regime, which emphasized Arab nationalism rather than Islamic identity, Iraq also managed to keep its small Arab Christian minority as part of the demographic and political landscape. Contrary to conventional wisdom Saddam Hussein's regime was not an exclusively Sunni system determined to suppress all Shiites. Saddam's regime was certainly Sunni-dominated but also boasted a co-opted Shiite presence even in the upper echelons of power. Saddam's paranoia ensured that no one group, sect, tribe, or person grew too strong. His security forces would indiscriminately purge anyone perceived as a threat.

Lacking democratic and popular legitimacy, Iraq had a coercive police state that functioned as a dictatorship. Saddam Hussein maintained power through the Baath Party and his tribal alliances, including with some Shiites tribes.[22] His own tribal pedigree from Tikrit played a crucial role in establishing what in essence was a Tikriti regime, with members of his clan and family holding critical position in the security bureaucracy and Baathist leadership. In many ways, the strongman managed to create the façade of a strong state—despite tremendous institutional weakness in terms of good governance—where all levers of power were concentrated in one hand.

Iraq certainly had sectarian tensions prior to the 2003 US invasion. Yet, the regime's ruthless suppression of dissent did not have to resort to "overt" sectarianism in order to maintain power. A critical division in the upper ranks of Saddam's regime was the political geography of tribes. What is often neglected in Saddam's power structure is the urban versus rural cleavage. The regional background of tribes was sometimes even more important than sectarian identity in the patronage network of the Baathist Party. As Nir Rosen argues, "Hussein punished urban Sunnis who became too prominent and suppressed Sunni Arab officers from Mosul and Baghdad in favor of more pliable officers from rural and tribal backgrounds."[23] This opened a window of entry for some Shiites close to the regime.

To be sure, a civic Iraqi identity was never in the cards. Under Saddam the country was far from being an example of good governance, where Shiites or Kurds enjoyed upward mobility. Rule of law and basic civil liberties were missing. But Iraq assured "coercive security" and economic capacity with its police state and oil wealth. The system lacked democratic legitimacy, but the fact that sectarianism was not officially encouraged also created space for an Iraqi national identity to be forged parallel to Arab nationalism. As a result, especially upper-middle-class, urbanized Sunnis and Shiites led a fairly well-integrated existence. According to some studies, nearly a third of marriages were between members of different sects.[24]

Saddam also used Islamic discourse in a pragmatic and opportunistic way. In the 1980s he co-opted Islam in order to maintain religious legitimacy against the Iranian revolution. He also embraced Islam toward the end of his reign as a rallying point against a potential US invasion. During most of his time in power, Saddam adopted a zero-tolerance approach to Shiite and Sunni religious networks that escaped Baathist control. The Shiite religious figures that left Iraq under Saddam found a welcoming home in Iran. Such dynamics only exacerbated the Baathist security concerns about Iranian infiltration after the Islamic Revolution in Tehran.

The 1980–8 Iran–Iraq war exacerbated sectarian dynamics in Iraq and across the Middle East. Yet, the vast majority of Shiite Iraqis maintained their loyalty to the Iraqi state during the devastating war against Iran.[25] National identity trumped sectarian identity in the army where the large majority of units were composed of Shiites. After the war, Saddam's invasion of Kuwait in 1991 and his defeat by American forces opened a new phase in sectarianism. Iraq's defeat by American forces was followed by a Kurdish uprising in the north and a Shiite uprising in the south. These rebellions were partly instigated by the United States in order to weaken Baghdad and secure the collapse of the regime on its own, without an American invasion of the country. These Kurdish and Shiite rebellions clearly revealed the ethnic and sectarian fractures of Iraq. Yet, Saddam was allowed to brutally crush both the Kurdish and Shiite insurgencies. Having seen how vulnerable his state was to internal ethnic and sectarian strife, the strongman entered his last decade in power with a deep sense of fear, insecurity, and suspicion.

American Mistakes in a Sectarianized Iraq

The US invasion exacerbated Iraqi sectarian divisions in three crucial ways. First, postinvasion Iraq witnessed the total collapse of governance, particularly in the security realm. Fully disintegrating the Baathist army proved to be a critical mistake with devastating consequences on the security and capacity fronts. This situation created predictable dynamics of state failure and sectarianism: communities turned inward for survival, protection, and subsistence. Second, US occupation authorities instituted sectarian identity as the core criteria for the political and administrative distribution of power in liberated Iraq. This fateful decision ended up empowering and entrenching sectarianism in unprecedented ways. It reflected a clear fact: American officials saw Iraq not as nation, but as group of minorities. Finally, the political vacuum that came with the collapse of governance paved the way for Iranian influence. Tehran became the most powerful actor able to shape military, political, and socioeconomic dynamics in Iraq, predictably in favor of fellow Shiites. The consequences of these policies continue to reverberate in Iraq and the wider region.

Overall, Washington proved utterly unprepared for the postinvasion phase in Iraq. The Bush administration naively believed that Iraqi authorities would easily build new institutions for democratic governance and that Sunnis, Shiite, and Kurds would share power peacefully. In any case, there was considerable reluctance on the part of the occupation authorities to engage in long-term "nation-building" in Iraq. Once the security vacuum emerged, instead of power-sharing arrangements, armed militia group filled the void and began to establish their sense of law and order. Millions of Iraqis naturally blamed the American occupation for their ordeal and turned to their own communities, sects, and tribes for physical security and well-being. It was this predictable collapse of security, not ancient tribal conflicts, that fueled tribalization and sectarian violence during Iraq's ensuing civil war under American watch.

The American occupation authorities—the Coalition Provisional Authority (CPA)—committed additional major policy mistakes that worsened sectarianism in Iraq. When the CPA created the Interim Governing Council (IGC) composed of Iraqi politicians, its members were selected by sectarian and ethnic quotas. By insisting that IGC membership rigidly adhere to Iraq's sectarian and ethnic demographics, the occupation authorities explicitly made sectarian identity the fundamental and "official" organizing principle of government for the first time in Iraq's history.[26] Not only each sect was allocated a specific quota in the governing council, but all Iraqi citizens were also instructed to declare their sect in state-issued documentation. Sectarianization thus became systemic and structural.

In many ways, this was an American attempt to create a fair sectarian balance for democratic representation, reminiscent of the system in

Lebanon. However, the Lebanization of Iraq with local cooperation proved a strategic disaster for the country. Sectarianization in Lebanon, as we will analyze, had already a spotty record. It had failed to prevent political conflict and was in fact largely responsible for two civil wars and systemic gridlock. Modeling Iraq after Lebanon carried predictably similar risks and soon produced familiar results. Instead of power-sharing based on political competition, competition for political power and economic resources turned into sectarian and ethnic conflict, pitting Sunnis, Shiites, and Kurds against each other. And since the Shiites had demographic majority, as long as they remained a united political bloc, their dominance of Iraqi politics could not be meaningfully challenged.

The policy of de-Baathification of Iraq's military and bureaucracy made things worse by disproportionately affecting the Sunnis, who were overrepresented in Saddam's Baathist regime. Sunni social and military elites were removed from positions of power and had no political recourse to rectify grievances. Not surprisingly, these dynamics rendered resentful Sunni groups highly susceptible to calls for armed resistance. The insurgency against the state and its foreign patrons grew increasingly sectarian and radical within this political context. In time, as security dynamics deteriorated, not just Sunni elites but the Sunni population at large found itself disempowered and targeted by the Shiite majority.

These sectarianized trends culminated with the rise of the Islamic State of Iraq (ISI). As we will see in the next chapter, the group was more radical and sectarian than Al Qaeda. The fact that Osama bin Laden decided to distance himself and his organization from ISI speaks volumes about the depth of their divergence. Al Qaeda's main strategic objective was to drive out foreign powers, while ISI was determined to target Shiites and non-Sunni minorities. At the end of the day, the ISI's reign of terror led to the purge of Christians and Assyrians from Iraq, while Shiites and Sunnis grew increasingly segregated geographically and politically.

It is not a coincidence that the primary remedy to sectarianization is improved security. Such an opportunity presented itself when the Bush administration decided to beef up the boots on the ground. The 2007 US surge only temporarily improved the security situation. The injection of tens of thousands of more American troops managed to significantly reduce sectarian violence. But increasing the number of American military presence on the ground was always a palliative measure for what had turned into a systemic problem. The temporary improvement in security failed to resolve Iraq's underlying sociopolitical dysfunction, resulting once again in sectarian implosion soon after the departure of American troops.

In the meantime, a major consequence of the American invasion was to offer Iran a historic opportunity to transform Iraq from an enemy into an ally. Shortly after the fall of Saddam Hussein in 2003, Iran became the major regional actor in Iraqi politics. Tehran worked with Shiite and Kurdish parties to create a weak federal state dominated by Shiites and amenable to Iranian soft and hard power. Tehran supported Shiite insurgent groups and militias and established dominance in the economic, religious, and informational domains. Iran's strategy has been to unite Iraq's Shiite parties so that they can translate their demographic weight into political influence, thereby consolidating Shiite primacy. The Islamic regime also encouraged its closest political and paramilitary allies to shape and dominate Iraq's nascent institutions. In many ways, the vacuum created by the American invasion and the disempowerment of the Sunni establishment came to be filled by Iranian proxies.

What about the Saudi role in this sectarianized conflict? Riyadh was concerned about the consequences of a US invasion of Iraq. It saw most of the Shiite political and religious establishment as cronies of Iran and remained reluctant to engage with the new political order after Saddam's fall. Believing that by invading Iraq and bringing a Shiite regime to power the United States had "handed the country to Iran, on a golden platter," as a senior Saudi official put it, Riyadh sought to attain alternative forms of influence by funding Sunni Arab organizations and politicians.[27] Relations between Baghdad and Riyadh deteriorated further under Prime Minister Nouri al-Maliki (2006–14). Maliki was not only extremely close to Iran where he spent most of his life in exile during the Saddam era but also one of the most sectarian of Iraq's Shiite politicians. Not surprisingly he was considered by Riyadh and other Sunni Gulf monarchies an Iranian proxy. His tenure in power exacerbated Sunni fears of Persian supremacy in Baghdad.

Saudi Arabia retaliated by mobilizing fellow Sunni rulers of the Gulf Cooperation Council (GCC)—Kuwait, Bahrain, Qatar, the United Arab Emirates, and Oman—to take a confrontational position vis-à-vis the Shiite leadership by supporting Sunni groups and militia in Iraq. Although vulnerable to Al Qaeda at home, particularly Kuwait and Qatar have turned a blind eye to their citizens funding radical Islamist groups opposed to Shiite supremacy in Iraq. Meanwhile, young Saudi volunteers showed up to join a Sunni insurgency in Iraq, saying they had been encouraged to fight the Shiites. Money flowed mostly from private charity and religious groups in Gulf countries and Saudi Arabia to Sunnis who took up arms. And not surprisingly, some of that money ended up with extremist groups like Al Qaeda in Iraq.[28]

For a brief period of time, the surge in US troops in 2007, a crackdown on Sunni fighters by the Iraqi government, and improved cooperation with Sunni tribes provided a respite, as the jihadist insurgency and sectarian violence seemed to be under control. Yet, it did not take long for the security situation to once again deteriorate parallel to the departure of US troops and the abuse and humiliation of Sunnis by the forces of Prime Minister Nouri al-Maliki. After 2011 a newer and more destructive form of the Islamic State in Iraq rose from the ashes of the insurgency. The civil war in Syria made things worse as the Islamic State in Iraq gained a new foothold in another collapsing state and turned into the Islamic State in Iraq and Syria (ISIS). As we will analyze in the next chapter on ISIS, seizing major cities like Mosul in northern Iraq, the so-called caliphate generated a new wave of sectarianized violence.

Sectarianism begets sectarianism. In response to ISIS threatening Baghdad and to the ineffectiveness of the Iraqi army, Shiite militias backed by Iran took matters in their own hands. They proved critical in saving Iraq from ISIS and gained legitimacy and popularity in the eyes of Iraq's Shiite majority. In today's Iraq, ISIS appears to be destroyed, at least on the surface. Iran still has the upper hand in the sectarianized dynamics of Iraqi politics and the country remains one of the main centers of gravity in the Saudi–Iranian geostrategic competition. Although the security situation seems to be relatively under control, the Iraqi state structurally is weak and good governance is clearly absent. For anyone taking the weakness of Iraqi state institutions and systemic corruption seriously, recent mass demonstrations cutting across sectarian lines were hardly surprising. They simply proved that the real problems in Iraq can no longer be analyzed with the same old tired refrain of ancient tribal conflicts and immutable blood feuds between Sunnis and Shiites.

Syria: A Sectarianized War of Attrition

Syria's descent to civil war is the bloodiest tragedy of the third wave of sectarianism that came in the wake of the Arab Spring. It all began in

2011 as a civil uprising demanding justice, jobs, dignity, and freedom. When President Bashar al-Assad responded to mass demonstrations with a brutal crackdown, civil unrest turned into an armed rebellion. As state institutions fractured and violence escalated, the conflict rapidly gained a sectarian dimension. Syria's implosion led to a regional explosion of sectarianism, due to the critical role Damascus played in the Sunni–Shiite balance of power between Saudi Arabia and Iraq. As they constantly jockeyed for influence in Lebanon, Riyadh and Tehran considered Syria the big prize that would tip the balance in one way or the other. In that sense, unlike in Libya or Tunisia, the stakes were extremely high for regional influence and supremacy. Syria was also the gateway to Lebanon where a microcosm of all sectarian problems in the Middle East had emerged since the 1970s.

The Alawite nature of the regime in Damascus was a source of historic and political resentment for Syria's demographically dominant Sunni Muslim majority. The Alawites, at about 1.5 million strong and representing 12 percent of the country's population, are considered a distant offshoot of Shiism. This minority rule, combined with governance problems on the capacity and legitimacy fronts, fueled sectarian dynamics in Syria and it did not take long for the uprising to turn into a sectarianized conflict with a clear regional proxy war dimension. Once again Iran and Saudi Arabia became the main protagonists with Turkey also quickly joining the pro-Sunni camp. As Iranian-backed Shiite militias rallied to defend Assad, Saudi-backed Sunni militants hijacked the rebellion for their own aims.

Bashar Assad had inherited the presidency from his father who had dealt with Sunni Islamist by brutally crushing them in the early 1980s. Hafez al-Assad ruled the country as a police state. He knew all too well that his Alawite sect was historically regarded as heretic by most Sunni Muslims. His regime was highly repressive but cognizant of the fact that blatant sectarianism would be a losing game for the small Alawite minority. In Baathist fashion and in similar lines to Iraq, the Syrian regime, under Hafez al-Assad Syria, adopted staunch Arab nationalism as its official ideology. At home, his regime dealt with Sunni resentment by co-opting wealthy Sunni merchant families and placing many Sunnis in high-profile government positions. He also courted Syria's Christians and other minorities who feared Islamic fundamentalism. While Assad appeased the Sunni majority with elaborate patron–client relations, Alawites held key positions in the army and security forces.[29]

With Arab nationalism its official ideology, in time, Damascus also turned into a key player in the Israeli–Palestinian question as well as the future of Lebanon, where Syrian forces became the main military power. Syria became a major foe of Israel and Assad a delicate player in the balance of power politics. As his relations deteriorated with Iraq, he always maintained strong political and financial links to Iran without burning bridges with Saudi Arabia. Being from a minority sect, the Assad family had to learn the art of survival in a context where they could not afford to lose powerful domestic and regional allies.

The political and military ascent of the Alawites, a rural and poor community centered in the Latakia province, had its roots in the French rule over Syria between the end of the First World War and 1946. The French mandate over Syria and Lebanon and the British one over Iraq and Palestine were in essence colonial arrangements. They just had a more "civilized" façade that reflected the spirit of the 1920s when Wilsonian principles were being articulated by the United States.[30] It is hard to determine the exact motivations of these European administrative systems as they became protectors of minorities in the Middle East. What is not disputed, however, is the widely shared perception of a malicious "divide and rule" strategy. After all, a united front of Arab nationalism would naturally have turned against French and British imperial interests and it should not come as a major surprise that exploiting existing divisions is a time-honored strategy for any external power.

In Syria and Lebanon, France was the historic protector of Eastern Christian Churches due to both humanitarian concerns to strategic calculations to break Syrian unity. The French desire to give autonomy to Muslim minorities such as Alawites and the Druze—whose eclectic faith combined a mix of Islamic, Christian, Greek, and pagan concepts—had similar imperialist tactical motivations. Unlike other ethnic and religious minorities in Syria such as Kurds, Armenians, Jews, and smaller Christian sects that were geographically more dispersed, Alawites were a politically and geographically united regional force. Their inclusion by the French in the colonial army not only helped break the Sunni vanguard but also allowed Alawite officers to become an integral part of the Syrian political and national fabric, probably for the first time in their communal history of isolation in the Western coastal province of Latakia.

The Baath Party takeover in 1963 provided another opportunity for Alawites' upward mobility in politics. With its socialist and Arab nationalist character, the party attracted the Alawite underclass and

Christian minorities willing to prove their patriotic commitment to the Arab cause. By the time Hafez al-Assad sidelined his rivals and took over political power in 1970, the army's officer class and the Baath Party's upper echelons were mostly Alawite.

Shortly after the Iranian revolution, regional dynamics pushed Iran and Syria into a strategic alliance. More than Shiite identity and sectarianism, it was common enemies such as Iraq, the United States, and Israel that shaped the alliance between Damascus and Tehran. Syria's friendship and enduring alliance with the Islamic Republic since 1979 proved a major strategic asset for Tehran. Without Syria serving as a land bridge, Tehran could not have turned the Lebanese Shiite militia Hezbollah into its strongest proxy force in the Arab world. In that sense, Iran saw supporting Assad as key to helping secure its regional interests in the Levant. The war between Iraq and Iran and the mutual hatred of Saddam Hussein further consolidated the ties between the two countries.

Given Syria's strategic importance for Tehran, it is not surprising that the Islamic regime saw the survival of the Assad regime as a major national security interest. Once the Syrian uprising began in 2011, the potential emergence of a Sunni government in Syria aligned with Saudi Arabia was not a risk Tehran was willing to take. This is why when the rebellion turned into a civil war, Iran was quick to offer conventional and unconventional military aid as well as intelligence training and cooperation to Assad. According to most estimates, Damascus received billions of dollars in loans, credits, and subsidized oil from Tehran. The Islamic regime also sent its own military advisers from the country's elite Quds Force and fighters from its proxy forces—Hezbollah, Iraqi militias, and Shiite fighters from Afghanistan and Pakistan—to fight the Sunni rebels. According to both US government reports and Iranian official statements, Tehran has also helped create a 50,000-strong Syrian paramilitary group to crush the rebellion.[31]

For Iran's rival, Saudi Arabia, the Arab Spring was a nightmare. Riyadh, as a conservative monarchy, was against any kind of revolutionary change. Concerned about instability at home, Saudi Arabia responded to almost all uprisings of the Arab Spring by supporting the autocratic regimes. Yet, Syria proved to be an exception. There, the uprising presented an opportunity to topple a leader and a regime allied with Tehran. Syria was worth taking a risk in order to change the balance of power in the region against Iran. Riyadh saw a major strategic opportunity to put an end to Iran's political, economic, and strategic influence in a country where the

Sunni population represented 75 percent of the population. By providing vast financial aid and weapons to anti-Assad militants, Saudi Arabia not only sided with forces promoting regime change but also encouraged all Gulf countries to do so. Iran's support for the regime and Saudi assistance to the Sunni opposition turned the Syrian civil war into a bloody proxy war and sectarian confrontation with great implications for the regional balance of power.

The radicalization of the Sunni opposition in Syria, however, presented a paradox for Saudi Arabia. Riyadh considered Al Qaeda and other jihadist affiliated groups as a terrorist threat not only in the region but also for the Kingdom. Remnants of Iraq's Al Qaeda gaining the upper hand in waging war against Assad therefore greatly complicated the Syrian picture for Riyadh. After all, the same extremist forces considered the Saudi regime as their enemy and posed a threat to the domestic stability of Gulf countries. The fact that these jihadists became the most lethal factions in the Syrian opposition led Saudi Arabia to support more moderate but less effective groups within the Free Syrian Army, composed mainly of defectors from Assad's military. In time, it became obvious to all external supporters of the Syrian rebels—Turkey, Gulf counties, the United States, the EU—that there was no single Sunni bloc united against Damascus. ISIS emerged in this context of chaos, where a shattered Syrian state structure and internal rivalries within the Sunni opposition created a political, economic, and military vacuum.

The rise of ISIS offered Iran the opportunity to claim that its intervention in Syria was against terrorism and jihadism. Tehran identified the defeat of ISIS in Syria as the best line of defense before the threat would reach its own borders via Iraq. Saudis, not surprisingly, blamed Assad and Iran's sectarian violence for the emergence of ISIS. According to Riyadh, jihadist violence in Syria was a product of the regime's carnage. The best way of fighting it was to have a new ruler in Damascus. Iran made things only worse by supporting the massacres of Sunnis and contributed to the rise of ISIS by sending its Shiite militias to Syria. In short, in the eyes of Riyadh the problem was the Damascus–Tehran axis. The Assad regime and Iran were responsible for the civil war that killed more than 500,000 people, displaced close to 8 million, and traumatized all the Sunni populations of Syria.[32]

It is clear that Riyadh wanted Washington to play a more active role in Syria in terms of countering Iran's influence on the ground. Saudi leaders were particularly angered by the Obama administration's decision not to intervene militarily after a 2013 chemical attack blamed on Assad's forces. Despite such disagreements, they agreed to take part in the US-led coalition air campaign against ISIS. The emergence of ISIS as a major disruptor in both Syria and Iraq provided a strategic and operational opportunity for the Saudi–American alliance despite continuing problems on the bilateral agenda such as the Obama administration's willingness to diplomatically engage with Iran on the nuclear question. To be sure, Saudi Arabia was also highly concerned about arguments that ISIS and the Kingdom shared a similar Wahhabi interpretation of Islam along dogmatic and fundamentalist lines.

Despite increased Saudi and American coordination in Syria, the balance of power in the conflict did not change in their favor. For a while it looked like Damascus was about to lose most of the country to rebels and ISIS. At the end of the day, however, growing Iranian direct and proxy support, combined with the Russian military intervention in support of the regime, became critical turning points in the Syrian conflict. Particularly after the Russian air force entered the picture in 2015, Assad regained the upper hand. Under intense bombardment, the opposition lost almost all its strongholds including Aleppo.

Today, the Syrian opposition is confined to a small region in the north. After major territorial gains in 2014 and 2015, ISIS is also defeated in great part thanks to Kurdish–American cooperation on the ground and intense American and coalition bombing. Having achieved its strategic objectives in Syria, Russia is seeking to finalize its military operations in the country. As of 2020, the situation amounts to an important victory for Iran and a major setback for Saudi Arabia. Ultimately the clear winner, however, has proved to be the sectarianized nature of this conflict with its bloody legacy. Assad has restored a tenuous sense of stability in a fractured state and deeply divided nation. Syria's tragedy is a clear illustration of the sectarianized bloodbath that came with state collapse. The worst phase of violence may seem to be temporarily over. But there is no prospect for good governance in Syria and therefore no clear end to sectarianization.

Yemen: Sectarianized Proxy War in a Failed State

Another bloody civil war that is emblematic of the third wave of sectarianism in the Middle East is still taking place in Yemen. The poorest state in the Middle East, Yemen has a very weak centralized state tradition due to all its internal divisions. The country is home to two major religious groups: the Zaydis, in the north, are closer to Shiite tradition while Sunnis are in the south and east of the country. Historically, however, it was not religion and sectarianism but tribal, economic, and regional cleavages that have been the main drivers of political and armed conflicts in Yemen. For instance, the civil war between North and South Yemen in the 1960s was primarily a political and ideological conflict. Similar to the civil war tearing apart the country today, the conflict reflected the regional power competition of the time with one crucial difference: back then Saudi Arabia and Iran were on the same side.

Tehran and Riyadh assisted the pro-monarchy forces against republican forces supported by Egypt and Iraq. It is quite telling that at the time, in a different regional and ideological context, the shared Saudi–Iranian strategic interests trumped their sectarian difference. Saudi–Iranian cooperation in the 1960s is therefore a useful reminder about the fallacy of overstating "ancient hatreds" among Sunni Saudis and Shiite Persians. Different contexts create different alliances and hatreds. Nothing is immutable. When national interests are aligned, sectarian difference is hardly a major impediment to the pursuit of common objectives. On the other hand, when there are strong ideological and political differences in defining national and geostrategic interests, as it is the case today between Tehran and Riyadh, sectarianism becomes a powerful instrument. Once again, the key factor to remember is the primacy of political and national interests over religious and sectarian identity.

In the 1960s Iranian and Saudi interests in Yemen were clearly aligned. When an Egyptian-backed military force managed to establish an Arab nationalist movement by overthrowing the king in Sanaa, the Zaydi royalist fled to their stronghold in the north near the Saudi border. Despite being Shiites, the Zaydi royalists received support from Riyadh. Once again, political interests trumped religious identity. The Yemeni civil war ended in a republican victory once Saudi Arabia and Egypt came to an agreement and began to focus on Israel as a larger strategic issue for both countries after the 1967 war.[33]

Ali Abdullah Saleh, a Zaydi general who came to power after a succession of coups in 1978, ruled Yemen for the next 33 years. His most important accomplishment, besides staying in power, was to unite north and south Yemen in 1990. When he tilted toward Iraq during the 1991 Kuwait war, he paid a price but still managed to survive a Saudi-backed southern civil war in 1994. His cooperation against Al Qaeda during the 1990s also helped him in getting support from Washington and Riyadh.

The Houthis, named after Hussein al Houthi, a Zaydi religious, political, and military leader, emerged in the late 1990s as a resistance movement against the corrupt rule of Saleh. After a series of military campaigns to destroy the Houthis, in 2004, Saleh's forces managed to kill Hussein al Houthi. Yet, the movement had modeled itself after Hezbollah and continued to wage a rebellion in the far north of the country. The Saudis helped the Yemeni army and air force but never succeeded in crushing this Houthi uprising. As Bruce Reidel argues: "For the Saudis, who have spent tens of billions of dollars on their military, this situation was deeply humiliating."[34]

The current civil war in Yemen is a product of the Arab Spring unrests in 2011 and the collapse of the already fragile central state structure. Shortly after the central government collapsed, the Houthis grew in power and began to expand their influence across northern Yemen. As Yemen broke down into civil war, a familiar pattern emerged. What is primarily a complex political conflict fueled by battles over territory, influence, and power gained a sectarian dimension. A proxy war ensued with the involvement of regional actors. Previously marginalized hardline sectarian groups gained influence and used religious identity as an effective instrument to militarily mobilize their communities.

The war took its current form in 2015 after the Houthis moved against a very weak central government in Sanaa that was backed by Saudi Arabia and other Gulf countries. Riyadh saw the Houthis' aggression as another sign of Iranian encroachment and launched a military campaign to help restore control of the country to their ally, President Abdu Rabbu Mansour Hadi. Most experts agree that Houthis are indeed receiving some financial and military support from Tehran. Yet, it is also clear that Houthis, whose rebellion goes back much before the Iranian involvement, are neither an Iranian creation nor exactly a proxy like Hezbollah in Lebanon.

Ironically, when Saudi Arabia intervened in Yemen in the late 1960s, the Houthis were on their side against forces supported by Egypt. Today, the political context is different, and the specter of Iran looms large in every Saudi political calculation.[35] One thing, however, has tragically not changed. The current conflict, as civil wars in the past, is once again devastating Yemen. More than 8 million people live on the brink of famine and according to the UN, the death toll since 2015 is more than ten thousand civilians. And sadly, the deterioration of security dynamics and the instrumentalization of sect by internal and external actors once again show a familiar pattern. As in the cases of Iraq and Syria, state collapse is worsening sectarianization and paving the way for Iran and Saudi interference in the form of proxy warfare.

Lebanon: The Sectarian Model in a Weak State

Lebanon is a microcosm of the Middle East with its sectarianism, shifting alliances, and delicate balance of power. Sectarianism is officially enshrined in the Lebanese political system and often considered the main reason behind the weakness of the state.[36] Confessionalism is officialized in the form of sectarian quotas designed to administrate a fragmented state. Lebanese politics is also a critical arena for the two intractable predicaments that have plagued the Middle East: the Arab–Israeli conflict and the Saudi–Iranian power struggle. Particularly, the Saudi–Iranian competition in Lebanon has created proxy dynamics instructive of how sectarianism from below is exacerbated by geostrategic rivalries from above. Syria, Israel, Saudi Arabia, and Iran are all critically important external actors worsening the sectarian fragility of the country.

Sectarianism favors the religious community over the Lebanese state and creates a system whereby the state's main function becomes to serve religious communities rather than the other way around. This system of confessionalism in the distribution of political power naturally creates a fragmented social and political reality. A civic understanding of equal citizenship and secularism takes second seat to communitarian and religious patronage. Lebanese sectarian divisions are structural, endemic, and frequently violent, as the civil war that lasted 15 years in the 1970s and 1980s tragically demonstrated. Yet, as we will see, the sectarian alignments in the country are not immutable and rarely reflect ancient hatred. To the contrary, they appear to be pragmatic and quite Machiavellian affairs, dependent on context and balance of power dynamics. Lebanon with the weakness of its state and its vulnerability to balance of power dynamics is, in that sense, not only a microcosm of the modern Middle East but also a rewarding study showcasing the primacy of strategic interests over religious fanaticism. To be sure, radicalization and violence can become an integral part of sectarian conduct, particularly once conflict gains its own momentum and logic. But in essence, nationalist and geostrategic competition more so than immutable religious conflicts define the changing sectarian configurations in the country.

Despite the obvious problem of state weakness that these dynamics have created, there is a silver lining to the country's sectarianism that can be analyzed in two ways. First is flexibility. The fact that sectarian alliances are not permanent and immutable creates ample space for constant political bargaining. The axes of conflict and coalitions are fluid. For instance, at the height of the civil war, the conflict primarily involved a Christian versus Muslim dynamic. Today, however, the confrontation is mostly between Sunnis and Shiites while Christians are divided between the two groups. More than timeless religious animosity, the primacy of changing political interests is on display. It is therefore a positive sign that politics and political choices are not completely controlled by the entrenched logic of sectarianism.

The second potentially positive dimension of Lebanese sectarianism has to do with distribution of power and the absence of a sole ideological or military hegemonic power. Whenever Lebanese power-sharing arrangements are combined with a modicum of political stability and security, the system creates space for a vibrant pluralism that is unmatched in Middle Eastern regional standards. This healthy liberalism, whenever it is able to find space, is the main engine for Lebanese economic success and a critical factor that keeps the country together despite the weakness of state institutions.[37]

The fragile peace in current Lebanese dynamics is predicated on a domestic and regional balance of power where Sunni and Shiite actors play competing roles. The Sunnis, Shiites, Maronites, and several different Christian denominations form the main confessional groups amounting to eighteen different sects. As far as external actors are concerned, Iran and Saudi Arabia are two primary states supporting their Shiite and Sunni proxies. The influence of Damascus always looms large in Lebanese politics as a by-product of Iranian influence in the country. For Iran, Lebanon is the most important arena where it can exert military and political influence to shape the Arab–Israeli conflict. This is also why Syria is critically important for Tehran as the main gateway to Lebanon. Hezbollah, the dominant Shiite force in the Lebanese political and military scene, is much more than an Iranian proxy. It is an Iranian creation and the crown jewel of the Islamic Republic.

It is mainly thanks to Hezbollah's success against Israel in the 2006 war that Tehran has gained some prestige in the Arab street as a genuine force of resistance against American and Israeli regional designs. Iran's achievements on the Arab–Israeli front seriously undermines Saudi Arabia's image as a status quo power that depends on American protection. Being upstaged by a non-Arab, Shiite power on the one issue—Israel— that is critically important for the Arab and Muslim world is a major blow to Riyadh's Islamic credentials. The Iranian vitriolic narrative about whipping Israel off the map comes in this context of winning hearts and minds in the Arab Sunni worlds at a time when capitals like Cairo, Amman, and Riyadh appear to be in peace with Israel and in line with American positions in the region.

Faced with Iran's regional influence, Saudi Arabia is often playing defense in countries like Lebanon and Syria. Trying to isolate and weaken the Syrian–Iranian axis in Lebanon has been a major Saudi strategic objective. Saudi Arabia does not have a military proxy that can balance the role of Hezbollah in Lebanese politics. However, the Kingdom has deep financial pockets and has used its economic power as a major leverage in Lebanon by supporting the Hariri family's construction empire. Today, Lebanon's increasingly weakened economy is chronically reliant on capital inflows from the Gulf. Three Gulf countries accounted for 76 percent of new foreign direct investment projects in Lebanon from 2003 to 2015.[38]

Lebanon's fragile peace managed to endure the Arab Spring. The war in Syria, however, and particularly Hezbollah's support for Damascus are a growing source of concern for Israel, Saudi Arabia, and the United States. These three external actors are in favor of a more robust military effort in containing Iran. Their action could easily destabilize Lebanon where weak governments are usually dependent on Hezbollah support. Saudi Arabia's ruler, King Salman, and his son and designated heir, Crown Prince Mohammed bin Salman, are pursuing a far more aggressive foreign policy than previous Saudi rulers in Lebanon, Yemen, and the Gulf.

Yet, the fact that the main rivalry in the Gulf is now a Sunni against Sunni affair—pitting the Saudi–UAE block against Qatar—speaks volumes about the primacy of politics over sectarianism and religion. For those who see sectarianism as the main cleavage in the Middle East, it is also highly ironic that the main conflict between Doha and Riyadh appears to be about Qatar's support for the Muslim Brotherhood, another Sunni political player.

These are additional reasons for putting nationalism and strategic calculation, rather than religion and sect, at the heart of what makes or breaks alliances in the Middle East. Lebanon is a case in point. Currently, dynamics in Lebanon seem to favor Iran's influence. Assad's survival and Hezbollah's structural power as a state within a state in Lebanon are major factors that trouble Saudi Arabia. Riyadh was clearly hoping to alter Lebanese dynamics in its favor by supporting regime-change in Syria. Yet this policy failed. Now that the Assad regime has managed to win the Syrian civil war, Saudi Arabia is looking to contain Iranian influence elsewhere in places like Iraq and Yemen. In short, there is no end in sight to the Saudi and Iranian regional competition and these dynamics do not bode well for Lebanon.

Conclusion

Sectarianism thrives when state institutions are weak. As the dynamics in these four countries clearly demonstrate, sectarian difference is regional reality. However, these sectarian and religious identities are not the main drivers of conflict. Institutional failure to provide good governance creates security, capacity, and legitimacy gaps. The Middle East has several states where state institutions have either collapsed or fail to provide even basic levels of security. Civil wars in Iraq, Syria, Yemen, and Lebanon have emerged not because of ancient sectarian hatreds but because state collapse fueled sectarianization.

The perception that Islam and immutable ancient hatreds between Sunnis and Shiites going back to the seventh century are to blame for the current troubles of the Middle East is therefore fiction. This mirage overstates the role of religion and creates a major disconnect between the West and the Middle East. In fact, what the West gets almost constantly wrong because of its obsession with Islam is the simple reality that both religious and sectarian identities are open to shifting strategic alliances and calculations in pursuit of power politics.

These sectarian identities are therefore hardly immutable. Instead of Islamic doctrine, all we need to look at is the political context in the region characterized by weak governance at the domestic level and a rivalry between Iran and Saudi Arabia at the regional level. The confluence of these two factors drives the sectarianized conflicts of the Middle East.

Neither of these two factors are religious problems in need of theological analysis. Instead they both require contextual and institutional focus based on the primacy of politics. Governance collapse is primarily a political problem. The rivalry between Tehran and Riyadh is also about political power and nationalism more so than sectarian identity. Their rivalry is not timeless, ancient, or irreversible. As we have seen Iran and Saudi Arabia were allies in the 1960s despite their sectarian differences. Why? Simply because they shared the same political and national interests.

It is therefore critical to have a good understanding of the local dynamics before jumping to conclusions about religious identity and ancient hatreds going back millennia. While religious and sectarian identities are important, they are not destiny. Lebanon and Yemen show us how these sectarian identities can adapt to new situations and be manipulated by changing national and strategic interests. In short, political interests and agendas often override sectarian allegiances. The West will only stop overstating Islam when it recognizes the primacy of politics over religion. Analyzing governance failure and competing nationalisms between Iran and Saudi Arabia, as we did in this chapter, is a step in this direction. Next, we turn to ISIS in order to see how similar dynamics of failed governance and rising nationalism played a major role in creating this monster that is almost always analyzed through the prism of religion.

4 THE ISLAMIC STATE IN IRAQ AND SYRIA

In the last two chapters we analyzed how the role of Islam can easily be overstated in analyzing Turkey and Sunni–Shiite regional tensions. Our third example, the Islamic State in Iraq and Syria (ISIS), raises a categorically different question: Is it possible to exaggerate the Islamic nature of an entity that calls itself the "Islamic State" and declares itself a caliphate? For a book criticizing the Western obsession with Islam, making the same claim about ISIS may seem absurd. ISIS is indeed categorically different than our previous examples. The movement is the quintessential embodiment of violent Islamist extremism. It is recognized as an extremely violent jihadist terrorist organization not only by the West but also by the majority of the Muslim world. And there is no doubt that ISIS takes its own Islamist identity and jihadist ideology very seriously. Most of the books focusing on ISIS do the same: they have lengthy chapters on how the movement justifies its violence based on Islamic theology. And the apocalyptic prophecy underpinning the movement's savagery gets particularly strong attention in the Western literature.[1]

Less ink is spilled, however, on a series of other questions such as: why ISIS emerged when it did; why did it have considerable success in seizing, holding, and governing large swaths of Syria and Iraq; who are ISIS supporters, and why have they joined the movement? Once you engage in this line of questioning a different picture tends to emerge and religion takes second seat to political, economic, and security dynamics. As in the case of the Sunni–Shiite sectarian tension in the Middle East, the key is to contextualize ISIS and analyze the environment where it came to life. This is the road I select in this chapter in order to show that it is indeed possible to overstate the role of Islam in analyzing the emergence and success of ISIS.

Let me be very clear about one point. My goal is not to argue against the role Islamic theology plays in the way ISIS justifies itself and its action. A specific interpretation of Islam is part of what ISIS is as a radical, violent, fundamentalist organization. Similarly, I see no need to contribute to an already crowded field of books about the peaceful nature of "true" Islam. To engage in a theological debate about what Islam stands for is beyond the purview of this book. As I emphasized earlier, it would be counterproductive for a book that is critical of essentialism to engage in "reverse essentialism" by waxing poetic about tolerance, peace, and justice as intrinsically Islamic. The premise of this chapter, and the whole book, is that Islam has no single interpretation. For some Muslims the violent fundamentalism of ISIS may very well represent "authentic" Islam, while for many others it is a perversion of an otherwise peaceful and progressive faith.

My objective is to show that governance and nationalism, as two political factors distinct from religion, are critically important for an accurate understanding of why ISIS emerged and gained traction. In that sense, ISIS is not an exception for the political framework I use to explain the Middle East. As we have seen in the last chapter, the Sunni–Shiite divide in the Middle East often gained a new dimension under two critical conditions: governance collapse and the competition between Saudi versus Iranian nationalism for geostrategic influence.

The main contention of this chapter is that the same framework—governance collapse combined with nationalism—also applies for an analysis of ISIS where religion takes second seat to political power. In other words, there would be no ISIS without failed governance in Iraq and Syria where Sunni populations developed a sense of nationalist victimhood. ISIS has become a vehicle for Sunni nationalism and grievances in two countries where Sunnis faced an existential challenge.

What this chapter seeks to analyze is the political context that led to the emergence of ISIS, not the religious meaning behind the movement or its theological self-justification. And once you focus on the political rather than the religious, one specific aspect of ISIS becomes abundantly clear: it is a product of collapsed state institutions in Iraq and Syria. Simply put, such an organization could not have emerged without the breakdown of governance in two critical Arab states. In that sense, ISIS is not the result of a sudden religious awakening in the Levant. It did not come to existence to fulfill the spiritual needs of Muslim communities in search of religious meaning and belonging. ISIS is the outcome of failed states and failed governance.

In this context of weak and disintegrating states, ISIS filled a major security, economic, and political vacuum by projecting a state-like image and performing government functions. The religious appeal of ISIS in the lands that it conquered is at best disputable. Neither Iraq nor Syria are known historically, politically, and culturally as countries prone to a puritan interpretation of Islam along fundamentalist lines. On the other hand, once governance collapsed, both countries had pressing priorities such as the absence of a modicum of security, a crumbling economy, and a quest for some sense of order instead of violent chaos and civil war.

ISIS savagely and effectively imposed this sense of order. It was a brutal, barbaric, and violent sense of order but it came to be accepted as part of a larger governance package that improved basic services such as the provision of water, electricity, and garbage collection. There was one additional factor that strongly contributed to the meteoric rise of ISIS in Iraq and Syria: Sunni disempowerment and victimhood. More than its violent implementation of Islamic fundamentalism, it was the Sunni identity of ISIS, and more precisely its ability to establish a state in defense of the Sunni cause, that proved crucial for its regional success. As we will explore in the following pages, governance and a sort of Sunni religious nationalism were the two key drivers of success for ISIS.

Religious Nationalism among Sunnis

The fact that Saddam-era Baathist officers with their secularist–nationalist backgrounds ended up as elite commanders within ISIS is an important fact that deserves scrutiny in the framework of Sunni nationalism. In fact, ISIS is the lethal product of Al Qaeda in Iraq (AQI) and Baathist remnants from the Saddam Hussein era joining their forces. The common denominator of these two ideologically very distinct groups is their Sunni identity. ISIS emerged in an environment where Sunni populations in Iraq and Syria felt embattled, brutalized, and besieged by Shiites and Alevites. And it certainly did not help to see Iran standing behind both regimes in Baghdad and Damascus. Such an existential threat perception in the eyes of Sunni communities in Iraq and Syria raised not only the question of sectarian but also of ethnic identity with the direct involvement of

Tehran in the civil wars of both countries. The emergence of Iran as a major actor raised the specter of Arab nationalism with a strong Sunni religious accent. This is what I refer to as Sunni religious nationalism.

What Baathists and ISIS had in common was their willingness to fight for Sunni primacy. As we will analyze in the following pages, it is quite possible that Baathist officers saw in ISIS the most efficient venue to defend Arab ethnic and Sunni religious nationalism against Shiite hegemony and Persian religious nationalism. Religion and nationalism were closely intertwined in this context. The union between Al Qaeda and Baathism in Iraq came to symbolize this fusion of religious nationalism in defense of Sunnis. Simply put, embattled Sunni communities were in search of protection and statehood. The Islamic State in Iraq, which later evolved into ISIS during the Syrian civil war, came to their rescue. If jihadists and Baathists could speak one common ideological language, it would clearly be the language of Sunni religious nationalism.

It is also in this context of Sunni nationalism that the ideological difference between ISIS and Al Qaeda gained significance. Unlike Al Qaeda, ISIS is not a borderless, transnational entity. It fashioned itself as a state, a "caliphate" on conquered lands against the clear directives of "Al Qaeda central" and Osama bin Laden.[2] This decision to achieve "statehood" on conquered lands was highly consequential in terms of imagining the disempowered Sunnis as a nation that deserves its own state for survival. In a world dominated by nation-states, ISIS had a political rationale based on governing and holding local territory. Defying Al Qaeda's universalism also meant defying its universalist ethos in favor of local realities of governing a Sunni nation at the heart of the Arab world where Shiism and Iran were on the rise.

By fashioning itself as the caliphate, ISIS was also clearly pursuing a historic claim over a traditionally Sunni geography. Territories ISIS was most interested in conquering were Baghdad and Damascus, the historic capitals of Ummayad and Abbasid caliphates, now in the hands of Shiite and Alawite regimes. In the eyes of ISIS, these were the same heretic and apostate regimes that disempowered, brutalized, and victimized Sunnis. And both regimes were clearly supported by "Persian" Shiites. Revengeful Sunni nationalism emerged in this anti-Iran, anti-Shiite, and anti-Alawite political context. And ISIS took this Sunni nationalism to its most violent and fundamentalist extreme.

The idea of labeling ISIS a Sunni nationalist movement is problematic for Islamic theology. The reason is simple: nationalism is anathema to

Islam's ideals of universalism, which seeks to unite all Muslims under one caliphate. ISIS, however, was a product of its time and place. Contextualization rather than theological reasoning is key to understand that in the caliphate ISIS envisioned there was no place for non-Sunnis. The hatred of Shiites gave ISIS a clear "raison d'état" which required thinking in Sunni "national" terms of *Sunnistan*. In other words, the caliphate had to be established on lands where Sunnis were stateless and without protection. As Juan Cole, a Middle East expert, correctly points out, ISIS in essence was a "form of nationalism appealing to medieval religious symbols."[3]

Defying Al Qaeda's universalism also meant defying global jihad. Statehood required priorities other than fighting distant enemies. Becoming a state meant monopolization of power, taxation, public administration, bureaucratic management, provision of services, fixing infrastructure, and law enforcement among many other activities of statehood. ISIS had certainly a global message and global aspirations. But it had much more urgent local priorities. It was primarily a local, indigenous, home-grown movement that identified local enemies and local objectives. The universalist ethos of borderless attacks targeting enemies afar could come later—once power was consolidated at home. Providing services to more than 8 million people in territories that corresponded to one-third of Iraq and one-third of Syria required taking local Sunni victimhood, frustration, and grievances very seriously. This is why ISIS should be primarily analyzed in the framework of Sunni nationalism and statehood rather than under the guidelines of Osama bin Laden's global jihad.

America and Al Qaeda in Iraq

One of the many disastrous unintended consequences of the American invasion of Iraq was the strengthening of jihadist extremism. This is a tragic irony for an enterprise legitimized and sold to the American people, at least partly, with the goal of fighting jihadist terrorism. It is important to remember that before the collapse of state institutions in Iraq, Al Qaeda did not have a presence in the country. Iraq was never a state with strong institutions providing governance with an optimal balance between security, capacity, and legitimacy. In fact, freedom, security, and prosperity never coexisted in Saddam's Iraq. Yet, the Iraqi state had control over its borders and jihadist Islam did not have a chance to emerge as a force challenging the dictatorial regime. The US-led invasion changed all this by causing the breakdown of already weak state institutions. It exacerbated all divisions within an embattled Iraqi society that already suffered for decades under oppression, war, and economic sanctions.

America's decision to dismantle the Baath Party and the Iraqi army exacerbated the security and economic situation by creating a major vacuum. The de-Baathification law promulgated by L. Paul Bremer, the top American decision-maker in Iraq, probably made sense at the time. The law had the strong support of Iraq's majority Shiite community and their religious and political leaders, as well as significant segments of the Sunni population who also suffered under Saddam. Yet, the decision proved to be a fatal policy mistake. About four hundred thousand members of the defeated Iraqi army were not only discharged and denied their pension. Perhaps even more consequential was the inexplicable decision to allow them to keep their weapons.[4] This proved a fatal mistake that ended up significantly exacerbating the sectarian dynamics of the civil war.

It did not take long for these mostly Sunni officers to become part of the deadly power struggle between nonstate actors. In the void left by the collapse of the Iraqi state, the main protagonists vying to fill the gap were Shiite militias taking security in their own hands and a violent jihadist Sunni movement, AQI, under the leadership of Abu Musab al-Zarqawi. Zarqawi had a clear strategy: to turn the Sunni insurgency into a sectarian war against Shiites. He pursued this vision with deadly efficiency by carrying out a long series of suicide bombings targeting Shiite religious symbols. Zarqawi was the ultimate sectarian entrepreneur. His method of suicide terrorism was consistently aimed at Shiite communities with the strategic objective of provoking them to retaliate against Sunnis. As we discussed in the previous chapter, the sectarianization of the civil war was not an unavoidable outcome. It had to be engineered.

There is no reason to doubt that the neoconservatives of the George W. Bush administration truly believed that freedom and democracy would flourish on Iraqi soil in the wake of the American invasion. It turns out they were naïve and utterly unprepared for the consequences of their actions. Instead of freedom, first a major vacuum and later chaos and civil war ensued. Iraq came at the brink of total destruction and disintegration. As the civil war gained a sectarian dimension, a parallel level of sectarianism took hold thanks to ethnic and sectarian quota system the authorities favored. Once again, the American objective was far from nefarious. The goal was to achieve a fair representation of differences in Iraq's political and administrative system. Yet, in a country with no institutional capacity or memory of power-sharing, such policies only strengthened a sectarian sense of belonging. At the end of the day, Shiites were empowered, Kurds marched toward independence, and Sunnis felt marginalized.

Having lost their privileged status, the Sunnis felt understandably threatened by the rise of the Shiite majority, particularly when they found themselves targeted by Shiite militias. The ascendancy of Iran in Iraqi politics and Tehran's strong support of Shiite clerics and religious militia alienated the majority of Iraqi Sunnis. As the country descended into civil war, these threat perceptions became existential. The military, political, and religious rise of the Shiites fueled alienation, frustration, and ultimately radicalization among Sunni communities. Washington and the new politics of Baghdad failed to take Sunni victimhood and marginalization fully into consideration. This created an opening for the AQI, which became the precursor of ISIS. Sunni jihadism not only connected with Sunni grievances and anxiety. It also exploited and weaponized these fears. The AQI leadership under the guidance of Abu Musab al-Zarqawi ignited this sectarian civil war in order to monopolize the Sunni cause and victimhood.

Although Zarqawi was killed by American forces in 2006, it took more time for a semblance of security to emerge in Iraq. In the years following the invasion, sectarianism and violence had taken a life of its own. A fragile sense of stability emerged only after a significant increase in US troop presence and the wise decision to politically and financially co-opt Sunni tribes in regions like the Anbar province in central Iraq. These policies managed to establish security, but in the absence of a functioning government in Baghdad and measures providing better services and jobs, Sunnis still felt marginalized. Security without capacity failed to create legitimacy for the Iraqi political regime.

By 2011 a combination of sectarianized politics in Baghdad under Shiite supremacy and civil war in Syria once again created fertile ground for Sunni extremism. As if the fractured state and sectarian dynamics of Iraq were not devastating enough, the implosion of Syria made things worse. Bashar Assad's minority Alawite regime brutally crushed what started as peaceful demonstrations. It soon became clear that Syria was much different than Tunisia and Egypt where dictatorships collapsed under popular pressure. In Tunis and Cairo, the police and military refused to use deadly force against demonstrators. In Syria, the regime and its coercive apparatus had no reluctance to do so.

The regional dynamics surrounding Syria coupled with the domestic power structure of the country was also different because of sectarian dynamics connected to the Sunni–Shiite balance of power in the Middle East. That these crucial factors were absent in Egypt and Tunisia proved to be a blessing for popular uprisings in these two countries. Syria would not be as lucky. When the Alawite regime of Damascus crushed a peaceful demonstration with familiar methods of coercive ferocity and torture, it calculated security would quickly be reestablished. Yet, the opposite happened.

What was possible in the early 1980s, when Hafez al-Assad's Baathist regime crushed the Muslim Brotherhood in the city of Hama and managed to end the rebellion, was no longer possible thirty years later. Pictures of tortured kids filmed by cell phones were now going viral on social media. The domestic, regional, international, and technological context was radically different than in 1982. Quickly crushing the rebellion with deadly force was simply no longer an option. As demonstrations and the cycle of violence spread nationwide, a sectarian civil war ensued.

The Genesis of ISIS

With Syria exploding, Sunni victimhood gained new regional ground. While Iraq had a Sunni minority, in Syria, Sunnis were more than 70 percent of the total population. If Iraq was a utopian endeavor for Sunni supremacy, Syria was where this vision could meet reality. ISIS emerged as the successor of AQI in this context of civil war in Syria. As an alternative to chaos, state collapse, and Shiite supremacy, the organization rapidly turned into a vehicle for empowerment, protection, and security in the eyes of an embattled Sunni community. Under the banner of its pseudo-state, ISIS fashioned itself as the caliphate. At the beginning, international analysts and American intelligence did not take ISIS seriously. Yet, it did not take long for the movement to give a sense of unity and purpose to different Sunni jihadist groups. United behind ISIS, Sunni jihadism rapidly conquered large swaths of land in both Syria and Iraq.

As it built a social base for support, ISIS attracted recruits not because of its ideological appeal but mainly because of its military and political prowess. Unlike Al Qaeda, by declaring a state, ISIS committed itself to governing. Once the enemies were defeated, ISIS monopolized the use of violence in conquered lands. Paradoxically, ISIS also improved the security situation by brutally enforcing its religious laws, based on an ultrafundamentalist interpretation of Sharia. For most of the Sunni communities living in lands administered by ISIS, the religious extremism of the organization was a small price to pay for some sense of order replacing chaos, desperately needed basic services, and the need to have a protective shield against Shiite militias. In Syria, ISIS quickly turned into the most effective Sunni resistance against regime violence. In short, a brutally imposed religious, social, economic, and political order under ISIS was better than deadly chaos in the hands of Shiite militias in Iraq or brutal regime reprisal in Syria. In time, as its financial resources increased, ISIS managed to improve its social and economic services. This helped the organization gain more legitimacy.

It is hard to overstate the differences between ISIS and Al Qaeda on this question of governance and gaining state-like legitimacy. The decision to declare a caliphate and to target regional and local enemies was critical in the divergence between ISIS and Al Qaeda. Osama bin Laden favored a completely different model of transnational, global jihad. His strategic priority was to target the West with terrorist attacks. The idea of a caliphate was premature and targeting local Shiite populations was divisive in terms of fueling sectarianism within the Islamic community. Before the emergence of ISIS, bin Laden was equally opposed to AQI leader Zarqawi's sectarian terrorist attack targeting Shiite religious symbols and communities for the same reason. For ISIS, however, holding territory, establishing a sense of order, and terrorizing the "near enemy" was a logical extension of its own political and contextual reality.

In the eyes of ISIS, this contextual reality was abundantly clear: Shiite supremacy in two failing states where Sunni communities felt targeted and were desperate for protection. This situation could simply not be ignored in the name of targeting the West. Faced with Shiite and Iranian ascendency, prioritizing the far enemy was simply not an option. Unlike Al Qaeda, the ISIS model could not be one based on transnational and borderless terrorism. The priority for ISIS was therefore to target local foes—Shiites, Alawites, Kurds, Yazidis—and territorial expansion by tapping into regional Sunni frustration and victimhood. In that sense, the model ISIS emulated was not Al Qaeda but more like the Taliban in Afghanistan whose leaders established a system of governance by mobilizing a sense of Pashtun "religious nationalism."[5]

It is this combination of violent religious nationalism and relatively competent governance that turned ISIS into a formidable force that managed not only to terrorize its enemies but also to co-opt Sunni tribes and populations by providing them protection, services, and a sense of order. The financing for such functions came from the taxation of local agricultural and economic activities, a big share of the illicit oil trade and smuggling in eastern Syria, and control of networks of contraband trafficking. In his demonization of Shiites, the leader of ISIS Abu Bakr al-Baghdadi exploited the deepening Sunni–Shiite rift across the Middle East as well as the regional cold war between Saudi Arabia and Iran. He depicted ISIS's mission as serving as the vanguard of persecuted Sunni Arabs in a revolt against Shiite regimes in Baghdad and Damascus.

The Baathist Paradox

Before leading ISIS as the self-declared caliph, Abu Bakr al-Baghdadi took charge of AQI in 2010 when the jihadist movement in Iraq was in relative decline. To reverse this loss of momentum, he prioritized the recruitment of experienced Saddam-era Republican Guard officers from the disbanded Iraqi army. Later, when ISIS declared the caliphate, these former Baathist officers became elite members of its military machine. They were instrumental in the group's rebirth from the defeats inflicted on insurgents by the US military in the 2007–2008 period. According to most security experts, it is the entry of these Baathist officers that significantly improved ISIS's fighting capacity and competency, fully displayed first in Syria and later in Iraq when ISIS forces shocked the world by conquering Mosul, the second largest city of the country.

By 2013, the majority of tactical and operational decision-makers within ISIS military councils were Iraqi Baathist officers. Battle plans were drawn according to their guidance and their military experience proved critical in almost all stages of combat. As the elite corps of military councils, Baathist strategists were also the ones commanding foot soldiers who mostly joined the movement from local Sunni communities and foreign fighters from neighboring countries in the Middle East and North Africa, the larger Islamic world, and the Muslim diaspora in the

West. When the US-led air campaign against ISIL began in 2015 it was estimated that half of the ISIS military council leadership were Baathist officers from the Republican Guards.[6]

The entry of these Saddam-era elements into the picture poses a dilemma and mismatch given the radically different ideological pedigree of Baathist officers and ISIS: Why would members of an Arab nationalist movement with secularist roots make common cause with a jihadist movement that practices a brutal theocratic model of governance? This question is central to the main argument of this chapter. The embrace of ISIS is the clearest evidence that the self-declared caliphate represented much more than just a jihadist ideological movement for these Baathist officers. There is probably more than just one reason why Saddam's soldiers joined the movement. But commonsense should take us in the direction of Sunni nationalism rather than jihadist conviction. This is not to say that all Baathist officers were hardcore secularists with no connection to Islam. It is clear that Baathism under Saddam had an opportunistic approach to religion.

In fact, during his last decade in power Saddam decided to co-opt Islam for political reasons. With the launch of the Faith Campaign in 1994, strict Islamic precepts were introduced. The phrase "God is Great" was inscribed on the Iraqi flag. Some Baathist officers recall friends who suddenly stopped drinking, started praying, and embraced the deeply conservative form of Islam known as Salafism.[7] But such sudden shifts are seldom motivated by purely religious convictions. Career-oriented opportunism and political motivations for upward mobility may have also played a role. In any case, it makes more sense to think of Baathism not as a doctrinal ideology but more as a network of patronage and clientelism for the Sunni ruling elite of Iraq under Saddam Hussein. In other words, for both Saddam and his followers what truly mattered was political survival rather than strict adherence to any ideology. And survival primarily depended on Sunnis having the upper hand in ruling the country. Despite the successful co-optation of Islam and Shiite elements, the essence of the Baathist regime was about Sunni supremacy. All instruments of power were monopolized by Saddam Hussein and his own Sunni tribe from Tikrit.

When this edifice of power crumbled in the wake of the American invasion, Baathist elements felt politically and economically marginalized. The loss of power and the urge to gain it back was probably a major motivation for many Baathist officers who joined the winning horse. Anecdotal evidence seems to point in that direction indicating some skepticism among ISIS hardliners about Baathist intentions in joining the movement. "They just want power" seems to be the impression true believers within ISIS formed of former Baathists joining the movement.[8] It is equally plausible that the leadership of ISIS exploited the economic and political desperation of Baathist officers in order to use their military expertise. If this is the case, it would demonstrate the political opportunism and pragmatism of ISIS in terms of forging an alliance with Baathist officers despite significant ideological differences. In other words, ISIS and Baathists had a marriage of convenience based on shared Sunni interests. Their alliance was far from a match made in heaven.

Shared interests are often formed thanks to shared enemies and threat perceptions. In the case of ISIS and Baathism there is no doubt that the shared nemesis was Shiism and the sectarian policies of Iraqi Prime Minister Nouri al-Maliki who managed to create a new pool of Sunni discontent after 2011. Maliki pursued what amounted to a second round of de-Baathification by firing the majority of Sunni officers who were reintegrated into the army during the "surge" of American forces in 2007 and 2008. The example of high-level officers such as Brigadier General Hassan Dulaimi is highly relevant in order to understand the problem. Dulaimi was an intelligence officer in the old Iraqi army who was recruited back into service by US troops in 2006 as a police commander in Ramadi, the capital of the long restive province of Anbar. Within months of the American departure in 2011, he was dismissed and lost his salary and pension. In an interview with the *Washington Post*, Dulaimi said some of his friends joined the Islamic State purely for economic reasons and that they soon gained high-level positions as administrators as well as strategists. "The people in charge of military operations in the Islamic State were the best officers in the former Iraqi army, and that is why the Islamic State beats us in intelligence and on the battlefield."[9] The influx of Baathist officers was on clear display in the immediate surrounding of Baghdadi, the ISIS leader. Abu Muslim al-Turkmani who served as his deputy in Iraq and Abu Ayman al-Iraqi, his top military commanders in Syria, both had Baathist military backgrounds.

These highly positioned former Baathist officers provided a critical filter against foreign intelligence infiltration to ISIL. Given the increasing numbers of Muslim recruits coming from Western countries between 2012 and 2015, the issue was of utmost importance for ISIL. Former

Baathist officers managed to insulate the top leadership of ISIL with their elaborate intelligence networks drawn from Saddam-era tradecraft. According to many former ISIS fighters at the lower levels, these former Iraqi military and intelligence officers became the eyes and ears of the organization.

Common Traits between ISIS and Baathism

In many ways, for Baathists, the partnership with ISIS was a pragmatic political enterprise rather than a deeply religious affair based on Islamic convictions. If ideology is not the answer, it makes sense to focus on other factors to explain this alliance. In addition to Sunni identity, the two groups had one more trait in common: how they approached power and use of force. Despite their ideological differences, a proclivity for violence and radicalism is part of both group's political culture. In that sense, a critical factor that united ISIS and Baathism was their rationalization of savagery. Both ISIS and Baathism broadly overlapped in their reliance on fear to secure the submission of people under their rule. ISIS carried out massacres, beheadings, systemic torture, barbaric methods of execution, and many other atrocities. Elaborate and cruel forms of torture were also not uncommon for Saddam's Baathist regime, which particularly in its last years decreed beheadings and systemic torture carried out by the Fedayeen unit.

The Islamic State's barbaric punishment methods followed the logic of terrorizing enemies while projecting strength to potential recruits. Similar factors were at play for Baathists radicals. In fact, by joining ISIS, Baathist officers may have just switched from one type of radicalism to another. Under this scenario too, more than ideological harmony, shared methods of repression and a certain common understanding of how to best subjugate opposing forces—both political rather than religious motivations—would explain why ISIS and Baathists joined forces. In any case, the decision to brutalize, traumatize, and terrorize its enemies in order to impress its sympathizers was a strategic choice coming from the top. Baghdadi's slogan of "victory through fear and terrorism" was a clear message to friends and foes alike. After the ethnic cleansing of Kurds, Yazidis, and Shiites from conquered lands, ISIS would prove that it adhered to a doctrine of total war by also rejecting any compromise with Sunni Islamist groups.

According to Fawaz Gerges, an expert on the Middle East and ISIS, the brutality of the organization partly stems from the rural background of most of its members. While Al Qaeda and other previous jihadist groups had leaders from the urban social elite and a rank and file mainly composed of lower-middle-class university graduates, "ISIS's cadre is rural and lacking in both theological and intellectual accomplishment. This social profile helps ISIS thrive among poor, disenfranchised Sunni communities in Iraq, Syria, Lebanon, and elsewhere."[10] Often a brutal logic of war trumped any constraints or need to rely on theology to justify action. ISIS promotional videos followed the same logic based on a cult of violence. Under Saddam, video scenes of Fedayeen training, marching in black masks, decapitating enemies, and, in one instance, eating a live dog had the same objective to project fear and intimidation.[11] In some ways, these videos were precursors of the ISIS propaganda machine that perfected the method with technical sophistication and a touch of Hollywood-like visual impacts.

Similar to the Sunni identity of ISIS transcending the borders between Syria and Iraq, there was also an element of transnationalism in the Baathist movement seeking to unite the Arab world behind the cause of Arab nationalism. The party established branches in countries across the Middle East and organized training camps for foreign volunteers from across the Arab world. Finally, it is also important to remember that prison conditions often become an incubator of terrorism and radicalization. The intermingling jihadists with Baathists during the American occupation at sites like Camp Bucca probably offered a toxic platform of ideological cross-fertilization. When ISIS embarked on an aggressive campaign to woo former Iraqi officers, such dynamics also facilitated Baathist integration in the movement.

At the end of the day, more than jihadism it was a shared sense of Sunni identity and nationalism against Shiite ascendency that fueled this lethal partnership. Other common factors such as the cult of violence, a certain level of transnationalism, or shared time in prison are also primarily political rather than religious drivers. All these dynamics provide clear evidence that it is indeed possible to overstate the role of Islam in the success of ISIS. What spurred the rise of ISIS was not a sudden need for radical Salafist Islam in Iraq and Syria. The institutional breakdown of Syria and Iraq, the quest for Sunni survival, and Sunni religious nationalism seeking revenge against Shiites are primary drivers behind ISIS taking over Sunni towns and cities with relative ease. Without disenfranchised Sunnis and the collapse of governance there would be no ISIS.

ISIS and Foreign Fighters

Having established the role of Sunni nationalism and Sunni grievances as crucial factors behind the rise of ISIS in two states with no real security, capacity, and legitimacy we can now move to the question of foreign fighters and their motivations for joining the movement. ISIS became a major pool of attraction after its territorial conquests in late 2014. Thousands have made the journey to Syria from the West, Russia, and, of course, the Muslim world itself. My goal in this chapter is not to provide an exhaustive study on their activities in Syria or who they are in terms of their national backgrounds. Not all of these individuals ended up as fighters for ISIS, but there is no reason to doubt that they were radicalized human beings. For the purpose of this study, the question I ask is more specific but also harder to answer: what is the role of Islam in their radicalization process?

Once again, as in the case of the Islamic identity of ISIS itself, it would be an understatement to say that those who joined the organization take their devotion to Islam very seriously. Not to do so would be absurd for both the organization and its followers. But the question I seek to answer is not whether foreign fighters who join ISIS are jihadists committed to their faith. We know they are. Instead, my objective is to understand the role Islam played in their journey toward radicalism. Are the individuals joining ISIS radicalized after reading the Koran or were they radicalized before they found religion?

In other words, as in the binary formula made popular by the French expert on political Islam Olivier Roy, are we dealing with the "radicalization of Islam" or the "Islamization of radicalism"?[12] We have just analyzed how the collapse of governance and Sunni nationalism—rather than a sudden Islamic awakening—led to the emergence of ISIS. Is it also possible that factors beyond religion also played a major role in the radicalization of jihadists? Is there room to argue that Islam provided only a superficial ideological cover for already radicalized individuals? My short answer is yes. It is very likely that there is a tendency to overstate the role of Islam in the radicalization process of those who ended up joining ISIS as foreign fighters.

Relative Deprivation and Frustrated Achievers Revisited

In analyzing who joins ISIS, it makes sense to revisit some of the arguments and concepts such as "relative deprivation" and "frustrated achievers" introduced in the first chapter. As we discussed earlier, stripped to its most basic form, the debate about the root causes of radicalization is polarized between two major camps. One group sees culture, religion, and ideology as primary drivers, while the other prioritizes economic and social factors. The correlation between socioeconomic deprivation and radicalism is strongly rejected by this culturalist camp for a simple reason: most terrorists are neither poor nor uneducated. In fact, the majority of terrorists seem to come from middle-class, ordinary backgrounds. Terrorism therefore has no socioeconomic roots or any obvious links to deprivation. It is a security challenge with strong ideological roots and the fight should be at the ideological and counterterrorism level.

For the other group focusing on the social and economic roots of the problem, priority should be given to development, education, and good governance. Instead of a single-minded focus on religion, Islam, and jihadist ideology, the struggle against radicalization should primarily target the social and economic context where terrorism finds acceptance. The fight against violent jihadist ideology can only succeed by addressing the popular anger that motivates it and this anger is about social, economic, and political injustice in the domestic societies and global context.

Both camps make valid points with major implications for policymakers. What we need in analyzing who joins ISIS is a pragmatic approach that can see the merits of both camps in order to forge a third way. The key is to transcend this binary debate in favor of a multidisciplinary approach that avoids rigid determinism. Understanding who joins jihadist groups such as Al Qaeda or ISIS requires going beyond socioeconomic factors or ideology as mutually exclusive drivers. There are many pathways to terrorism. Similarly, radicalization is a complex phenomenon with multiple causes. Any attempt to generate a profile is bound to be reductionist unless various social, cultural, economic, political, and psychological causes are factored in. This is why dismissing the economic and social roots of radicalization on the grounds that most terrorists have middle-class backgrounds is simplistic and misleading. And it is equally wrong and reductionist to argue that ideology, culture, and religion play no role in the radicalization process.

For a multidisciplinary and open-minded approach, the place to start is to accept that ideology becomes much more important when socioeconomic, political, and psychological aspirations are on the rise. For many Muslims in the West, as well as in the Islamic world itself, there is a major tension between growing expectations and the dismaying realities on the ground. The tension and radicalization fueled by rising expectations are of course not new. There is a vast academic and political literature explaining the history of revolutions with rising expectations.[13] What is new today is the unprecedented scale and scope that globalization brings to the equation. Easy access to information makes the political, economic, social, and cultural contrast between the West and the rest of the world visible and touchable at an extraordinary scale. This brings unprecedented power and fervor to relative deprivation. As a result, expectations, resentments, and frustrations play out at a new level. The social and psychological dimensions of this tension coupled with the question of belonging, identity, purpose, and meaning add further complexity to the predicament. Thus, the challenge goes well beyond the simple issue of economic deprivation. Deprivation is now increasingly relative to growing social, psychological, political, moral, ideological, and identity-related needs, aspirations, and expectations.

The concept of relative deprivation can also help us understand why most radicalized individuals who venture into terrorism seem to have middle-class economic backgrounds. Aspirations, expectations, and ambitions increase with upward socioeconomic mobility. The quest for success, meaning, and purpose is also often the product of a life where economic subsistence is no longer the primary concern. The real challenge is the perception that the road to "further success" is blocked. Frustration tends to increase when rising aspirations remain unfulfilled. For instance, individuals who are educated and ambitious but see no real prospects for their social and economic upward mobility due to systemic obstacles beyond their control—such as racism, cronyism, corruption, bias, and rigid class structures—can easily turn into "vulnerable frustrated achievers" tempted by radicalism. Educated but unemployed youth in the Arab world or in the European Muslim diaspora potentially present such a demographic group venturing into patterns of radicalization.

Their frustration is not purely economic. It has strong political and social dimensions. Providing jobs and economic benefits without creating outlets for political and social participation fall in this important category of relative deprivation. Education without employment or employment without a sense of political empowerment fuels the dynamics of humiliation, alienation, and frustration. This is why the growing numbers of educated but unemployed youth are particularly alarming for those who are concerned about the rise of frustrated achievers in the Arab world—and among Muslim minorities in Europe, where there are additional identity issues exacerbating the problem. In addition to studies focusing on how rising expectations may cause revolutions, there is a growing body of literature that looks at frustrated achievers with high ambitions and high levels of individual dissatisfaction.[14]

Based on this methodology focusing on relative deprivation and frustrated achievers, it makes sense that a small country like Tunisia, which has not only high levels of educational attainment compared to the standards of the Arab world but also very high unemployment rates, provides disproportionately high numbers of recruits to ISIS. Similar dynamics of relative deprivation are at play in Europe, where significant portions of Muslim populations are young, frustrated, and relatively educated but often unemployed and uprooted from any sense of belonging. For instance, a small country like Belgium—with serious national identity, unemployment, and Muslim integration problems—provides the perfect example of a toxic breeding ground where, like Tunisia, a disproportionately high number of ISIS recruits have emerged. In that sense, concepts such as relative deprivation and frustrated achievers provide excellent analytical tools shedding light on links between socioeconomic factors and ideological radicalization.

Tunisia and Belgium may be special cases, but the interconnected nature of the world thanks to information technology and globalization creates a widespread and acute awareness about opportunities elsewhere. We live in a global context and globalization itself further complicates the problem of relative deprivation. Poverty is no longer an absolute concept in the context of globalization. Deprivation in an interdependent world immediately turns into relative deprivation thanks to easy access to information and comparison. Rising inequality and a heightened awareness of such inequality go hand in hand. The scale of frustration is compounded by a demographic explosion and weak state capacity in large parts of the Middle East and North Africa. The absence of opportunities relative to expectations is particularly acute in the Arab world and larger Islamic world. Socioeconomic decay in the Islamic world often creates considerably more frustration than in other parts of the developing world for historical and civilizational reasons as well. And this is where culture, ideology, and socioeconomic dynamics merge to form a combustible mix.

Seen in this context, relative deprivation can also help us understand the role religion plays in radicalization. Among Islamists, there is a sense of nostalgia for the golden age of Islam from the eighth to the twelfth century during which Arab civilization was much more advanced than the Christian West in terms of its scientific, architectural, philosophical, and military achievements. This historic success of the Islamic world relative to Europe is a source of Arab pride and anguish given where the Middle East is today. The West, and particularly Europe, remains a point of reference and comparison for the Middle East for reasons having to do with geographic proximity, historic rivalry, and recent patterns of immigration. Past achievements combined with present inferiority fuel a sense of frustration and victimhood. The legacy of colonialism and military subjugation is particularly relevant because they create feelings of injustice and resentment in the eyes of progressive intellectuals as well as right-wing populists.

These factors, combined, make Islam a religion that shares the feelings of frustrated achievers at the civilizational level. In other words, Islam as a religion is a microcosm of relative deprivation. The gap between Muslim expectations and opportunities in the Middle East is enormous and this makes Islam a frustrated achiever. The Muslim faith had once created a great civilization that far surpassed the West but today it has not much to boast about in terms of economic, political, and cultural success. This exacerbates frustration among growing cohorts of urbanized, undereducated, and unemployed Muslim youth who are increasingly making comparisons between their civilizational failure and the success of the West. The scale of youth frustration is compounded by a demographic explosion, growing expectations, weak state capacity, and diminishing opportunities for upward mobility in most parts of the Islamic world.

There is therefore a certain way to discuss the role of history, culture, civilization, and religion in connection with social, economic, political, and ideological dynamics when we discuss the complex roots of radicalization. In analyzing the issue of who joins ISIS, the key, once again, is to understand the context rather than the religious texts. In other words, as Dalia Mogahed puts it: "It is not the interpretation of Islamic text that drives the brutality of ISIS—it's the group's desired brutality driving its interpretation of the texts."[15] In what appears to be a sequencing question, radicalization often precedes the turn to Islam to find meaning and direction in channeling preexisting frustration, resentment, and humiliation.

Radicalization versus Terrorism

The prioritization of radicalization as a "process" with all its implications in terms of sequencing provides a better paradigm and framework to analyze the root causes of terrorism for a number of reasons. First, radicalization more accurately reflects the political and ideological dimensions of the threat. No matter how diverse the causes, motivations, and ideologies of terrorist organizations, all attempts at premeditated violence against civilians share the traits of violent radicalism. Second, while terrorism is a deadly security challenge, radicalism is primarily a political threat against which noncoercive measures should be given a chance. There is nothing preordained in the potential transition from radicalism to terrorism. Most terrorists start their individual journey toward extremist violence first by becoming radicalized militants. All terrorists, by definition, are radicals. Yet not all radicals end up as terrorists. In fact, only a small minority of radicalized individuals venture into terrorism. Focusing on the journey of radicalization amounts to preventing terrorism at an earlier stage before it is too late for noncoercive measures. This effort at prevention can be conceived of as a first line of defense against terrorism.

Moreover, radicalism, unlike terrorism, has social dimensions involving large segments of society. One can identify radicalized societies where acts of terrorism find sympathy and even some degree of support. Yet, there are no "terrorist" societies. The relative popularity of certain terrorist networks in the Islamic world can only be explained within the framework of radicalized societies where extremist violence finds a climate of legitimacy and support. Such radicalized societies are permeated by a deep sense of collective frustration, humiliation, and deprivation. Not surprisingly all these conditions are only exacerbated when there is a collapse of governance. Failed and failing states provide the ideal social habitat for radicalization. No wonder they are also easily exploited by terrorist groups. The collapse of social and economic order in Iraq and Syria, which enabled the emergence of ISIS, fits into this framework where the organization exploited all the political, social, and economic dynamics of frustrated, brutalized, and victimized Sunni populations.

As far as the economic background of terrorists is concerned, it is important to remember that effective terrorist groups always rely on a division of labor between young and uneducated "foot soldiers" and ideologically trained and well-funded elite operatives. While terrorist masterminds and operative leaders tend to come from professional or middle-class backgrounds, foot soldiers are often from lower socioeconomic strata. One should also not be confused by the fact that at the highest level, complex terrorist operations require major organizational skills. The more complex a terrorist operation, the more likely the perpetrators are to be well-trained elites.

All these factors only reinforce the importance of addressing the question of relative deprivation, frustrated achievers, and radicalism as a social milieu. At the end of the day, what we should really be focusing on is not the decision of a particular individual to become a terrorist. Rather, we should be looking at the social conditions that make dissident movements more likely to turn to terror and—more importantly—the circumstances under which terrorism finds popular acceptance. This is why the economic and social context within which a jihadist movement like ISIS takes root is profoundly important. Without societal support, most terrorist movements are doomed to fail. It is not a coincidence that prosperous and democratic countries have an easier time overcoming terrorism compared to impoverished and politically unstable countries where terrorism becomes a systemic problem.

The most successful terrorist groups usually seek failing or failed states in which to set up shop. Failed or failing states such as Afghanistan, Sudan, Somalia, Syria, and Sierra Leone easily turn into terrorist havens and are often engulfed in a vicious cycle of civil war, political violence, and radicalism. When thinking about terrorism, we have to remind ourselves that it is primarily within a radicalized social, economic, and cultural environment that the engineers of terrorism can freely recruit thousands of frustrated achievers. The challenge is to avoid an exclusive focus on either economic development or Islamist ideology. The best policy prescriptions will be ones that include a combination of both.

This is why an effective strategy against the root causes of radicalism should take the socioeconomic dimension of collective frustration very seriously. Little can be done in the short term about deeply rooted cultural and psychological grievances. But quite a lot can be done in the social and economic sphere with a program emphasizing development and good governance. An agenda based on human development with equal emphasis on education reform, democratic reforms, and socioeconomic advancement can address the cultural and ideological as well as economic root causes of radicalization.

Islamization of Radicalism

The limited amount of evidence and data available seems to validate the point that Islam is not the main reason why the foreign fighters who ended up joining ISIS were radicalized at the first place. ISIS's sophisticated outreach campaign via social media appeals to disaffected Muslim youth around the world by presenting the movement as the most powerful vanguard of a project that delivers both glory and salvation. The brutality and savagery of ISIS have a perverse appeal to those in search of individual or collective revenge for their sufferings. The caliphate that ISIS has embraced as the primary identity for itself provides both religious utopia and political reality. In that sense, it is a marketing success for youth in search of meaning, belonging, and glory. Territorial expansion, military success, the methodical use of violence, the ability to deliver economic benefits and services, and the idea of serving a higher cause are all factors that resonate with a radicalized youth.

There is no reason to doubt the religiosity of foreign fighters. Yet, there is enough evidence to show that Islam alone does not explain their radicalization process. As Olivier Roy aptly summarizes, what we are facing is not the radicalization of Islam as the main path to jihadism but rather the Islamization of preexisting forms of radicalism.[16] Evidence shows that those who have joined ISIS rarely become radicalized by reading sacred texts. In other words, their path to radicalism is seldom a result of theological reasoning and convictions. According to released ISIS records containing details for more than four thousand foreign recruits, while most of the fighters are well-educated, 70 percent state that they have only basic knowledge of Islam.[17] If Islam was the source of their violence, disaffected Muslims who understand Shariah would certainly be more prone to radicalization. Instead, the data available seems to show that Muslims with little knowledge of Islam may be more susceptible to radicalization and violence.

According to many reports, typical ISIS recruits had ordinary backgrounds with no clear allegiance to Islam. The case of two Muslims from Britain, who ordered books such as "The Koran for Dummies" and "Islam for Dummies" from Amazon to prepare for jihad abroad, is an often-cited example validating the Islamization of radicalism rather than a process of radicalization by reading Islamic texts.[18] And those who claim advanced knowledge in Shariah are reportedly less likely to want to become suicide bombers, according to a study by the US military's Combating Terrorism Center, an academic institution at the US Military Academy. As the reports concludes,

> If martyrdom is seen as the highest religious calling, then a reasonable expectation would be that the people with the most knowledge about Islamic law would desire to carry out these operations with greater frequency. However, despite the religious justification that IS uses for suicide missions, those with the most religious knowledge within the organization itself are the least likely to volunteer to be suicide bombers.[19]

At the end of the day, the role religion plays in radicalization needs to be analyzed with an open mind. Individual stories, the complex nature of human psychology, and diversity of backgrounds defy easy generalization and categorization. Instead of macro-scale explanation, researching micro-level, individual paths to radicalization is a much more promising avenue to address the challenge. The search for meaning, adventure, and self-worth and the zeal that comes with rebellion and conversion are all factors in need of more attention. Studying this complex picture will help us appreciate the multiple drivers of the disturbing journey from radicalization to terrorism. This situation does not absolve Islam or jihadist ideology, but religion is seldom the sole factor behind radicalization.

ISIS and Governance

At its height, between 2014 and 2016, ISIS governed large swaths of land in Syria and Iraq including Mosul, the second largest city of Iraq. A population of close to 8 million lived in the conquered territories of the self-declared "caliphate." ISIS established a theocracy and ruled brutally in accordance with the strictest ultrafundamentalist interpretation of Islamic law. The Western focus on ISIS has understandably been on its barbaric violence, jihadist theology, doctrinal scripture, and particularly its apocalyptic vision preparing for the last battles heralding the end of days. Yet, any entity that calls itself a state also needed to perform some basic functions of governance. By 2013, ISIS was already issuing pamphlets that laid out the exact governance activities it would undertake in territories that would come under its military and economic control. These included the provision of key public services and a system of taxation. Behind its savagery, often overlooked is the fact that ISIS managed to establish a sense of order where none existed. Given the low starting points, it also had considerable success in providing basic services.

It is important to remember that what ISIS replaced in conquered territories was a broken system of collapsed institutions under civil war-like conditions. By the time ISIS emerged as a force able to conquer and hold land, large parts (mostly Sunni) of Iraq and Syria were under conditions of extreme sectarian strife. State institutions had no capacity to regularly provide basic services such as running water, electricity, sanitation, healthcare, or education. This state of affairs was hardly surprising given the absence of security. Without security, as we previously noted, achieving capacity and legitimacy turns into impossible objectives. What ISIS managed to achieve, at its most basic level, was the monopolization of coercion by neutralizing its enemies and instituting codes of conduct. The set of rules established were based on an ultrafundamentalist interpretation of Islamic law and were enforced brutally. In practice and implementation some of these punishments involved beheadings, slavery, amputations, and other cruelties that terrorized people and assured the subjugation of all enemies through fear.

In addition to its fighting force of around thirty thousand people, ISIS had a much larger bureaucracy that kept its state functioning. One element of relative success in its administration system has been the organization's willingness to work with the local Sunni populations, including civil servants who remained in place. Salaries were paid on time, organizational discipline was established in providing services, and rules were enforced with punitive measures. Given its proclivity for violence, ISIS quickly replaced chaos with order and managed to combine its coercive power with institutional capacity in providing what people urgently needed: protection, water, electricity, sanitation, health services, garbage collection, improved traffic, fixed potholes, and so on.

Security combined with capacity allowed ISIS to enjoy a certain level of "legitimacy" in the eyes of Sunni communities. Of course, it is important to emphasize that the sense of legitimacy the organization gained came with the reign of terror that targeted all the enemies of ISIS. Order came with brutality and savagery against non-Sunnis and all the other enemies of the movement. But once territories were conquered and enemies eliminated, ISIS had to govern by co-opting the Sunni populations under its rule. According to Mara Revkin, who has studied the ISIS system of governance,

> When ISIS captures a new area, its first priority is to win the trust and cooperation of civilians, who are an essential source of information, labor, and other material resources that are necessary for territorial expansion and state-building. In order to do so, it offers civilians a social contract that provides three main categories of benefits: justice and accountability, protection, and services. Access to these benefits is conditional on compliance with two main obligations: exclusive allegiance to ISIS and material support for governance and jihad through either tax payments or military service.[20]

Normally, one would have expected at least some parts of Sunni populations in Syria and Iraq to resist the rule of ISIS. The kind of sectarian war, chaotic violence, and brutal regime repression that existed may be one of the probable reasons why such resistance did not occur. The reluctance to take on a violent jihadist movement is another likely factor. However brutally enforced, the sense of order ISIS established came to be willingly or unwillingly accepted and, in some places, probably welcomed compared to the worse alternative for Sunni majorities. The need for a Sunni sense of security trumped sectarian war and suffering at the hands of Shiite militias in Iraq or Alawite reprisal in Syria. Once security was established, this relative "success" paved the way for the provision of previously absent or sporadic basic services such as electricity and water. State institutions able to provide basic governance, particularly security and capacity, were absent in most of the territories conquered by ISIS. When the organization began to improve the security situation and the provision of basic services, it therefore had a distinct advantage of starting from a very low point. What ISIS achieved in terms of governance, therefore, always needs to be compared with the alternative. Not surprisingly, the higher levels of legitimacy enjoyed by ISIS in the early stages of its rule, in time, deteriorated as people grew accustomed to the new order.[21]

After all, it was impossible for an entity like ISIS to turn into a normal state. By 2015 ISIS was under heavy attack from a very powerful international coalition and its revenue sources based on taxation and smuggling could no longer expand. Therefore, just as its citizens began to expect better services, the question of survival reemerged with all its urgency. As the security situation worsened so did the economic and financial capacity of the organization. Not being able to provide security or services just when expectations were on the rise and the constant pressure of war ultimately brought the end of ISIS. The organization maintained its hold over Raqqa, in northeastern Syria, until 2018. But already by 2015, it could no longer maintain the provision of essential services and had to resort to heavy taxation and conscription.

According to the New York Times that recovered fifteen thousand pages of internal ISIS documents, the system of governance established by the organization combined bureaucracy and brutality in an efficient way. The documents confirmed that ISIS relied primarily on tax revenues from almost all economic activities under its territories ranging from agriculture to finance and services. An intricate and all-encompassing extraction system was put in place and the incomes obtained dwarfed the revenues from black market oil sales.[22] Such heavy taxation, combined with an equally aggressive system of conscription proves that, contrary to conventional wisdom, ISIS depended on domestic governance much more than external funds or foreign fighters. When countries like Turkey with previously an open border policy with ISIS changed course, international recruitment and oil smuggling further declined. ISIS increasingly came to realize that its success, as a state-building and governance project, dependent on cultivating strong partnership with local tribes and ordinary citizens under its rule.

Such reliance on the domestic populations came in the form of what Mara Revkin rightly describes as a "social contract" based on mutual obligations between state and society.[23] In other words, ISIS would provide security, protection, justice, and services. In return for this protection and services, the citizens of the caliphate would pay their taxes and have duties such as military service. Their model of repressive governance was therefore based on the familiar structure seeking security, capacity, and legitimacy in a theocratic framework. The nature of the ISIS social contract is modeled after what Prophet Mohammed himself is believed to have drafted as a constitutional treaty for governing the city of Medina in 623. Containing more than a dozen articles, "documents of the city" were issued after almost all ISIS urban conquests.

"Document of the City" (*Wathīqat al-Madīna*)	
Art. 1	"We [the Islamic State] bear responsibility for restoring the glories of the caliphate and obtaining retribution for the oppression and injustice suffered by ... our Muslim brothers."
Art. 2	"... We do not make accusations without evidence and proof ... We show mercy to a Muslim, unless he has apostasized or given aid to criminals."
Art. 3	"The people in the shadow of our rule are secure and safe ... Islamic governance guarantees to the *ri'aya* their rights. The wronged will be given justice against a violator of his right ...."
Art. 4	"We order that the fimds that were under the control of the Safavid* government (public funds) must be returned to the Muslim people. These funds will be spent in the *maslaha* [interest] of the Muslims and no one is permitted to reach out his hand to loot or steal ... or else be brought before the sharia judiciary ... Whoever steals private property in the form of money, furniture and [other] goods from a private place without doubt will have his hand cut off, and anyone who collaborates with armed gangs who engage in brigandage will be subject to ... deterrent punishments."
Art. 5	"Trafficking and dealing alcohol or drugs, or smoking, or other taboos, are prohibited."
Art. 6	"Mosques are the houses of God ... We urge all Muslims to build them and pray ...."
Art. 7	"Beware of employment with the Safavid government and the *tawaghit*** ... He who repents of sin is not guilty of sin. To the apostates of the army and police and the rest of the unbelieving apparatus we say that the door of repentance is open to anyone who wants it. and we have designated specific places to receive those wishing to repent subject to conditions ... For those who insist on remaining apostate. there is no alternative but death ...."

"Document of the City" (*Wathīqat al-Madīna*)

Art. 8	"Councils and associations and banners [bearing the names of other groups] are unacceptable."
Art. 9	"God commands that you join the society [the Islamic State] and renounce factions and strife … Division is one of the traps of the devil …."
Art. 10	"Our opinion regarding … polytheistic and pagan shrines is that of the Prophet [who prohibited them]."
Art. 11	"To the virtuous and dignified women: … Dress decently and in loose tunics and robes …Do not leave the house except out of necessity …."
Art. 12	"Establish Islamic governance and … release the people from the shackles of rotten positive laws …."
Art. 13	"We listen to the council of the small and the great and the free and the slave. and there is no difference among us between red and black, and we judge ourselves before others."
Art. 14	"In conclusion we say: You have experienced a secular system and the eras of monarchy and Republicanism and Safavid rule … Now is the era of the Islamic State and the era of the Imam Abu Bakr al-Quraishi and you will see the vast difference between a secular government that saps the resources of the people and that muzzles their mouths and tramples on their rights and dignity and a Quraishi Imamate that has made the divine revelation a way of life."

The language of the above document is remarkable for two main reasons. First and foremost is the definition of enemies as "Safavids." ISIS uses the term Safavid in reference to Shiites in Iraq and Syria who are backed by Tehran. The fact that Shiism became the official religion of Iran under the Safavid dynasty is not lost on Baghdadi and other ISIS ideologues. Similarly, that Safavids are not Arabs is common knowledge in the Middle East. The Turco-Persian ethnic roots of Safavids make them foreign elements in the Sunni Arab lands of Iraq and Syria. What this chapter describes as Sunni religious nationalism, in defining the ideology and appeal of ISIS to all its adherents, finds no better description than the identification of the nemesis as Safavids with their Persian ethnicity immersed in Shiite heresy.

The real enemy in the eyes of Sunni religious nationalism is not just Shiism that has place, albeit illegitimate, in the Arab world due to the large Arab Shiite populations in Iraq, Lebanon, Bahrain, and even Saudi Arabia. The identification of the real threat as Safavids places Iran and its non-Arabic Persian "otherness" at the center. This paves the way for an ethnic as well as religious demonization of the enemy. This is why ISIS easily appealed to Sunni Arab nationalist groups as well as Sunni jihadists. Even secularists such as former Baathist military officers found a comfortable ideological place within ISIS precisely because the organization effectively combined the language of religion with the language of nationalism. The result was not only a discourse but also a political context of Sunni religious nationalism. This aspect of ISIS seldom receives the attention it deserves while discussions of apocalypse and the "ends of days" dominate the theological lens of analysis.

The second factor that makes the "document of the city" remarkable is its commitment to a new system of governance that will improve material conditions and the political system without too much elaboration on theology. To be sure, Islamic law and the need for compliance is conveyed in strict terms. Yet, there is also a very modern aspect to the document that in some parts reads like a political campaign document making promises to citizens. The last article of the text, for instance, is particularly important because it speaks of how people suffered under secular systems, Republican and Monarchic eras, as well as under the Safavids and that "Now is the era of the Islamic State ... and you will see the vast difference between a secular government that sap the economic resources of the people and muzzles their mouths and tramples on their rights and dignity and the new Quraishi Imamate that has made divine revelation a way of life." This message is as religious as it is economic and political with the promise of a "new morning" in Sunnistan with justice and improved governance under the caliphate. It has a clear message of religious nationalism that could be summarized as "Make Sunni Islam in Arab lands Great Again." This is why, behind the brutal façade of theology and jihadism, Sunni religious nationalism and the promise of improved governance in the shattered lands of Syria and Iraq were so integral to the success of ISIS.

Conclusion

"The reality is that Islamic state is Islamic. *Very* Islamic ..." as Graeme Wood famously argued in *The Atlantic Magazine*.[24] It is hard to overstate this point. ISIS is of course Islamic. But, Islam is not the main reason why the organization managed to attain a relative sense of legitimacy in the territories it ruled. The coercive bureaucratic machinery of ISIS established security, introduced taxes, engaged in arbitration and conscription, and provided services, food, and medicine while it also fixed roads, telephone lines, the electrical grid, and water pipes. A sense of order replaced chaos, and such efficiency was perhaps much more important than jihadist violence in creating a sense of legitimacy. This is why the Islamic State was much more than an apocalyptic theocracy based on scripture. ISIS was also about Sunni nationalism, Sunni disempowerment, and a semblance of effective governance in parts of Syria where order had collapsed and chaos reigned. Today, those who insist that ISIS is defeated should think twice before premature celebrations. In parts of Iraq and Syria where failed governance and Sunni victimhood still prevail, all the conditions that led to the emergence of this monster are still there.

5 THE WESTERN DISCONNECT

The Western obsession with Islam, as we have seen so far, creates a major disconnect with the political, economic, and social dynamics of Turkey, the Sunni–Shiite sectarian divide, and ISIS. Similarly, the lazy culturalism fueling the overstatement of Islam fails to correctly identify the dynamics behind authoritarianism in the Arab world and misunderstands the root causes of radicalization and terrorism. In sum, the myopic fixation with religion creates a major deficiency in the Western approach to critical problems in the Middle East. It would not be so tragic if overstating Islam was just an analytical fallacy or a mere problem of sloppy conceptualization. But faulty diagnosis often leads to wrong prescriptions.

Overstating Islam has counterproductive and sometimes dangerous policy consequences. When journalists and analysts insist on looking at the Middle East through the prism of Islam, public opinion naturally reflects the same tendency. When wide-ranging and highly complex issues such as radicalization, autocracy, violence, terrorism, and underdevelopment are all analyzed as indirect products of Islam, average citizens show a similar bias and see Islam as the defining problem in the Middle East. Public opinion reflects such results. Politics and populism have become inseparable in our democratic systems. When public opinion and the media are consumed by alarmism about Islam, why should politicians not quickly follow the same path? As much as politicians shape public opinion, they are also highly under the influence of public sentiments. A chain reaction, with clear implications for electoral politics, appears in this vicious cycle.

Elections are essential to democracy and mass opinion determines electoral results. The media has a tremendous responsibility in shaping this political environment. Alarmism about Islam in the media has a major impact on Western politics. Even pure idealists, a rare breed in politics, who want to campaign, govern, and lead without catering to masses have to adapt to social reality in order to change it. The experience of former American President Barack Obama offers an instructive tale. Obama was far from being a naïve idealist. He pursued American national security interests against terrorist networks with unprecedented lethality with an aggressive expansion of drone use. And lest we forget, Osama bin Laden was killed in Pakistan at his orders. Yet, Obama came under heavy criticism for not using the term "radical Islamic terrorism" in defining the terrorist threat he so efficiently targeted during his two terms in power.

The more generic and sterile concept of "extremist violence" failed to satisfy those who strangely argued that we need to clearly define the ideological nature of the threat in order to fight it more effectively. This argument hardly stands to scrutiny since it suggests that a president who ordered the assassination of Osama bin Laden despite considerable risks to relations with Pakistan or significantly increased the use of drones against jihadist terrorists is somewhat clueless when it comes to defining the threat the United States is facing. Obama's rationale in his reluctance to use the term "jihadist Islam" or "Islamist terrorism" was clearly lost in translation in the eyes of his detractors.[1]

In reality, he was one of the few politicians who correctly understood that references to Islam, jihad, and Muslims were exactly what jihadists wanted to hear and see from the superpower. By not overreacting to terrorists and refusing to use a narrative demonizing their religion, Obama was in fact skillfully avoiding a trap. The fact that America's adventure in Iraq ended up creating more jihadist recruitment and radicalization was a lesson he took to heart. He was also reluctant to further polarize relations between the Western world and Muslims, by injecting the name of Islam in the fight against terrorism. Unlike many of his Western counterparts, he understood that for terrorists, the clash of civilizations was good for business. His reluctance to refer to radical Islam was a clear indication that Obama also understood the problem of religious polarization.

Obama was an exception. There is no shortage of populist politicians who prefer to exploit the anxiety and fear that Islam creates in the West. In that sense, what followed the Obama administration reflects the norms of traditional populust alarmism. And this does not bode well for the future of relations between the West and the Islamic world. Once populist politicians come to power they have the legitimacy and power to turn their convictions into action. President Trump's bias against Islam, his attempts at a travel ban on Muslim majority countries, and his support for declaring the Muslim Brotherhood a terrorist organization are clear examples that the clash of civilizations is alive and well. The Western misunderstanding of the Middle East sooner or later impacts policymaking. It is seldom confined to just the media, public opinion, and political climate.

Islamophobia versus Overstating Islam

What happens when journalists, analysts, politicians, and even academics believe Islam is behind most problems in the Middle East? What are the consequences of this obsession with Islam in Western circles? The easy and short answer of Islamophobia is not necessarily the correct one. Something more sophisticated and subtler than bigotry is at play when one questions the compatibility of Islam with democracy, secularism, modernity, and gender equality.

Overstating Islam displays an essentialist bias. But it does not amount to Islamophobia. Those who believe Islam is at war with progressive values can defend their viewpoint in the framework of a legitimate intellectual discussion. Islamophobia, on the other hand, is a form of racism and hate speech. It has no intellectual pretense or need for rational argumentation. It often ends up considering Islam and Muslims as sources of evil. Unlike the more nuanced orientalism that overstates Islam, Islamophobia embraces an extremist approach. Instead of pointing out problems with Islamist politics, it demonizes Islam as a faith system that should find no tolerance in the West.

The problem is primarily one about the difference between identity and ideology. The question of Western reaction becomes more complicated when the focus shifts from Islam as a religion to Islamism as a political ideology. There is a clear difference between the two since the first refers to Islam as a faith, while the second is about a political agenda and therefore favors a path for political action. The challenge begins when Islam, political Islam, and Islamism are used interchangeably. Such blurring of the lines has become inevitable in our age of political polarization over identity. Essentialist assumptions are clearly responsible in fueling identity politics. According to essentialists, Islam is an intrinsically political religion that wants to govern, regulate, and dominate all aspects of life. There is therefore no need to make a distinction between Islam and political Islam. "Islam is a way of life" is their ultimate orientalist cliché.

Essentialism and orientalism are not political tools used by politicians to mobilize masses or shape policy. They are merely intellectual trends confined to academia and philosophy. Yet, terrorism changed the whole picture. 9/11 turned orientalism and essentialism into a popular way of looking at what is wrong with the Middle East and Islam.

In that sense, more than theoretical, intellectual, or theological debates, it is the violent extremism of Al Qaeda, ISIS, or other jihadist groups that poisoned the debate about Islam in Western circles. A very legitimate fear of jihadist terrorism fueled an alarmist brand of politics that demonizes Islam. The view that Islam is a political religion that not only rejects modernity and democracy but also promotes violence became conventional wisdom in this context of angry populism.

To be sure, terrorism should not legitimize the bias toward Islam and the path to Islamophobia. But understanding why Islamophobia resonates with the masses is a critical step in tackling the problem. In the eyes of large masses in Europe and the United States, political Islam is a confusing term because jihadist terrorists claim to act in the name of Islam. And in a Western world traumatized by jihadist terrorism or the savagery of ISIS, the words of terrorists have more influence than those who seek to distinguish between Islam, political Islam, and extremist violence. The progressive circles who believe there is a difference between Islam and political Islam are often limited to their own echo chamber. The same goes for the nuanced argument that "jihad" means different things in different contexts.

Contextualizing is never easy when passions run high and the threat perception is existential. As a professor who has been teaching a course on Islam and the West for more than fifteen years in American and European universities I am highly familiar with this problem. The institutions I teach are often home to well-informed, progressive students. Yet, when the topic is jihadist violence and radicalization, the question that I most frequently face is invariably the same: Where are the moderate Muslims who are supposed to represent "real" Islam? Why are average Muslims not speaking up against terrorism? The fact that they often are is not registered in an age defined by sensationalism in the media. Images of Muslim masses yelling "Death to America!" fit the conventional wisdom much more nicely than Muslim voices who preach peace, tolerance, and interfaith dialogue.

Despite such polarization that feeds Islamophobia in the West, it is counterproductive for Muslims to overreact to legitimate Western concerns about security. The belief that political Islam—or even Islam itself—leads to violence, sectarian conflict, jihadism, and terrorism should not be quickly dismissed as Islamophobia. In a world where there are very few secular and democratic Muslim countries, and in a global context where the overwhelming majority of terrorist attacks on European and American soil are perpetrated by jihadists who claim to act in the name of Islam, questioning what is wrong with the Muslim faith may appear simplistic, biased, or even bigoted. But it is hardly surprising. The Western reaction to Islam is largely based on fear, anxiety, and skepticism because of understandable factors. If Muslims today faced terrorist attacks on their soils perpetrated by Christian groups who used religious language and justification to defend their acts, their reaction would probably be not that different than the current reaction to Islam in the West. The intolerance toward Jews and Judaism in the Muslim world due to the situation in Palestine is a case in point.

Be that as it may, some will argue that questioning the compatibility of Islam and democracy or arguing that Islam fuels violence provides intellectual ammunition to an already powerful anti-Islamic camp. This may very well be the case. Yet, once again, it is important to reemphasize that such views are to be expected in a post-9/11 world where Al Qaeda and ISIS have turned the clash of civilizations into a self-fulfilling prophecy. Questions about the true essence of Islam and anger with Muslims who fail to speak up against political Islam are only to be expected when a sense of civilizational conflict dominates politics. It is also important to remember that freedom of speech requires tolerance for all kinds of views, including deplorable tendencies toward bias, prejudice, and bigotry. Disdain toward Islam and Muslims falls in this category. Such views are unpleasant, but they are legitimate expressions of frustration and should be stomached in any society where the freedom of expression is under constitutional protection. Islamophobia should therefore be tolerated in the context of a liberal democracy.

My goal here is not to legitimize or minimize anti-Muslim politics. Islamophobia is a major challenge, not a negligible nuisance that should be accepted as the new normal. It is certainly real, on the rise, and widening the disconnect between Muslims and the West. This is exactly why questions and criticisms about Islam have to be handled with patience and understanding instead of moral outrage and righteous indignation—even when such questions may end up providing some ammunition to racism. Trying to understand where Islamophobia is coming from is not to condone it. To the contrary, it is a necessary step to fight it more effectively with more convincing arguments. Constantly complaining about the Islamophobia industry or engaging in reverse essentialism by defending Islam as an intrinsically peaceful, democratic, and tolerant religion will not convince skeptics.

Adopting arguments based on theology to counter Islamophobia will only focus the debate where it already is: the realm of religion, culture, and civilization. We need to move from culturalism to the realm of politics. Arguments about the intrinsic justice and fairness of Islam are a dead end that will only widen the distance between the Islamic world and the West. There will always be differences in the interpretation of theology. Instead the focus should be on how political, social, and economic dynamics can change cultural and ideological predispositions. A more nuanced discussion, one that recognizes problems in the Middle East but goes beyond religion, will have a better chance of starting a dialogue.

At the end of the day, the problem with overstating Islam is not Islamophobia but faulty analysis. As we analyzed earlier, attempts to understand the Middle East by linking most problems to Islam are firmly rooted in the simplistic and often lazy methodology of cultural determinism. Cultural determinists tend to inflate the role of religion and civilizational identity at the expense of political, economic, and social factors. Yet, their reductionist and one-dimensional approach should not be mistaken for Islamophobia and bigotry. Most cultural determinists in the West indeed believe Islam is not compatible with democracy. But this bears little importance for the rise of Islamophobia. After all, people who vote for xenophobic parties or who engage in Islamophobia by targeting Muslim immigrants are not particularly worried about Islam's compatibility with democracy. They have a problem with liberal democracy itself.

The Political Economy of Identity Politics

The real challenge we are facing in today's political conjuncture is identity politics. We live in an age where political ideologies and norms of liberal democracy have retreated in favor of innate, primordial differences. Nationalism, ethnic identity, religion, race, and gender are all parts of these identity dynamics. Identity politics, especially at the hands of populist politicians, is by its own nature divisive. In the absence of compromise and the search for common ground, the *tribalization* of politics can get quickly very polarizing.[2] Consensus is elusive and collective action for the greater good has become a relic of the past. What Sigmund Freud aptly conceptualized as the "narcissism of small differences" can have the most devastating consequences. Today, in our age of identity polarization no difference seems too small and the stakes are often defended and presented in existential terms. The posttruth environment and social media keep generating more polarization and discord. There is obviously no common ground when we can't even agree on what is fact and what is fiction.

In the eyes of cultural determinists "identity" is a much more powerful driver of world events than ideology. In a world where identity politics dominates, political and ideological differences are increasingly shaped by who we are rather than what we think. In other words, identity trumps ideology. In practice, this means right-wing and left-wing politics are now primarily absorbed by identity issues. The left, for instance, is no longer fully dedicated to socioeconomic solutions to the problems of the working class. Instead it appears to be more concerned by multiculturalism, gender rights, the LGBT community, political correctness, and affirmative action. The quest for equality has been replaced by the cult of diversity.

The right, on the other hand, is busy embracing populist nationalism and religion—traditional identities—as a reaction to cultural relativism. It defends "core" and "pure" notions of identity and traditional values against what it perceives to be the loss of sovereignty and the hegemony of globalism uprooted from nation, religion, and tradition. As a result, politics today increasingly appears to be centered around the question of primordial identity rather than political ideology. Globalist versus nativists, internationalists versus "America firsters" provide a binary paradigm.

When you scratch the surface, it becomes obvious that some of the cultural and identity problems that polarize politics still have social and economic roots. Particularly the rise of nationalist and nativists populism with its anti-immigration agenda is a clear product of worsening economic dynamics. Nativist frustration seems to go parallel with the grievance of large societal segments that no longer have a path for upward mobility. This is particularly the case for the lower-middle-class and unskilled labor in a globalized economy. In that sense, identity politics needs to be placed in a proper socioeconomic context. It would be a grave mistake to see it as fully detached from material realities.

Identity politics turns into angry nativism mainly because globalization creates winners and losers. Those with advanced education and technical skills have a much better chance of economic success in a global world economy where national borders impose no protectionism. Knowledge, creativity, and entrepreneurialism are highly rewarded in an interdependent world of free trade and global finance. The opening of trade and finance, increasing foreign direct investment to countries like China and India, and the adoption of export-led growth by emerging markets had a tremendously positive economic impact on countries that played their cards right. Hundreds of millions have been lifted from abject poverty in the developing world thanks to globalization and rising productivity levels.

Countries like China, India, Vietnam, and Indonesia, with low labor costs and a welcoming environment for foreign direct investment, witnessed unprecedented improvement in living standards. Unqualified workers in the West, however, experienced the opposite. Especially in uncompetitive manufacturing sectors, they lost their job security because of automation, technological progress, and high labor costs. Blue-collar workers in Europe and the United States who used to enjoy lifetime employment and decent incomes now risk unemployment or much lower incomes. Naturally, they became the relative losers of globalization and free trade. These segments of society, mostly composed of blue-collar workers, gradually turned against globalization and globalist elites.[3] Urban, liberal, cosmopolitan upwardly mobile progressives in favor of multiculturalism and immigration have become their enemies.

It should not come as a surprise that the losers of globalization are opposed to open borders, free trade, immigrants, and the loss of national sovereignty. Suffering from stagnant wages, growing income disparity, and a sense of socioeconomic injustice, they are angry with establishment politics. They are unable to reap the economic benefits of globalization—other than having access to cheaper consumer products—and blame rootless business elites and the unpatriotic, morally corrupt political establishment for not representing their values, interests, morals, and national identity. Their economic and cultural insecurities in a globalized world fuel resentment. And they express their anger with the system in the language of reactionary nationalism, religion, and civilization. The 9/11 terrorist attacks came to torment the West in a context where these economic, political, and social dynamics were already well under play. In that sense, identity politics and the clash of civilizations found fertile socioeconomic ground.

All these factors were already in place before capitalism had a global systemic crisis in 2008. It is critically important to understand how the global financial crisis and the ensuing "Great Recession" exacerbated identity politics and populist antiglobalization movements.[4] The most serious crisis of financial capitalism since the 1930s was bound to have societal ripple effects. The way many Western governments dealt with the crisis—by imposing austerity measures that squeezed the middle class while bailing out the financial institutions responsible for the crisis—led to an even more powerful backlash against mainstream "establishment" politics. Worsening income disparity, wage stagnation, and the painfully slow economic recovery became crucial economic factors that reinforced the already powerful reactionary populism. With additional factors such as masses of Muslim refugees, civil wars in Syria and Libya, jihadist terrorist attacks in Europe and America, a perfect storm emerged as Middle Eastern realities and a global recession converged. All these factors created an even more virulent type of nativism and xenophobia.

Add to the social, economic, and political dynamics associated with globalization the threat of political Islam and jihadist terrorism and you have a combustible mix. The situation turns even more toxic when political Islam and jihadist terrorism are associated with Muslim immigrants, and Muslim immigrants are associated with open borders and globalization. What we end up with is a wave of angry nationalism against Islam. In many ways, the current state of affairs in the West can be summarized as "the clash of civilizations meets the new wave of nativist populism." Populist, xenophobic parties, the Christian right, and reactionary nationalists have formed an unholy alliance against Islam. Together, they form a powerful type of religious nationalism.

For religious nationalists, the West is above all a Judeo-Christian civilizational construct. Ideals such as democracy, liberalism, and pluralism are irrelevant, especially when it comes to countering the Islamic threat. This is why most nativist populists are most comfortable when they rally around the nation, its flag, and its religion. They extol conservative values centered around patriotism, family, God, and individual responsibility. Nationalism and sovereignty are core principles of this populist backlash infused with symbols of religion and civilization. After Brexit; the electoral victory of Donald J. Trump; the steady rise of xenophobic parties in Germany, France, Italy, Holland, Denmark, and Sweden; it became disturbingly clear that Western Europe and the United States were highly vulnerable to the power of nativist populism and religious nationalism. This means that the West is no longer immune to the kind of angry nationalism that brings back not too distant memories of fascism.

There is an important difference between today and the 1930s, however. In the interwar era, fascism stood mainly against communism. Socialism, as an economic and political project, appeared to be on the march both at home and internationally. It was the age of ideologies. The right defended nationalism and religion while the left embraced socialist ideals for the working class. Class conflict was rampant. When identity trumps ideology, everything is different: today the right no longer targets communism and the left no longer defends socialism. Instead, culture wars dominate politics. Nationalism with religious flavors is rampant at the global level. A reactionary type of populist nationalism with antiglobalization flavors is often embraced by both right-wing and left-wing parties. In this new environment of identity politics, the clash between Western values and Islam is the favored topic of religious nationalists. And even centrist parties are playing into the hands of populist extremists in their attempt to co-opt some of their anti-immigration agenda. In other words, the wave of angry nativism and religious nationalism is gaining ground by moving the right further toward anti-immigration, xenophobic populism, and Islamophobia.

The clash of civilizations thus gained a noxious dimension in this new global context where identity dominates at the expense of ideology. For instance, today, when President Trump gives a speech in Poland in defense of Western civilization and asks: "Do we have the confidence in our values to defend them at any cost? Do we have enough respect for our citizens to protect our borders? Do we have the desire and the courage to preserve our civilization in the face of those who would subvert and destroy it?", it is clear that he is not talking about defending Europe from Russian aggression, authoritarian fascism, or socialism.[5] Or when he asserts in the same speech that "the fundamental question of our time is whether the West has the will to survive" he doesn't need to define the nature of this existential threat. Everyone understands that he is talking about Islam. When identity so clearly trumps ideology and the narrative of a civilizational clash becomes the norm, one can afford to be vague instead of bluntly targeting a religion practiced by more than 1.3 billion people.

Political Islam and Nationalist Populism

The virus of religious and populist nationalism is certainly not confined to the West. It is on the rise at the global level. It is a global phenomenon against globalization. China and India with Xi Ping and Modi, respectively, are as much a part of populist nationalism as Brexit, Trump in the United States, Putin in Russia, Orbán in Hungary, Chávez–Maduro in Venezuela, Lula–Bolsonaro in Brazil, Sisi in Egypt, Erdoğan in Turkey, Mohammed Bin Salman in Saudi Arabia, or Duterte in the Philippines. The Arab world, where identity problems are compounded by weak states and civil wars, is no exception to this global wave of nationalist populism. Yet something strange occurs when nationalist populism takes place in the Muslim world. The nationalist anger and populism of Muslim countries seem to belong to a different category than the rest of the world. The reason is simple: Islam. The ground tends to shift from populist nationalism to Islam. The perception of a civilizational clash defined by religion once again intervenes and dominates the Western perception.

Under the spell of Samuel Huntington and the clash of civilizations, the West remains obsessed with Islam in its analysis of the Middle East and fails to understand the populist power of Turkish, Saudi, Persian, Egyptian, or Sunni (Iraqi and Syrian) nationalism. The fact that Islam in Western eyes immediately generates the perception of a security threat in the post–9/11 world is partly to blame here. As a result, religion gets much more attention than populist nationalism. And often, what is clearly populist nationalism is seen as political Islam. This is why as we have done with cases on Turkey, the Sunni–Shiite divide, and ISIS, we need to unveil what is behind the Islamic façade and expose the power of nationalism with its socioeconomic roots related to governance problems. Changing our lens will allow us to see that what appears to be Islamism in the Middle East is often not that much different than the nationalist populism so clearly on the rise at the global level.

The Western tendency to overstate Islam naturally dominates the bulk of Middle Eastern analysis and nationalism gets short shrift. As discussed earlier, such Western focus on Islam does not necessarily amount to Islamophobia. Yet, it is my contention that our Western obsession with Islam is potentially more dangerous than Islamophobia because of its appeal for the mainstream. While Islamophobia has no intellectual impact and mass appeal, overstating Islam has both. The focus on Islam resonates because unlike hate speech it comes under the veneer of political analysis. While Islamophobia is naturally considered racist, overstating Islam can appear analytical. It can even enjoy intellectural legitimacy and credibility in the eyes of academics, journalists, and politicians. Overstating Islam can therefore resonate with the political center in ways that are unimaginable for Islamophobia.

This is exactly why an exclusive political, social, and cultural focus on Islam is sometimes even more dangerous than Islamophobia. Without demonizing Islam in an extremist way, it provides ammunition to those who wish to normalize, rationalize, and legitimize the portrayal of Islam as a dangerous, overly political, exceptional religion. In short, if not challenged the right way, overstating Islam may at some point seamlessly converge with Islamophobia. The best way to address this growing Western disconnect with the Middle East is to challenge faulty analysis and sensationalist alarmism.

Understanding the power of nationalism in the Middle East and the magnitude of governance problems is a step in the right direction because it debunks the myth that everything is about Islam. Challenging this fallacy by bringing politics, governance, and nationalism back in our analysis has also clear prescriptive advantages. Addressing political, social, and economic challenges is a much more realistic endeavor than the ambitious project of religious reform. Trying to improve governance with institutional and structural reforms has also a stronger connection with regional realities on the ground compared to the alternative of cultural fatalism that sees the Middle East as a region beyond redemption because it has somehow beholden to an Islamic curse.

Focusing on nationalism in the Middle East instead of religion has one additional clear advantage: similarity with contemporary Western reality. Nationalism is a political force that the West is tragically familiar with in its dark past and disturbing current dynamics. Religion, on the other hand, is buried too deep in medieval times. Secularism has come a long way in Europe and even in the United States despite much higher levels of church attendance compared to the old continent. For a secular Europe and America, political Islam in the Middle East harks back to memories of an irrational, dogmatic, barbaric Middle Age. On the other hand, angry nationalist populism is a global phenomenon today and is often analyzed in the framework of economic problems and governance failure. The Middle East should be no exception. Political Islam, after all, is the Muslim version of anti-Western and antiglobalization religious nationalism. Egypt, Iran, Saudi Arabia, and Turkey are just a few examples of countries where religious nationalism is rampant. If Western countries shift the prism through which they look at the Middle East from Islam to populist nationalism, they will see all the problems they have in common. They will also realize that solving these Middle Eastern problems requires rational rather than religious solutions such as good governance with improved security, better capacity, and stronger legitimacy.

As we have seen in the context of Turkey, Sunni–Shiite sectarianism, and ISIS, problems in the region go well beyond just an Islamic predicament. Contextualizing the domestic context of and itemizing the socioeconomic challenges greatly improved our understanding of diverse dynamics at play in each different case. The methodology of prioritizing religious nationalism and institutional factors related to governance constituted an alternative lens to Islam in each distinct case. Perhaps most importantly, contextualizing this diversity allowed us to see that there is no Islamic monolith that shapes all political, social, and cultural dynamics in the Middle East. But what happens when we engage in a generic discussion of Islam without a national or regional context? The Western disconnect is more at this cosmic level of generalities. It lacks national, political, and economic context. This is the issue we turn next in order to explain the relevance of nationalism in an Islamic world composed of very diverse nation-states.

Understanding Nationalism in the Islamic World

Islam does not exist in a vacuum. It adapts to changing political, social, and economic conditions at the national, regional, and global level. Like all enduring religions with a claim for universality, its relevance often depends on flexibility and openness to different interpretations. Today, the context of the Islamic world is characterized by dozens of nation-states with their own version and understanding of the same faith. There is simply no singular Islamic world. Even within the same country there are significantly diverse approaches to the practice of Islam. Muslim citizens of different social, economic, political, and cultural backgrounds practice the same faith in different ways with diverging interpretations.

Socioeconomic factors are only a small part of the diversity. The Islamic ideal of a seamless relationship between God and believers also helps the diversity of religious opinion. Unlike Catholic Christianity, there is no Vatican, no pope, and no centralized ecumenical clergy in Islam. This further strengthens the relevance of nationalist interpretations and the influence of individual nation-states in shaping the religious arena according to their political interests. We are dealing with a multiplicity of actors that speak in the name of Islam and none can claim the monopoly of supreme theological authority. Not surprisingly, this situation creates a sense of theological disharmony. Sometimes one even gets the chaotic sense that anyone who is remotely credible can come up with a fatwa (religious decree).

The Western perception of an Islamic monolith is surprisingly oblivious to the power of nationalism in the Islamic world. This creates a major disconnect with the diversity of Muslim nations and fuels the erroneous assumption that Islam uniquely provides the essence of political identity in all Muslim countries and particularly in the Arab Middle East. This Western blind spot about divisions within the Muslim world is ironic. After all, it is the West itself that invented nationalism and the nation-state. One would normally expect a stronger Western tendency to explore how nationalism and nation-states can shape Islam. The failure to do so is partly because most Western analysts pay too much attention to political Islam and its discourse of "unity of all Muslims"—the umma—at the expense of how governments in a Muslim world divided between nation-states instrumentalize Islam in pursuit of their political, strategic, economic, cultural, and diplomatic interests.[6]

Part of the reason why the West tends to neglect the power of nationalism in the Islamic world is that Islamists themselves seek to transcend the nation-state politically and theologically. Conservative Islamic principles believe sovereignty should be in the exclusive possession of God (*al hukm l'il-allah*) and not the nation, the nation-state, or the individual.[7] Islamists have a *supranational* agenda that yearns for the unity of the umma. Such unity of the Muslim community defined the early centuries of Islam. These were times when powerful Islamic caliphates single-handedly represented not only Islam but also all Muslims united under the sovereignty of God.

The era of the Umayyad and Abbasid caliphates, from roughly the seventh to the thirteenth centuries, is considered the golden age of Islam. Most pious Muslims, particularly in the Arab world, remember these centuries with great nostalgia as the only period in history when Islam surpassed the West in terms of its scientific, architectural, and philosophical achievements. In the eyes of many Islamists, this era was also, not coincidentally, the only period in Islam's history when all tribal, ethnic, and sectarian divisions were transcended in the name of the unity of the Muslim community. The dream of once again reuniting all Muslims under a single roof is therefore the ultimate objective of Islamists.

Yet, such longing for a united "ummah" (Muslim community) is today an Islamist fantasy. It is confined to the utopia of fundamentalism. The reality of the Islamic world is national and nationalist divisions; sectarian or sectarianized conflicts; and the primacy of autocratic states using and abusing Islam in pursuit of political power. There is no singular Islamic world and no Muslim community that speaks in unison. The Middle East, the birthplace of Islamic unity, is today the epicenter of these fault lines and divisions. Since the fall of the Ottoman Empire and the emergence of postcolonial Arab states, the region also witnessed the most polarizing of ideological, political, national, and geostrategic competition between regional and international actors. While the West takes the fantasy of Islamic unity too seriously, it fails to see the reality of nationalist divisions in the Middle East.

Political Islam as Nationalist Reaction

The West also makes a mistake when it thinks of political Islam and its Salafist version as simply a project to return to the seventh-century

Islamic norms and political traditions. Political Islam certainly glorifies and romanticizes the golden age of medieval Islam. Yet, in essence, Islamism is a nationalist reaction to Western military, economic, and cultural domination. It seeks to put an end to Islamic decline and find ways to restore Muslim glory, dignity, and power against European imperial and military encroachment.

The founding ideologues of political Islam are often considered as Islamist "modernists" and "reformists."[8] One can also see them as Muslim religious nationalists. Their vision of success against the West is based on a reconstructed Muslim nation under a strong state that protects the principles of the faith and strives to unite the whole community. Like most nationalisms, Muslim nationalists also embrace a narrative of victimhood and lost glory. They define their enemies and project their ideals in pursuit of economic, political, and cultural success. In that sense, there is more than meets the eye in terms of how political Islam emulates nationalism based on a similar narrative and political vocabulary.[9]

Every nationalism has an opposite identity, sometimes referred to as "the other" against which it defines itself. For Islamists this other is often "Western secularism." The power of Western secularism certainly posed a threat to Islamists. Yet, although all Islamists had a problem with Western norms of secularism, none took issue with a sense of reactive nationalism defined along Islamic lines of "Muslim nationalism" as a project of revival and resistance to Western political, cultural, and economic hegemony. To be sure, ethnic nationalism was divisive for the Islamist project. Ethnic divisions reminded most Islamists of the tribal fragmentation that characterized pre-Islamic Arabia. The ideal of uniting all Muslims under a caliphate rejected ethnic divisions in the Muslim world by embracing an Islamic–Muslim sense of belonging. Despite its rejection of ethnicity, however, political Islam adopted nationalism with an Islamic facade. It conceptualized a Muslim nation that surpassed ethnic divisions under a state that protects the fundamentals of Islam. "Making Muslims and Islam great again" would have been a great slogan summarizing this Islamic nationalist vision.

Despite its problems with ethnic nationalism, today, political Islam continues to operate in a global context characterized by Islam's division into dozens of nation-states. Islamist political parties and their Islamist ideologies displayed considerable pragmatism in adapting to this fragmented picture defined by local conditions. In time, this divided reality of the Muslim world of nation-states led most Islamists, even purist Salafists, to drop their utopia and see the world as it is, rather than how it should be. This represented the triumph of politics over religion.[10] Even the Muslim Brotherhood, the most successful Islamist movement in the Arab world, which is supposed to transcend borders in the name of Islamic unity, has accepted the primacy of politics over religion. Nothing challenges the myth of an all-powerful Islamic monolith more so than Islam's inescapable adaptation to the political reality of nationalism and nation-states. This is why, instead of obsession with Islam, we need a better understanding of how nationalism and religion interact to form a powerful force in politics.

Religious Nationalism

The concept of religious nationalism deserves special attention because it debunks the myth of an immutable, eternal, and monolithic Islam. The sacred nature of religion is often at the service of the state and nationalism. This creates a symbiotic relationship between nationalism and religion.[11] Particularly in the Middle East, nationalism and Islam joined forces in anticolonial, anti-imperialist, and anti-Western movements of independence. In the 1960s, the wave of Arab nationalism in the Middle East was not militantly antireligious. To be sure, its secularist version had disdain for political Islam and the Muslim Brotherhood. But, Arab nationalism often co-opted mainstream Islam and more importantly it gained legitimacy in the eyes of pious masses thanks to its pragmatic embrace of religion.[12]

Although this partnership is in theory counterintuitive for a secularist conceptualization of nationalism, in the Middle Eastern context secularism has never been a sharp dividing line between religion and state. Religion has almost always been at the service of the state. Even the most secularist Muslim country in the Islamic world, Turkey, has conceptualized the Turkish nation as a Muslim one. And as we have seen, Turkish secularism is not based on separation of Islam and state. The religious establishment is at the service of the state. This is why the secular–Islamic dichotomy that dominates Western analysis of Turkey and the larger Middle East is based on faulty assumptions. Drawing too sharp a division between Arab nationalism and Islamism would similarly overlook the mutually reinforcing historical dynamics between the two. All these dynamics make religious nationalism a powerful conceptual tool that bridges the gap between Islam, state, and nationalism in the Middle East.

The nation-state is a relatively modern invention with roots in the early nineteenth century. Religion, on the other hand, and particularly Islam, evokes deeply rooted theological tradition. It is no wonder that when religion is perceived as the driver of conflicts, as in the case of the clash of civilizations, we tend to focus on ancient tribal conflicts and neglect modern politics and national interests. The focus is on the irrational, dogmatic, medieval, and impulsive. This creates a sharp dichotomy between the modern and traditional as well as between secular and religious. The rejection of secular modernity is also the prism through which the West looks at the religious Middle East. The problem with this binary lens is that it fails to see the interplay between the modern and traditional as well as the secular and religious. These sharp dividing lines often fail to capture the hybrid nature of religious nationalism. As Jocelyne Cesari puts it: "Modern political conditions have altered religious concepts of community, law, and tradition."[13]

Although the West invented nationalism, it has a strange disconnect when it comes to non-Western nationalisms. This tendency is even more pronounced in the case of the United States. Americans often use the more positive term patriotic, infused with a healthy dose of American exceptionalism, for their civic understanding of American identity and ideals. They consider patriotism as a defense of American values associated with human rights and individual liberties enshrined in the constitution. Overall, Americans consider themselves very patriotic and hold patriotism in high esteem. Nationalism, on the other hand, has a more negative connotation in their political vocabulary and is associated with other countries' ethnic, parochial, and potentially fanatical inclinations. In short, while American patriotism is positive, the nationalism of other countries has potentially dangerous implications.[14]

In addition to considering nationalism in other countries as provincial and hostile compared to the innate universalism and goodness of American patriotism, there is perhaps an even more consequential American failure to detect the power of nationalism when the threat perception is focused on the more global and systemic forces such as communism and jihadism. Once again, the United States seems to suffer from this blind spot about nationalism more than Europe. There is, indeed, an American tendency to overlook nationalism whenever there are larger systemic and ideological threats behind the scene. For instance, during the Cold War, Washington was obsessed with communism and failed to grasp the underlying nationalist spirit behind anti-imperialism in places like Vietnam during the decolonization process. The fact that communism and socialism often managed to converge with nationalist movements due to a common threat perception of neocolonialism, neoimperialism, systemic dependency, exploitation, and capitalism was somehow lost to most American cold warriors.

The United States committed a similar mistake in Iran when it failed to understand that Mosaddegh was an Iranian nationalist and not a pro-Soviet communist, as British intelligence projected him to be when he decided to nationalize the Iranian oil industry. In Egypt, Nasser's flirtation with the Soviet Union created similar concerns in the 1960s. As the Cold War ended, nationalism gained higher visibility in the 1990s, especially in the Balkans and Caucasus. The breakup of Yugoslavia, Kurdish nationalism, and border conflicts in the former Soviet Union such as the one between Armenia and Azerbaijan signaled the bloody return of ethnic nationalisms. However, 9/11 once again caused the pendulum to swing in the direction of a global and systemic threat perception. Jihadist terrorism quickly turned into the new global threat. And this perception of Islamism as a systemic challenge to the West, as in the case of communism, managed to mask the driver of angry nationalism behind it.

Today, the Western obsession with Islam resembles the Cold War hysteria about communism. The fear that political Islam is on the march overshadows the role nationalism plays behind the religious scene in the Middle East. The parallels between the Western approach to communism during the Cold War and to Islam today are striking. In each case, there is a blind spot when it comes to nationalism. The fact that both political Islam and communism are in theory inimical to nationalism in their postnationalist utopia has probably contributed to this situation. Interestingly, if you take communist and Islamist *manifestos* seriously, they claim to transcend the nation-state. Once again, the West seems to have focused on the text rather than context. In effect, neither political Islam nor communism were independent of the national context and the nationalist environments they operated in. Once in power, it did not take long for communism in Russia and in eastern Europe to gain a nationalist character. Wherever Islamist parties come to power they also rapidly turn from idealism to realism by adopting nationalism.

Power politics, economic dynamics, and nationalist and territorial rivalries with neighbors transcend the ideals of Islamic unity. The Islamist experience in Iran, Sudan, Turkey, Tunisia, and Egypt has shown how Islamic ideals of unity are quickly compromised by the reality and power of nationalism. With few exceptions, most Western analysts fail to see the nationalization of political Islam. They are captivated by the message, narrative, and fundamentalist texts of political Islam. And such focus on Islam, Islamists, and fundamentalist texts often comes at the expense of the wider social, political, and economic context.

Today, this obsession with Islam is even more consequential than anticommunist hysteria during the heyday of the Cold War. The clash of civilizations between Islam and the West has deeper cultural roots and popular resonance than the clash between capitalism and communism. The primordial nature of identity can often be more organic and galvanizing than the constructed and imposed nature of ideology, especially in the case of communism. In other words, demonizing Islam is more dangerous than demonizing communism. Vilifying a popular religion means antagonizing hundreds of millions of pious Muslims and what they genuinely consider sacred and "Holy."

Targeting an imposed political ideology is different than targeting religious identity. Islam is a belief system and unlike communism it enjoys an organic and *"authentic"* legitimacy. Religions tend to outlive political ideas, and this means denigrating a faith can have much more devastating consequences than fighting a political ideology. This is why the clash of civilizations paradigm is so dangerous. And it is even more so when religion is intertwined with nationalism. The marriage of religion and nationalism can be much more lethal than the mobilization of just religion or nationalism in isolation from each other. This is also why those who constantly talk of a clash between Islam and the West should keep the power of religious nationalism in mind, particularly in an age where terrorism came to exacerbate an already polarized context.

To be sure, the clash between the West and communism carried the risk of catastrophic war, particularly under scenarios of nuclear war between the United States and the Soviet Union. Yet, there were also certain patterns of predictability based on rational action in a bipolar configuration of the world. Theories of deterrence and mutually assured destructions mitigated the risks of miscalculation between the two superpowers who were by definition state-actors rationally calculating risks behind their actions. The civilizational clash between Islam and the West, however, has reached current levels because of nonstate actors engaged in terrorism. And terrorism, by nature, is a much less predictable type of asymmetric violence aimed at terrorizing civilians and political targets. It has no rules of conduct like the Geneva convention.

Perhaps more importantly, the era of clash of civilizations exacerbated by jihadist terrorism involves potentially suicidal, often irrational, nonstate actors that may not be deterred. All this makes our current era potentially much more dangerous than the somewhat predictable norms of Cold War ideological conflict. Compared to the geopolitical and ideological struggle between capitalism and communism when the rules of the game were defined by state actors, symmetric deterrence, balance of power, and mutually assured destruction, the civilizational clash between Islam and the West is therefore highly unpredictable. Such conditions further aggravate the alarmist approach to Islam. Understandably, there is a sense that we are dealing with irrational, nihilist actors who cannot be reasoned with. The sense of Western anger is compounded with media reports of Muslim support for jihadist terrorist attacks and organizations like ISIS or Al Qaeda or ISIS. This situation naturally creates the sense that the threat posed by Islam is irredeemable and intractable.

What is often overlooked is the possibility that such tacit support for jihadist attacks may very well be caused by religious nationalism and an anti-imperialist anger against the West, or more precisely against the United States. It should not take a huge leap of imagination to see how anti-Americanism could translate into a perverse sense of satisfaction when America comes under attack. Palestinians who have allegedly been dancing in celebration of the 9/11 terrorist attack or Pakistanis who fail to condemn Osama bin Laden are not all radical jihadists. They are probably average conservative nationalists.

In short, the line between political Islam, jihadism, and anti-Western imperialist nationalism may not be as sharp as we imagine it in the West. Religious nationalism or nationalist religiosity is where these lines intersect. All these factors point us to a clear conclusion: understanding why there are strong pockets of Muslim support behind jihadist terrorism requires less obsession with Islamic theology and more analytical focus on religious nationalism. While the former is pure religion, the latter is primarily political.

To recap, political Islam may have a problem with secularism, but it does not have a problem with co-opting nationalism or adapting to national contexts. The Western approach to the Middle East is reluctant to analyze religious nationalism because it considers political Islam and nationalism as mutually exclusive rather than mutually reinforcing forces.

This creates an analytical failure in need of urgent correction because it leads to a dangerous fascination with Islam, theology, and civilizational identity at the expense of politics and nationalism. In short, it is politics not religion that will help the West to better understand the Middle East. Finally, putting an end to the belief that Islam is the main problem will also help debunk the myth that a reformed, modernized, or moderate version of the same faith can provide miraculous solutions. This part of getting the Middle East wrong is what we will analyze next.

An Islamic Reformation?

Faulty assumptions often fuel misguided prescriptions. If Islam is the heart of most problems, as it is often assumed in the West, it should also hold the key to most solutions. A diverse group of Western intellectuals are therefore lured by the promise of an Islamic reformation that will pave the road to a Muslim enlightenment in the Islamic world. Their model is not surprisingly Western-centric. Europe's own history with the Protestant Reformation is their intellectual inspiration and blueprint. Simply put, they are looking for a Muslim Martin Luther who will save Islam from dogmatism and intolerance. There is an unmistakable level of cultural determinism in this approach that prefers to see the Protestant Reformation as the precursor of enlightenment, secularism, liberalism, and democracy in Europe.

The intellectual footprints of Max Weber who famously linked the emergence of capitalism to the Protestant ethic are clearly visible in such thinking.[15] Despite their faulty assumptions and reductionist methodology, it is hard to blame the proponents of an "Islamic Protestantism" for logical inconsistency. Given their obsession with Islam as the problem, it is only normal that they expect miraculous solutions from an enlightened, progressive, moderate, and repaired version of the same faith. Not surprisingly, this view is also popular among liberal Islamists who are convinced the "correct" interpretation of Islam would bring back the golden age of Islam.

The quest for an Islamic reformation is problematic on several fronts. For starters, there is a problem of false analogy. Islam and Christianity are both monotheistic, Abrahamic faiths. But they are quite different in terms of institutional and organizational structures. As mentioned above, unlike the Catholic Church that was the primary target of the Protestant

Reformation, Islam does not have centralized hierarchical clergy with a Muslim pope seating on top of the Islamic ecclesiastic structure. There is no supreme religious authority that needs to be challenged. The caliphate that Ataturk abolished in 1924 had no comparable power to the Vatican because Islam never recognized a supreme clerical authority between believers and God.

The ideal of a seamless relationship between God and believer is at the heart of Islam. In that sense, Islam has an institutional structure that is already close to what Martin Luther wanted to achieve with the Protestant Reformation. Instead of an institution like the Catholic Church with all its religious functions, the defense of Islam and Muslims was the duty of the state. It is also important to note that even the caliphate, as a religious institution, had lost its power and appeal in the eyes of Muslims after the end of the golden age. The last time the institution of the caliphate had an all-powerful religious and political meaning in the Middle East was in the thirteenth century during the Abbasid era.

This is not to say that the Islamic world and Islam as a religion are already perfect and therefore there is no need for reforms. It just means that the nature of the problem and the context is different compared to Christianity and Europe in the sixteenth century. In fact, several reform movements have already emerged in the Muslim world in the past two centuries. Unlike the Protestant Reformation that targeted the Catholicism, these Muslim reformers had a different approach however. Their target was not theology or religion itself. In the absence of a religious structure like the church to challenge, Islamist reformists targeted the only meaningful institution with the institutional power to generate political, cultural, and social change: the state. Only the state had significant authority to shape society and religious norms. The Muslim effort at reforming Islam, therefore, had to deal with political authority more than religious doctrine. The same principle applied to efforts at secularist reforms as in the case with Ataturk in Turkey or Bourguiba in Tunisia. Their target was the political realm of the state more than the religious paradigm of an Islamic reformation.

Trying to understand this difference between Islam and Christianity when it comes to questions of modernization, reform, or secularism is important for the contextualization of the challenge. Since Islam doesn't have a church or ecclesiastic structure, it is often argued that the clash between church and state—that eventually led to secularism in the West—has no real equivalence in the Islamic world. Because Islam is all too powerful, it is supposed to control the state that it helped create with the emergence of the Muslim faith. The argument is also often used by orientalists to make the argument that Islam is a much more political religion than Christianity, which was born as a stateless religion and therefore did not develop a legal body of regulations for running a state. The implication of such thinking for secularization in the West is clear: Christianity is not as political as Islam and is therefore more "secularizable."

Yet, there are also very clear limits to such views based on essential differences between Islam and Christianity. Even a cursory historic overview would point out that Christianity became a highly political religion despite its origins as a stateless religion. It did not take an eternity for the faith to become a state religion and develop highly political ambitions in terms of influencing governance. By the fourth century the capital of the Eastern Roman Empire, or Byzantium as it came to be called, had become the seat of the Greek Orthodox Church. The emergence of the Holy Roman Empire and the power of the Catholic Church and the Papal States were also clear symbols of political and financial power starting with the ninth century. Needless to say, the Crusades are a clear indicator of how the church used its religious power for political, military, and financial ends. The political power of Christianity should therefore give some pause to the idea that Islam is an exceptionally political religion.

The Question of Secularism

It is not the realm of God and the realm of Caesar that harmoniously paved the way to secularism in the West.[16] The argument that Christianity is "secularizable"—while Islam is not—is once again based on religious determinism. Those who believe secularism is a product of the Protestant Reformation are at least recognizing that Christianity had to go through significant political upheaval in order to come to where it is today. Yet, whether Protestantism is the main reason behind the secularization in Europe is debatable. To answer this question we have to consider the multilayered and complex nature of secularism. French-style anticlerical secularism (laicism) aimed at total separation between state and church, which inspired Muslim countries like Turkey and Tunisia, was a product of a revolutionary clash with the Catholic Church. On the other hand, many European states with Protestant-majority populations don't share the anticlerical and militant character of French laicism. To the contrary, they have state churches and their secularism is therefore more accommodating of religiosity.

Beyond the question of how secularism historically emerged in Europe, there is also the critical question of the secularization of society, which is different than secularism as a political project. This sociological aspect of secularism is perhaps even more important than the question of theological or political change because it is an evolutionary process that reflects society's changing relationship with faith. For instance, the fact that church attendance rates in today's Europe are very low is a product of societal secularization and has little to do with religious wars that took place in the sixteenth century. Social, economic, political change and particularly upward mobility, educational advancement, and industrialization are strong drivers of secularization. Even in the United States, where church attendance is still considerably higher than in Europe, the level of religiosity seems to go down in more urban, prosperous, and educated segments of society.[17]

Therefore, we are once again facing the shortcomings of cultural and religious determinism in discussing the question of an Islamic reformation. Arguments about structural differences between Islam and Christianity, Islam's supposedly more political nature as a religion, or the quest for a Muslim Martin Luther to reform the faith all display the same misleading tendency to overstate religion and theology at the expense of social, political, and economic dynamics. At the end of the day, Europe's secularization took centuries and is a product of political, economic, cultural, and societal evolution. If the ultimate objective of Western advocates of an Islamic reformation is secularization, enlightenment, modernization, and democratization in the Islamic world, they should start by recognizing that European secularization, enlightenment, modernization, and democratization took much more than the reformation. In any case, the often-repeated mantra of "Islam is a political religion" should perhaps guide us in the direction of political rather than theological reform.

The fact that so many analysts and pundits insist on fixing Islam rather than focusing on politics speaks volumes about the Western disconnect. A progressive interpretation of Islam that fully rejects radicalism and violence is of course a laudable objective. But instead of fantasies about reforming Islam, the West should recognize that a progressive approach to Islam is much likely to emerge with good governance and democratization. The political objective should be inclusive institutions and the rule of law.

Political Islam as the Western Disconnect

Some will argue that even if Islam is not the real problem, Islamists who embrace political Islam is a major predicament in the Middle East. The same circles point out that democratic openings in the Muslim world always help Islamists who end up winning elections. This is a legitimate concern in need of deeper analysis and reflection. Is political Islam, instead of Islam itself, the real impediment to democratization in the Middle East? Especially after the Arab Spring and the electoral victory of the Muslim Brotherhood in Egypt, the view that Islamists are to blame for the failure of the democratic experiment has gained currency not only in Western circles but also among status quo forces in the region. And shortly after the military coup in Cairo, there emerged concerted efforts in Saudi Arabia, the United Arab Emirates, and Egypt demanding from Washington the designation of the Muslim Brotherhood as a terrorist organization.

Only a minority of Western experts tend to see the Muslim Brotherhood as a terrorist group.[18] Yet, there is more or less consensus on the fact that Islamists will win elections and establish autocratic systems under a "one vote, one man, one time" scenario. Such pessimism turns democracy in the Arab world into a dangerous and unrealistic project for the West. Free elections, it is believed, will be exploited by Islamists in pursuit of a fundamentalist, autocratic, antimodern, theocratic project. So why support democracy if the result is guaranteed to be antidemocratic, antiliberal, and anti-Western? The fact that the US Congress still has serious debates about the designation of the Muslim Brotherhood as a terrorist organization speaks volumes about the threat perception.

Such thinking conflates political Islam with radical extremism. A deeper analysis of the political dynamics in the Middle East should lead us in a less alarmist direction about the differences between the two. In fact, there are reasons to believe that the best way to deal with organizations like the Muslim Brotherhood is not to exclude but to include them in the system with incremental steps toward liberalization and democratization. Given autocratic dynamics in most parts of the Arab world plagued with corruption and dysfunction, political Islam often provides the only populist vehicle of opposition to the regime. The absence of a pluralistic political system, individual rights and liberties, and good governance creates major openings for Islamist parties.

Since most autocratic regimes in the Middle East are reluctant to fully suppress religion, Islamists have institutional advantages with their networks of mosques, charities, and civil society organizations. In autocratic environments, Islamists are often the only ones with social and political mobilization power thanks to their grassroots level social welfare networks and conservative ties that resonate with the masses. Much better organized than any other political force, they are also highly effective with their religious discourse against injustice and tyranny. Not surprisingly, the domestic tyranny they are complaining about is associated with autocratic secularism supported by the West. Even in Saudi Arabia where the regime strongly maintains its Wahhabi religious legitimacy, the kingdom is highly insecure when it comes to the Islamist challenge and religious accusations of subservience to the United States. When there is no space for national opposition movements, political Islam can therefore serve as the voice of religious nationalism against Western imperialism.

Even under relatively more liberal autocracies such as Jordan, Morocco, or Egypt (under Mubarak) Islamist movements can connect with masses and establish large pockets of genuine popular support compared to the weaker civil society organizations. Often co-opted by the local regimes and sponsored by Western regimes, secular NGOs in the Middle East are seldom able to break their narrow elitist circles. The fact that these autocracies do not allow freedom of assembly or speech, and instead prefer to play the game of cosmetic liberalism with token gestures of tolerance for "loyal" dissent, turns Islam into the only authentic and organic voice of opposition. The religious-political discourse that Islamists adopt by asking for "justice" against corruption and tyranny becomes a very effective voice in this context. The "Islamization of the opposition" that goes hand in hand with the "politicization of Islam" is what we end up with in this social milieu.

Although there is increasing control of religion in autocratic regimes, the mosques and Islamic charities are often the only social outlets not fully suppressed by the coercive apparatus. The fact that repressive regimes in the Middle East tend to suppress the secular, progressive, and liberal voices is not only a major problem but also a critical part of the autocratic strategy. Prodemocracy voices, activist labor unions, independent TV networks, newspapers, and journalists are perceived as a major threat in repressive systems of the Arab world for a simple reason: if not suppressed, such movements can develop into popular opposition parties that will challenge the regime's claim that the only alternative to enlightened autocracy in the Arab world is the anti-Western, antimodern, antisecular Muslim Brotherhood with its fundamentalist, anti-Israel political agenda.

These repressive regimes are therefore masters of presenting a binary picture to the West as the only alternative: it is either secular autocracy or political Islam. There is no third option. The regimes are in fact much more concerned about democratic–liberal alternatives than the Islamist networks whose presence is sometimes carefully cultivated and manipulated. Islamists are often co-opted, monitored, and presented to the West as the only other option—as a clearly undesirable choice for the West compared to the "progressive" and "enlightened" autocratic local partners in power.

Under such circumstances, the secular alternative in the Arab world is caught between repressive regimes that allow no democratic space for dissent and popular Islamist movements with their anti-Western agenda. As a result, liberal movements are struggling for relevance and influence. Making things worse is the fact that the secular and educated middle classes that should normally support democracy are understandably concerned that Islamists would be the main beneficiaries of free elections.

As a result, it is not only the West that is anxious about political Islam. The local intelligentsia is also reluctant to roll the dice when it comes to free elections. The alternative of cosmetic liberalism, supported by enlightened autocrats in the Arab world, has therefore genuine popular appeal for those who fear the tyranny of majority. The educated, secular, progressive, pro-Western segments of society as well as religious or ethnic minorities who would normally welcome a more democratic system are therefore not willing to take huge risks. They believe post–Arab Spring dynamics in Egypt proved that Islamists will inevitably win elections. The stark choice therefore seems to be one between secular autocracy and Islamization via the ballot box.

In effect, this means they have to choose between two types of repression: one with secularist and the other with Islamist tendencies. What happened in Egypt is a case in point. A transition to democracy with free elections led to an Islamist victory. And in power, the Muslim Brotherhood failed to establish good governance, inclusive institutions, and the rule of law. With no constitutional liberalism and effective checks and balances, the secular autocracy of the old regime was replaced by a democratically elected Islamist autocracy. In many ways, this was illiberal democracy in action. Eventually, the more liberal and secular segments of Egyptian society supported a military coup and the country returned to an even more repressive type of autocracy.

As we focus on the role of Islamist parties and movements, this is why it is important to acknowledge the acute tension between electoral democracy based on majoritarian, populist politics and constitutional liberalism with effective checks and balances. As Shadi Hamid, author of an insightful study on Islam and illiberal politics in the Middle East, argues: "popular participation in conservative Arab societies will lead to less, not more political freedom."[19] Hamid makes his case by citing polls that illustrate the conservative and religious nature of societal demands in the Arab world. He asks: "what if a majority of citizens in a given country want to pass legislation that bans alcohol, segregates the sexes at various levels of public schooling, empowers clerics, or 'Islamizes' the educational curriculum? These are all things that, at some level, restrict or constrain individual freedom and liberty."[20] He also reminds us that Islam is an exceptional political religion with a Holy text that represents the direct word of God with no room for interpretation.

Hamid's approach challenges what political scientists call the inclusion–moderation thesis—based on the view that Islamists will moderate their ideology as they participate in the political system. The inclusion–moderation argument enjoyed strong political support during the "Freedom Agenda" of the Bush administration. Defending Hezbollah's participation in Lebanese elections in 2005, George W. Bush popularized the idea of the "pothole theory," saying that: "I like the idea of people running for office. There's a positive effect …. Maybe some will run for office and say, vote for me, I look forward to blowing up America …. I don't think so. I think people who generally run for office say, vote for me, I'm looking forward to fixing your potholes."[21] Contrary to such optimism, Hamid argues there is no need for Islamists to moderate their political views. If Islamist parties such as the Muslim Brotherhood have a social and political agenda that is shared by the majority of voters, why should the party move to the center? To the contrary, once in power, they will be free from the pressure of repressive secularism and implement their autocratic religious agenda with no boundaries.

The Arab awakening in 2011 and the arrival of the Egyptian Muslim Brotherhood to power after winning elections in 2012 provided a real-life test of the inclusion–moderation thesis. Hamid's argument that democratization leads to more conservative and illiberal policies once the Islamists are elected to power came to fruition with the Egyptian experiment. It has now become conventional wisdom to argue that the Brotherhood brought its own demise by following autocratic and incompetent policies. Are we therefore to conclude that Islamist political parties are unfit to rule democratically and that Islam is incompatible with democracy?

The fact that many in the West seem to think so proves the disconnect that stems from overstating Islam. Even if there is ideological harmony between Islamists and the majority of the population, this situation should not preclude the fact that to govern effectively and to keep winning elections Islamists eventually need to find solutions to social, economic, and political problems of governance. Had the Muslim Brotherhood in Egypt proved better at providing social and economic services and establishing a better balance between security and freedom, it would have gained more popular legitimacy. This is why inclusion–moderation worked with the AKP's first ten years in Turkey (between 2003 and 2013) or seems to be working with political Islam's moderation in Tunisia. As we have seen in Turkey, the success and moderation of political Islam came in great part thanks to the Islamists' participation in democratic elections since the early 1970s.

Before we succumb to gloom and doom about the future of democracy in the Middle East and reach sweeping conclusions about the essence of Islam and Muslim culture in the Arab world, we need to remember the conditions under which the Muslim Brotherhood was ousted from power. There was no quietism, passive acceptance of autocratic rule, or collective inertia as millions of Egyptians took to the streets to protest the Islamist government. Egyptian society proved more pluralistic and complex in its political, social, economic, and cultural demands. The reason why millions took to the street had a lot to do with the need for democratic governance and competence—in short political and economic performance—rather than Islam or Muslim culture. The failure to provide democratic and competent governance generated a backlash against the Islamist government. The way Egypt's experiment in Islamist inclusion ended abruptly with a bloody military coup requires analytical scrutiny before we reach a conclusion about the incompatibility of Islam with democracy.

Imagine an Egypt under a political or constitutional liberalism with an independent judiciary assuring the rule of law. Imagine an Egypt where freedom of speech and assembly, as well as all other individual rights and liberties associated with democratic liberalism, are constitutionally protected, where there is separation of powers, a free media, and a strong civil society, where diverse political parties are free to operate and compete in free and fair elections. The inclusion of political Islam to a system where norms of liberal democracy have been gradually introduced and genuinely internalized by the citizenry would have certainly produced a very different outcome than the one in 2013.

Like most illiberal electoral system, the Egyptian system of 2013 where the Muslim Brotherhood won the elections was prone to create a "winner takes all and captures all institutions of the state" situation. Under a liberal and democratic system along the described lines, the Muslim Brotherhood's electoral victory would have most likely led to moderation. And if it didn't, the ideological rigidity and political incompetency of the party would be punished in the next elections. It would be up to the party to learn from its mistakes. This imaginary scenario in the context of Egypt is more or less how Turkish Islamists moderated their position in their journey from Erbakan to Erdogan. The key condition is to establish the rules of the game and apply them judiciously.

The view that democratic politics under a truly liberal system could have eventually encouraged moderation should not be dismissed. As discontent with Morsi grew stronger, it became clear that the Brotherhood would lose support in the next election. We will never know what would have happened if the army had stayed out of politics. Maybe the Islamists would have lost the next election and learned from their mistakes. There is also a least a slight chance that some moderation could have occurred in the face of mounting protests with the fear of losing elections. In any case, had proper checks and balances been in place and some norms of constitutional liberalism been established, the inclusion–moderation hypothesis could have worked. The absence of a national consensus on the rules of the game was what doomed the Egyptian experiment.

More than a failure of compatibility between Islam and democracy, the tale of Egypt and the Muslim Brotherhood is about a governance failure at the systemic level. We should always remember that liberal democracy is about a set of rules rather than a set of values. If Egypt had checks and balances against arbitrary rule, a clear separation of powers with an independent judiciary, and a national consensus on the rules of the game—in short, functioning political institutions underpinning the rule of law—popular opposition to the Muslim Brotherhood would have resulted in a very different outcome. At the end of the day, whether the inclusion–moderation scenario can work depends in great part on the kind of political system the Islamists are included into. The key question should be the following: Are there institutional arrangements that can stop the tyranny of majority? And this is a debate about politics, institutions, good governance and the rule of law—not a question about the compatibility of Islam with democracy.

Islam and Economic Development

Another commonly held orientalist view that contributes to the Western disconnect with the Middle East is the argument of Islam as an obstacle to economic development. Is Islam an impediment to growth? Can we explain the relative absence of economic success stories in the Muslim world by analyzing the role Islam plays? Once again, one must avoid sweeping generalizations about Islam since there are Muslim countries such as Turkey, Malaysia, and Indonesia that have managed to grow at respectable rates in the last few decades.

Is the problem, once again, the Arab world? Has religion anything to do with Arab economic underperformance? Is the divergence between the Arab world and better performing Muslim countries such as Turkey, Malaysia, and Indonesia due to different interpretations of Islam? Can a more progressive interpretation of Islam lead to higher growth and productivity rates? These are all legitimate questions. Even if we disagree with cultural determinism, the role religion and culture play in economic growth needs to be seriously analyzed. For instance, the question of Islam's compatibility with capitalism is very relevant for the Weberian school, which famously claimed a clear causality between Protestantism and the rise of capitalism in Europe.[22] Although this "Calvinist" manifesto, as Fukuyama calls it, has been somewhat discredited with the rise of capitalism globally, the culturalist viewpoint of economic development has still some currency among analysts who strongly believe "Asian values" based on discipline and hard work explain a great deal about the success of countries like Japan, South Korea, Singapore, Taiwan, and even China.

However, the consensus among most development economists is that economic growth is intimately linked to the implementation of the right economic policies and the presence of critical factors such as the rule of law, good governance, and inclusive institutions. Property rights and the enforcement of contracts are particularly important elements for market economics. These structural elements are believed to be much more important than the abstract category of culture in promoting economic development. The divergence between culturalism and structuralism is once again highly evident. In the eyes of most economists any reference to culture as an explanatory category is a sign of empirical weakness and intellectual laziness. Yet, once again structuralism and culturalism can find some common ground when we focus on politics, economics, governance, and political culture as a whole. The key is to avoid determinism and to probe the interdependence between economics, politics, institutions, and culture.

The question then becomes: What is the role of political culture and political economy in the emergence of institutions or in the adoption of the "right" economic policies? Does religion play a role in this context of political culture and political economy? From a strictly religious and culturalist perspective, one could argue that Islam has an advantage compared to Catholicism when it comes to capitalism. After all, Islam is a religion founded by a merchant and its holy scripture, the Koran, is full of praise for successful tradesmen. There is no stigma attached to profit-making as long as taxes owed to the state are paid and community welfare is taken into consideration. Most importantly, private property is sacred, according to the Koran. Islam's positive approach to commerce, profit-making, and private property stands in sharp contrast with the Bible and traditional Catholic views about money making and the guilt associated with being wealthy.

These Catholic norms were certainly important. However, they did not stop Italian city-states such as Genoa and Venice from adopting capitalist institutions and dominating the Mediterranean trade starting by the twelfth century. In that sense Max Weber was once again wrong when he argued that the birth of capitalism in Europe had to do with Protestant asceticism. Was there something in the culture and religion of these Italian city-states that enabled capitalist achievements? More than Italian and Catholic values, the success of these merchant states can be explained by institutional factors. Their invention of corporate institutions such as banks, bills of exchange, and joint-stock companies laid the foundations of financial capitalism. Such economic and financial innovations more than any other religious abstract factor allowed Italian city-states to outcompete their rivals, to develop incentive structures for trade, and to accumulate enough capital to take financial risks in pursuit of greater profits.

Political economist Timur Kuran notes that the rise of these Italian merchant states marked the end of the golden age for Arab civilizations between the eighth and twelfth centuries. What followed was what he calls "The Long Divergence" between the West and the Islamic world in terms of growth performance.[23] During the Arab golden age per capita income was much higher in the Muslim Middle East than in Europe. In questioning what led to the decline of the Muslim Middle East relative to Europe, Kuran's "Long Divergence" finds that religion had indeed a role to play not in the cultural sense but in terms of defining a legal and political framework for capital accumulation. Kuran argues that although the Koran encouraged trade and commerce at the individual level there was another body of religious law under the umbrella of Sharia that prohibited larger scale financial partnerships and thus the emergence of joint-stock companies. As a result, commercial partnerships in the Islamic world never gained scale and scope. Commercial partnerships were often formed among family members and could not outlast the death of partners.

Joint-stock companies that Italian city-states first developed had much greater scale and reach. Their tolerance for risk-taking was also much higher. Sharia inheritance laws coupled with polygamy were important obstacles to wealth accumulation. Islamic law required that upon a husband's death his wealth should be distributed to his children and surviving widows. Compared to the Roman law where the eldest son inherited all the wealth, the Islamic legal framework hindered capital accumulation. The fact that Islamic law prohibits charging interest rates should also be seen as another obstacle for finance and trade. Yet, from at least the fourteenth century onward, sharia law allowed "fees" that could accompany money lending, getting around the ban. All these factors constituted legal rather than strictly cultural impediments and they did not exist in the Western legal framework.[24]

Timur Kuran argues that in addition to Islamic legal hurdles, there were also institutional complications. For instance, Muslim welfare foundations, called "waqf," compounded fiscal problems. The waqf functioned as a charity that helped the poor and was therefore tax exempt. In time, merchant families began to organize their commercial enterprises as waqf charities in order to avoid taxes. Deprived of important tax income, this system tuned into a predicament for both Arab Kingdoms and the Ottoman Empire as they faced growing fiscal deficits. It is important to note that most of these historical factors rooted in Islamic legal customs and traditions have eroded in time. By the nineteenth century Muslim states adopted more pragmatic interpretations of Sharia law that allowed the formation of joint-stock companies. The drive for Westernization, especially in the late Ottoman era, created room for financial and commercial capitalism. In fact, today, most Islamic banks in the Arab world follow the same practices of non-Islamic banks. They just adapt and describe them in accordance with Islamic legal traditions. Interest rates, for instance, are conceptualized as profit sharing. The historic and legal factors rooted in Islamic law therefore fail to explain the modern-day absence of strong economic development in the Muslim Middle East.

So, if not Islamic tradition, what explains the Arab economic predicament? We have already noted how oil revenues and strategic rents in the Middle East create unearned income, precluding the development of organic linkages between taxation, civic consciousness, demands for accountability, and representation. There is more to the oil curse than just political problems with democratization. Reliance on energy resources is also a major curse in economic terms. Most nonindustrialized oil-rich countries fail to develop productivity-based capitalist systems with vibrant private sectors and entrepreneurialism. In that sense, energy resources and overreliance on strategic rents (in the form of foreign military and economic assistance) often lead to an absence of sustainable growth.

In most rentier states the economy largely depends on energy exports since there are no other sectors where any significant economic production takes place. This is mainly because the discovery of oil and gas resources changes the incentive structure of the economy at the expense of nonoil sectors.[25] The result is that most investments go to the energy sector while there is little or no market incentive or know-how for diversifying the economy to areas such as manufacturing or agriculture. Moreover, the absence of private property rights—the most basic requirement of capitalism—when most of the economy and resources are controlled by the state is a fundamental obstacle to the emergence of an independent business community.

Since oil and gas wealth accrues to the state, the public sector dominates the economy with a bloated bureaucracy. Inefficient state-owned companies are often the only employers. Because the energy sector is capital intensive, it does not create the much-needed employment opportunities for a young and growing population. This demographic dynamic with a major youth bulge is a common challenge for most Arab states.[26] Energy-dependent growth models therefore result in massive rates of youth unemployment and underemployment. Finally, there is also the fiscal health dimension of the oil curse. Public sector job programs meant to buy political peace in rentier states also create public deficits and jeopardize the fiscal stability of the whole system in the long run. Especially when energy prices are low, the spending habits of welfare states create structural deficits. As a result, the boom and bust cycles that come with commodity dependence are a major problem.

If oil and gas explain the structural problems of rentier economics in energy-rich countries, what explains poor economic performance elsewhere in the Middle East? After all, not all Arab countries are resource abundant. Egypt, the largest Arab state with its almost 90 million population, is the pacesetter of the Arab world. Bereft of abundant oil and gas revenues, Egypt is an energy importer. As noted earlier, most Middle Eastern countries have geostrategic value. Proximity to oil transportation lanes and to Europe creates geostrategic rents. Most energy-poor Arab countries have workers who send remittances from oil-rich countries or from Europe where they migrated in the 1960s as workers. These funds significantly contribute to domestic fiscal balance. And perhaps most importantly, most Middle Eastern countries, and especially Egypt, have access to foreign security and economic assistance.

The European Union is particularly concerned about immigration from North Africa and has therefore a lot at stake in regional stability. The EU contributes billions of euros for economic and social stability in the form of foreign assistance.[27] The United States is equally concerned about peace and stability in the region for multiple reasons, including the security of Israel. This is why countries like Egypt and Jordan that have signed peace agreements with Israel are rewarded with generous security and economic assistance.[28] At the end of the day, access to multiple sources of "unearned income" is a form of geostrategic rent that keeps energy-poor countries fiscally afloat. On the negative side, such easy access to "strategic rent" creates dependence and a lack of incentive to engage in private sector-friendly structural economic reforms. In such an economic environment there is obviously no organic connection between economic performance, taxation, accountability, and civic consciousness.

This is why the roots of economic underperformance in the Arab world are political and institutional rather than religious and cultural. In fact, political economy alone goes a long way in explaining the absence of democratization and sustained growth in the Middle East. In nearly every Arab Muslim country, the main enemy of the free market and private sector is a predatory government and its fiscal capacity to maintain coercion and unaccountability. Most Arab regimes often rely on a nationalist anti-Western discourse rather than just Islamic legitimacy. Many states in the region such as Egypt, Algeria, Morocco, and Syria have emerged from their decolonization struggles with understandable anger against the West since the primary colonizers were Europeans. Militaristic and autocratic regimes espoused nationalism and rejected checks and balances and the rule of law. Good governance remained elusive. As the public sector dominated the economic environment, corruption and heavy cronyism became the norm at the expense of entrepreneurship and private sector development.

The international context of the Cold War also helped entrench autocratic politics. Many Arab states saw the Soviet model of centrally planned socialism as a shortcut to economic power and prosperity. They failed to guarantee private property rights and created massive public sector monopolies in the name of national independence and economic modernization. The ruling power elite monopolized economic patronage mechanisms and tightly controlled investments and financial decision-making.

Even after the Cold War, most of the autocratic regimes in the Middle East failed to liberalize their trade and financial regime. Unwilling to privatize their state-owned enterprises they did not open their economies to foreign direct investment. Cronyism and systemic corruption continued as ruling elites rejected the promarket liberal "Washington Consensus" preached by the World Bank and the International Monetary Fund and instead embraced state capitalism. Without the rule of law, transparency or entrepreneurial dynamism and economic systems in the Middle East are still highly regulated by bloated bureaucratic structures and regulations. A handful of families dominate productive sectors and get the public sector contracts thanks to their crony connections with the political elite.

Turkey stands as a major exception in the Middle East thanks to its transition from a public sector-oriented semi-socialist system to an export-led growth model after its promarket reforms and privatization drive under former World Bank economist Turgut Özal. This transition from what political economists call an import substitution industrialization model—where protectionism and state-owned enterprises dominate the economy—to a private sector-friendly and free trade model has been key in Turkey's economist transformation since the mid-1980s. Yet, even in the case of Turkey, the road to economic success has been very bumpy. After a relatively strong performance between 1983 and 1993 under Özal's leadership, Turkey went through the lost decade during the 1990s when high inflation, high debt, endemic corruption, and political instability plagued the system. After the worst financial crisis in its modern history and a major overhaul of its banking system in 2001, the Turkish economy bounced back and had a stellar performance between 2003 and 2013 under the AKP, which continued Özal's market-friendly reforms with stricter fiscal discipline.

During the golden decade of the AKP, the state's budget remained balanced and inflation under control, EU-oriented reforms helped attract foreign direct investment and crony capitalism was constrained. As a consequence, Turkey's GDP more than doubled. Most importantly, Turkey's economic performance was fueled by high productivity, a diversified economy, and strong export rates to Europe. Turkey has no oil or gas and therefore it is not plagued by rentier dynamics of energy dependence or foreign assistance. It is also important to note that whatever the reason for the Turkish breakthrough, Islam has not impeded it. To the opposite, there is a strong consensus about how the devout bourgeoisie of Anatolia—mostly small and medium companies close to AKP—fueled Turkey's export-led growth. Turkey's strong economic performance came to an end due to governance failures and autocratic politics since the corruption scandal of 2013. With the end of the peace process with Kurdish nationalists in 2015, the absence of the rule of law, the monopolization of power under the erratic leadership of Recep Tayyip Erdoğan, and a failed military coup attempt in 2016, political dynamics went from bad to worse. By 2019, high inflation, low growth, and increasing unemployment rates were the main reasons behind AKP electoral defeat at municipal elections across the country. Once again, more than religion, the economy and failing governance proved their critical role in shaping political outcomes.

Conclusion

We live in an age of culture wars where the clash of civilizations has come to define relations between Islam and the West. In addition to jihadist terrorism that fuels the civilizational clash, the global financial crisis of 2008 exacerbated identity politics. Times of economic hardship hasten the search for scapegoats. The prolonged recession empowered xenophobic, anti-immigration political parties by unleashing a backlash against the proglobalization establishment. This rising trend of angry nationalism in the West made Islam, multiculturalism, immigration, and refugees easy targets. Political parties that campaigned against Muslim immigration are now in power in Austria, Italy, Poland, and Hungary, and they define the contours of public debate in Britain, France, and Germany.

This is a polarized global context where disinformation is abundant and even a basic agreement on facts is absent. Identity politics, angry nationalism, and backlash against multiculturalism fuel Islamophobia. As Gideon Rachman, from the *Financial Times*, observes:

It is now getting on for 20 years since the attacks on New York and Washington of September 11 2001. But suspicion and hatred of the Muslim world, inflamed by 9/11, has not faded with the passage of time. On the contrary, Islamophobia, as it is often called, is now a central part of politics in most of the world's major power centers— from the US to the EU, China to India.[29]

In this chapter, we analyzed how the tendency to overstate Islam fuels such Islamophobia and ends up creating a major disconnect between the West and the Middle East. The tendency to see all problems—ranging from autocracy and terrorism to underdevelopment—is a clear result of such faulty analysis. Prescriptions such as the need for an Islamic Reformation fall in the same category of simplistic religious and cultural determinism. One important thing the West can do to improve its understanding of the Middle East is to dig deeper into problems beyond their Islamic façade. Most of the disturbing developments in the region have political drivers that are in fact similar to challenges faced by the West. Yet, despite the rise of nationalism in America and Europe, the West strangely is oblivious to the rise of nationalism and socioeconomic issues in the Middle East. The rise of nationalism and the collapse of governance are much more powerful drivers of conflict in the Middle East than Islam. Is there a way out? Having established that Islam is neither the main problem nor the main solution for the Arab predicament, we now turn to what could offer a promising path for inclusive governance and political reforms.

6 WHAT IS TO BE DONE?

In previous chapters we analyzed the overstatement of Islam in the specific context of Turkey, Sunni–Shiite sectarianism, and ISIS. We also took a close look at the Western disconnect with the Middle East on issues such as democracy, radicalism, and development. The main objective in these chapters was to go beyond the "clash of civilizations" paradigm and to show that most of the challenges in the Middle East are of institutional nature and connected to nationalism more than Islam. We are now shifting from prognosis to prescription. This last chapter will focus on how the West can help the Middle East solve some of its most urgent problems, ranging from civil wars to entrenched autocracy and governance failure.

It is always difficult to be precise when we talk about "Western" efforts. What is the West? For the purpose of this chapter aimed at formulating policy recommendations, I include in the category of the West three main actors: the United States, the European Union, and Japan. This trio will play a major role in providing the vision and strategy for the path that I propose in pursuit of governance reforms in the Middle East. All three have major stakes in the future of the region as well as significant resources that can be mobilized in pursuit of their common interests and shared democratic values. Yet, the United States, the EU, and Japan have so far failed to show a sense of unity of purpose and determination in pooling their influence in the same direction. The strategic coordination between these three actors—in terms of what needs to be done and how to do it—will therefore prove critical to achieve a modicum of success.

Any Western effort to provide policy recommendations for the Middle East should start with a sense of humility. The complex challenges of the region are beyond easy solutions. Most observers are highly pessimistic about the possibility of positive change in the short run for understandable reasons. After short-lived euphoria following the Arab Spring, today, the region is facing civil wars in Syria, Libya, and Yemen; chronic authoritarianism in Egypt, Saudi Arabia, Iran, and Algeria; fragile states in Iraq, Lebanon, and Jordan; and cosmetic liberalism in monarchies such as Morocco, Kuwait, UAE, Qatar, Oman, Bahrain, and Kuwait. With Turkey as an illiberal democracy bordering on autocracy and Lebanon a fragile state plagued by structural dysfunction, Tunisia remains the only democratic experiment in the region. Yet, this small country's relative success is not likely to provide a regional model for positive change.

What makes Middle Eastern problems uniquely challenging is the simultaneous presence of daunting characteristics. The list is well known: entrenched authoritarianism, vast energy resources, excessive defense spending, failing economies, the youth bulge, structural unemployment, civil conflicts, failed states, proxy wars between regional actors, geostrategic competition between external actors, terrorist organizations, sacred places for Islam, Judaism, and Christianity, and geographic proximity to European countries terrified by the specter of Muslim refugees. No other region in the world can boast a similar confluence of haunting attributes. The simultaneous juxtaposition of all these geostrategic, political, economic, military, and religious factors creates a Middle Eastern exception to democracy and structural deficits in terms of good governance.

Given such dynamics, the words optimism and Middle East hardly come together. Yet, all the problems in this region have primarily political roots. This should give us not only hope but also a sense of direction for political reforms. As we explained in previous sections, to portray the Middle Eastern predicament in religious, cultural, and civilizational terms is misleading. Autocracies, repression, civil wars, and sectarian conflicts in the region are not products of cultural proclivities, religious mindsets, or ancient hatreds going back millennia. The region may be exceptionally challenging. But these challenges have institutional, economic, and sociopolitical origins. They therefore require political solutions instead of culturalist gloom or visions based on Islamic reformation.

The Problem with Friendly Autocrats

The region is not a monolith. States in the Middle East have diverse histories, political systems, security challenges, and economic problems.

Any Western strategy in dealing with this complex region needs to contextualize the local institutional dynamics. In the eyes of the West, however, there is an opposite tendency to generalize the challenge. And this feeds into a simplistic threat perception. For the West, the most urgent national security challenge coming from the Middle East remains the same one: terrorism associated with jihadism.

One can add the fear of Muslim refugees as a close second behind jihadist terrorism. The Muslim identity of these refugees represents a challenge to security and identity of Europe. Populist politicians on both sides of the Atlantic who thrive on polarization and constantly exploit Islamophobia naturally exacerbate the problem. At the geostrategic level, the threat posed by the Iranian regime is also fundamentally about the Islamic anti-American nature of the regime. Iran is a rogue actor because of its support for proxy terrorist organizations such as Hezbollah and Hamas.

Since the West is highly alarmed by radical Islam, terrorism, and Muslim immigration, the authoritarian regional dynamics in the Middle East are overlooked. There is a major premium placed on stability. The fact that such stability is provided by repressive regimes is not ideal. Yet, there seems to be no good alternative to these friendly autocracies that deliver counterterrorism cooperation and much needed political control over restive young populations. Autocracies, after all, are better than failed states that cause massive refugee and immigration problems for Europe.

As a result, when governments in Egypt and Saudi Arabia present themselves as stable allies against terrorism and radicalism there is a Western tendency to believe them. The same autocratic, coercive regimes are wrongly perceived as strong states and good stewards of socioeconomic and political stability without which the West would be flooded with millions of Muslim youth. This makes the relationship between Middle Eastern autocracy and the West an interdependent one. To tackle this dysfunctional partnership, what is required is nothing less than a paradigm change in the Western definition of national security.[1]

Most of the autocratic states in the region are repressive regimes where security comes at the expense of capacity and legitimacy. These countries may appear as strong partners against jihadist terrorism but in fact their repressive institutions create more problems than that solved by fueling radicalism. Their police states end up crushing not only radical Islamist groups but also pro-Western, moderate, secular opposition movements.

Under such autocracies political Islam and mosques turn into the only venue for dissent.

Repressive regimes make sure there is no democratic alternative to Islamism and present a binary choice for the West: friendly autocracy or radical Islam. However, this is a false choice because these friendly autocratic regimes are behind the Islamization of society and politics. Heavy-handed police brutality, systemic injustice and corruption, growing income disparity are all part of the autocratic package these regimes offer their average citizens. It is the social, political, and economic conditions they endorse and create that fuel political Islam.

With the exception of mosques and Islam, such regimes leave no room for freedom of speech, political liberties, and collective action. The Islamization of the opposition and the politicization of Islam are net results when all other political avenues are shut down.

Instead of seeing these repressive friendly autocracies as stewards of security and stability, the West should reconsider its understanding of security and take a closer look at the political consequences of relying on such regimes for stability. The security such regimes provide is only a temporary illusion that masks the undercurrent of massive societal discontent, resentment, and radicalization. Behind the façade of stability lies the oppression of masses and the Islamization of the opposition and society. Prioritizing short-term political stability requires answering a critical question about the long-term ramifications of such repression: Is the Islamization of society and opposition in Western security interests?

Political dynamics in the Middle East will go from bad to worse when Islamist groups willing to play by the rules are crushed. No one should be surprised if the criminalization of Islamist movements ends up fueling violent extremism and jihadism. These dynamics are already present in Egypt, a place where the Muslim Brotherhood is now declared a terrorist organization. This demonization of the most popular Islamic movement in the Arab world that espoused elections, ran for office, managed to win, and was eventually subject to a brutal military coup only after a year in power is now pushing millions of brotherhood sympathizers and members outside the system, creating fertile ground for their radicalization. The most powerful political organization in the Arab world is now forced to operate underground as a result of brutal repression. When Muslim Brotherhood activists are jailed, brutalized, and tortured, is it surprising to see radicalization? If such shortsighted and violent crackdown continues, Egypt under Abdel Fattah al-Sisi will manage to achieve what decades of authoritarianism under Hosni Mubarak failed to produce: a convergence between the Muslim Brotherhood and jihadist terrorism.[2]

Imagine the consequences of turning the Muslim Brotherhood into a terrorist organization. The brutal crackdown of the most powerful and relatively moderate Islamist group in the Arab world, on the grounds that it is a violent extremist group, can turn into a self-fulfilling prophecy. An Islamist movement with mass following and genuine popularity that played by the rules of electoral politics could eventually turn to jihadist violence to defend itself. It could also embrace violence against the external underwriters of its jailers. This scenario would present an even more daunting security challenge for the West than terrorism perpetrated by Al Qaeda or ISIS. After all, these jihadist extremist groups never reached the level of mass societal support and political legitimacy that the Brotherhood enjoys. Is it in the Western security interests to turn a relatively moderate Islamist party like the Muslim Brotherhood into a terrorist organization? Is the victimhood narrative among Islamists—their complaints about Western support for the tyrannical Arab regimes—in the interest of American and European security? This is what I mean by changing the way we think about security. There should not be such major logical gaps between national and "rational" security.[3]

Our friendly autocrats are supposed to be stable allies against terrorism. They may look friendly and stable in the short term. In reality, they are often weak states plagued by structural governance problems. They are producing long-term insecurity for the West by suppressing secularist prodemocratic dissent, leaving no room other than political Islam for protest, and now, in the case of Egypt, brutally crushing and thus radicalizing political Islam toward a jihadist extremist direction of violence. The radicalization of millions of Egyptian Muslim Brotherhood members is potentially a much more dangerous development than terrorist groups operating on the fringes. Providing a larger pool of recruits for jihadist violent extremism is certainly not in the European or American national interest.

This is why long-term security for the West can only come in the form of inclusive governance in the Middle East. Reliance on friendly autocracies creates more problems than it solves by fueling the radicalization of large societal segments in the Arab world. The friendly autocratic partners such as Egypt and Saudi Arabia that the West needs for national security reasons in fighting terrorism or containing unfriendly autocracies like Iran would be much better security partners for Europe and the United

States if they took incremental steps toward liberal and democratic reforms.

I am not advocating a starry-eyed promotion of democracy without considering its consequences in realistic terms. Fighting terrorism will always be of vital importance for the West. But in the absence of a strategy that deals with the underlying causes of radicalization and extremist violence, counterterrorism amounts to fighting the symptoms of the predicament. The West needs to identify and prioritize the regional political, economic, and institutional problems that fuel radical Islam. The ideology behind terrorism certainly matters. Yet, without a deeper political analysis going beyond the superficial and generic façade of jihadism, Salafism, or radical Islam, it will be impossible to develop effective policy prescriptions.

Jihadist terrorist groups, such as Al Qaeda, have their ideological origins in friendly autocracies. Difficult questions need to be asked: Why has such extremist violence ideologically emerged in Egypt and Saudi Arabia? Is there a connection between autocratic repression and the radicalization of religion and society? If the Western perception overstates the Islamist façade of the threat, without addressing the political, social, and economic dynamics fueling radicalization, there will be no need to change course. There will also be no need to question the repressive policies of friendly allies.

Focusing on the religious dimension of radicalization—rather than on the repressive nature of political systems under which such radicalization occurs—also fuels the elusive search for an Islamic model of moderation, tolerance, peace, and justice. Many repressive states in the Middle East are happy to assume this role in defense of an "authentic" and moderate Islam against radicalism. They love the narrative of a "peaceful religion" hijacked by extremists, but they are reluctant to acknowledge their role in radicalizing society and fueling such extremism with their crackdown on all venues of democratic dissent. The Western obsession with radical Islam empowers these false hopes of creating a liberal, reformed, modernized Islam as the solution.

From Erdoğan who once was hailed as the best hope as a "Muslim model" for democratization in the Middle East, to Mohammed bin Salman, who until the grisly assassination of journalist Jamal Khashoggi was the darling of Western pundits as the "reformer of Islam" in Saudi Arabia, to Abdel Fattah al-Sisi in Egypt who fancies himself as the "bulwark against the radical Islam" of the Muslim Brotherhood, we are faced with the same dynamics: a Western obsession with the need to fix, contain, moderate, reform, and democratize Islam.

The first step in the right direction would be to recognize, as suggested in this book, that Islam is not the main problem. An Islamic solution based on reforming religion is not only unrealistic but also misleading. From the backlash against multiculturalism fueled by Islamophobia to supporting autocratic regimes in the Middle East that present themselves as security partners against radical Islam, the fear of Islam only exacerbates the political situation in Europe, the United States, and the Middle East.

The Arab world primarily suffers from governance problems that require political solutions. Only when the imperative of political reform is established will the West have a better chance of understanding, analyzing, and helping the Middle East. The sooner the focus shifts from a civilizational clash to the political, economic, and social realm with an honest debate about the causes of radicalization, the better. This transition will not be easy, especially in times defined by identity politics, culture wars, rampant disinformation, and polarization.

Getting to Inclusive Governance

Most of the challenges in the Middle East are products of failed or failing institutions. The national context of each Middle Eastern state is different. Local dynamics, not generic and monolithic threat perceptions should inform our analysis in favor of reforms. Such diversity is also a stark reminder that no one-size-fits-all solution exists. Civil wars, weak states, sectarianism, autocracy, and cosmetic liberalism are complex drivers of instability.

However, such diverse complexity should not come at the expense of a clear vision about what needs to be done. Almost all countries in the Middle East suffer from a deficit of freedom, transparency, capacity, and legitimacy.[4] Any improvement in the political and security situation will have to address fundamental problems related to governance failure. And external actors willing to help the region will need to show a sense of unity by coordinating their efforts in the same direction. They should therefore formulate a grand strategy guided by the long-term objective of inclusive governance.

The reason why inclusive governance should be the end goal is simple. Almost all Middle Eastern challenges have their origin in coercion without inclusion. Power-sharing mechanisms and representation procedures are, by and large, absent in the Arab world. This is a common source of dysfunction that fuels conflict at the domestic and regional level. There is basically no representation and participation of citizens in decision-making, no constitutional systems that protect individual rights and liberties, and no institutional checks and balances against strong rulers. Repression and arbitrary rule is the regional norm at the expense of inclusiveness and the rule of law.

The solution of inclusive governance, however, should not be conceptualized as pressure for democratic elections. Instead of a big rush for the ballot box, the gradual liberalization of autocratic regimes through incremental governance reforms—such as instituting freedom of speech and assembly—will be paramount.[5] The law of autocracies will have to be replaced by the rule of law. Constitutional changes improving rights and liberties will prove key in achieving inclusive governance. Legitimate channels of political participation will require the empowerment of political parties, the independence of the judiciary, and the active participation of civil society organizations in this carefully planned transition to constitutional liberalism.

This vision has to unite external actors and help coordinate their long-term strategy. More importantly, the real challenge is to ensure that this reform agenda is owned by local actors. Inclusive governance cannot be imposed or exported by outside forces. Steps in the right direction will only come if there is local ownership of the reform agenda. Autocratic regimes need to see incrementalism toward constitutional liberalism as a political process they can control and benefit from in terms of improving their legitimacy. Instead of panicking about regime survival, they need to be incentivized to see these reforms as the only way they can remain in power without facing destabilizing social revolutions. In short, they need to see that without inclusive governance, they will never achieve long-term security, capacity, and legitimacy. Just like Western powers who need to reconceptualize their understanding of national security, nothing short of a mental shift is required in how local regimes will have to reassess their structural problems.

What outside forces can do is provide stronger incentives and assistance to local actors who are willing to engage in meaningful political reforms. Instead of continuing with assistance to friendly autocrats, military and economic support should be based on strict conditionality for an agenda aimed at achieving inclusive governance and long-term democratization with incremental steps. The underlying principle should be the Hippocratic oath of "do no harm," which in the context of the Middle East means to limit unconditional military sales and financial support for repressive regimes. It is absolutely critical for external assistance to be coordinated, targeted, and most importantly conditional toward the strategic objective of inclusive governance.

The first step in establishing this unity of effort is to bring together a group of like-minded and influential external actors. This group should be composed of actors that themselves are practicing inclusive governance and therefore are able to agree on the need for institutional reforms for democratization. Their familiarity with notions of constitutional liberties, rule of law, representative government, and separation of powers should at least create a sense of common interest based on common practice.

This is why the European Union, Japan, and the United States should take the lead in the effort to come up with a joint program. The unity of the trio will be critical. Too often, regional states have relied on divisions between donor countries to play one actor against another in ensuring political, military, and financial support. For any chance of success, the external forces pushing for liberalization, openness, and good governance should not allow the exploitation of their tactical differences and instead focus on their joint strategic objective of inclusive governance.

This Western effort for inclusive governance in the region will have to be realistic in terms of what it can achieve. What I propose is a long-term strategy with an ambitious vision but only with incremental steps. There is little Western leverage with energy-rich states other than using conditionality in military sales. The United States and European countries greatly profit from their defense contracts with countries like Saudi Arabia. They also apply no political conditionality to such sales. Thinking about long-term security in terms of inclusive governance— along the lines described above—may bring moderate levels of Western conditionality to military exports.

Admittedly, such conditionality with wealthy Gulf monarchies will prove an uphill struggle. The West will have more leverage with energy-poor regional states such as Egypt, Jordan, and Morocco. Yet, even then conditionality will have to be couched in very realistic, long-term, and incremental steps. Excessive demands will naturally push these countries to turn to China and Russia, as fellow autocracies that apply no conditionality in their economic assistance or military sales. It is also no secret that countries like Egypt and Jordan can always rely on financial assistance with no strings attached from wealthy Gulf allies. Given all these challenges, it is therefore all the more important for the United States, the EU, and Japan not to let small tactical differences turn into a lack of strategic coordination in foreign assistance and military sales.

The long-term challenge for good governance in the region is about institution building aimed at power-sharing. As the United States discovered after the invasion of Iraq, this is a monumental challenge. Yet, postwar reconstruction by an invading military power is a radically different paradigm than economic and political assistance for inclusive governance in the context of peace. A most critical dimension of this strategy should be to avoid creating the perception of an American agenda that would trigger conspiratorial accusations of neoimperialism. This is why the United States, the EU, and Japan should work with international development assistance organizations and ideally opt for housing their multilateral initiative under the World Bank umbrella. This will help avoid the optics of an imperial agenda and boost the multilateral and neutral image of the effort at inclusive governance.

The initial steps for planning this effort will require quiet and effective interagency coordination between the trio. Joint working groups will have to be formed to coordinate not only between Washington, Brussels, and Tokyo but also with multilateral institutions specialized in the field of social and economic assistance. The goal will be to learn from the experience of institutions such as the World Bank, the International Monetary Fund, the World Trade Organization, the United Nations Development Program, the European Bank for Reconstruction and Development, the Asian Development Bank, and the Arab Development Bank. What this new approach to the region needs to convey, however, is a departure from business as usual. A fresh start with an urgent sense of commitment is needed. It is clear that the existing approaches, with their record of mixed success and failure, will have a hard time to change expectations.

A New Impetus: The Mediterranean Governance Reform

Since messaging and public diplomacy greatly matter, it is important to name this new effort in terms of what it exactly wants to achieve. A new initiative, named "Mediterranean Governance Reform" (MGR), can convey a fresh sense of commitment in a common geography shared with the West. The bulk of planning, preparation, and funding for this new project will have to come from the trio's coordination. However, given its wealth of experience with governance and development coupled with a relatively more positive image compared to other multilateral institutions, the MGR should be housed under the organizational umbrella of the World Bank. The joint strategy of the trio supporting this new project will be "conditional assistance for inclusive governance."

The MGR will have "inclusive governance metrics" based on security, capacity, and legitimacy criteria. In practice this will mean a scoring system that will assess country performance in all three areas as a condition for further financial assistance. For instance, a high score in security—measured in terms of the government's ability to monopolize the use of violence—but a low score in legitimacy—measured in terms of the accountability, transparency, and representativeness of the political system—will lower the average score of good governance. Capacity will be measured with metrics looking at socioeconomic data progress. Inclusive governance criteria will be based on simultaneous progress and good performance in a way that security will not come at the expense of legitimacy.

The long-term goal will be to boost inclusive governance with mutually reinforcing improvements in all three areas of security, capacity, and legitimacy. Inclusive governance will therefore see the legitimacy of the system as integral to its security and capacity. This vision will not only promote economic development and security but also pave the road of conditional assistance for incremental steps toward constitutional liberalism strengthening the rule of law. In practice this means the protection of political liberties such as freedom of speech and assembly, checks and balances against arbitrary executive action, and assurances for judiciary independence will all be part of long-term MGR strategic objectives.

We should also be realistic about assistance. Official development assistance, in the form of foreign aid, can never match foreign direct investment (FDI) from the private sector. Yet, it is well known that FDI goes only to countries that have some basic standards of security, productivity, and institutional stability and maturity. This is why the MGR will seek to qualify the countries it works with for a governance standard allowing them to attract more FDI rather than dependency on external assistance. To this aim, structural economic and political reforms will need to be coordinated and integrated. FDI to the region will also have to be encouraged with tax incentives for investing companies, particularly when there is proof of job creation. In other words, tax exemption mechanisms for foreign investors who create jobs should be prioritized. Public and private sectors in target countries should work together with the goal of improving exports, productivity, and employment opportunities. The experience of the World Bank with economic development and governance reform coupled with the International Monetary Fund's model of conditional assistance for structural economic and financial reforms can serve as useful models for the MGR.

Coordination between the European Union and the World Bank will be particularly important for MGR. Thanks to its geographic proximity to the Middle East and its institutional memory with a myriad of initiatives—ranging from the Barcelona Process to the Mediterranean Partnership Program—the EU has considerable experience with regional assistance to countries such as Egypt, Morocco, and Tunisia. The EU could provide guidelines for inclusive governance criteria based on its enlargement process. Although EU membership will certainly not be possible for Middle Eastern countries in the MGR program, the Copenhagen criteria applied to countries such as Turkey for its membership negotiations could provide a model for liberal constitutional reforms in pursuit of inclusive governance. Some of the conditional assistance mechanisms for the MGR could therefore emulate the EU enlargement model as an aspirational framework.

In short, MGR will make its assistance to countries in the Middle East and North Africa (MENA) region conditional on their progress in inclusive governance, based on simultaneous progress in security, capacity, and legitimacy. However, to succeed, MGR will have to go beyond just conditional assistance as a reward. To further incentivize entrenched autocratic regimes to adopt constitutional liberalism, stronger incentives need to be presented. MGR will therefore have to offer a much more prestigious and rewarding enticement, conducive to massive flows of FDI at the end of the road. In that sense, instead of official assistance, the strategic objective for MGR will be to qualify these countries into a much more advanced platform where they will have access to significant flows of FDI. In practice, this means MGR will serve as a conditional assistance platform for eventual graduation into the Mediterranean Union (MU)—a new international organization modeled after the European Union.

Eventual membership in the MU will be an official stamp of approval by the World Bank and the EU for a country's inclusive governance performance and its ability to receive FDI. A paradigmatic change for the international standing of a country, MU membership will come with additional economic and security incentives such as "privileged partnership" agreements with both the EU and NATO; free trade with the United States and Japan; much higher FDIs thanks to tax incentives provided by the trio to firms investing in MU countries, and access to low-interest funding from the World Bank. Planning for the creation of the MU as a long-term project for the next 10–15 years should also be part of strategic coordination between the EU, the United States, and Japan. Qualifying countries to the MU will be the ones that pass the MGR security, capacity, and legitimacy criteria. As a result, MU membership, unlike membership in the moribund organization currently titled "Union for the Mediterranean," will be a prestige project that provides exceptional political, economic, and security benefits.

The Need for Prioritization and Gradualism

Defining what needs to be done is in many ways the easy part. The real challenge is figuring out how to achieve inclusive governance when civil wars, repression, dictatorship, police states, corruption, and illiberalism are the hallmarks of the Middle East. Idealism about changing the Middle East needs to be balanced by realism. And in devising a realistic strategy, the place to start is always prioritization.[6] Entrenched and challenging as it is, the problem of authoritarianism is not causing a humanitarian crisis and mass casualties as civil wars do. This is why finding political solution to civil wars has to become a top priority in the contexts of Yemen, Libya, and Syria. These countries are now failed states. In the absence of security no progress in governance can be registered. There will be no progress toward economic development and inclusive governance in failed states as long as some sort of monopolization of violence by a central authority remains elusive.

When we are dealing with failed, failing, or highly fragile states, unable to establish a sense of order, liberalization, democracy, rule of law, representation, and economic development can only be wishful thinking for a future that may never come. As illustrated in previous chapters, failed states and civil conflicts provide the ideal breeding ground for sectarianism, proxy wars, jihadist groups, and terrorism. They are also at the heart of refugee problems as the millions of displaced Syrians, Libyans, and Yemenis would attest. This is why the first step for the West is to speak with one voice and to engage in a concerted diplomatic effort to bring the civil wars to an end. There has to be consensus and unity of effort among external actors to prioritize this strategic objective before pushing for an agenda of inclusive governance.

Ending civil wars will primarily require a new sense of diplomatic commitment on the part of the United States. Washington will have to take the lead in the context of Yemen to bring Iran and Saudi Arabia to the table. In the context of Syria, a new approach needs to converge the United Nations Geneva process with the Astana Process. Russia, Iran, and Turkey are the main actors in the latter and have come to a certain point in ending the hostilities between the regime and the Syrian opposition forces now confined to the small pocket of Idlib. Yet, the effective absence of Saudi Arabia, the United States, and the EU in the Astana process means there are clear limits to the legitimacy to any diplomatic breakthrough. Since the regime of Bashar Al-Assad has managed to survive the civil war with a Pyrrhic victory, any diplomatic negotiations and postconflict reconstruction efforts need to deal with this reality on the ground. Under a new impetus with reengaged American diplomacy, all regional actors— starting with Saudi Arabia and Iran—will have to be at the table and given a stake in the reconstruction of a post–civil war Syria. A similar framework of international diplomacy but this time under the lead of the European Union should be applied for Libya and Yemen.

Ending civil wars will prove to be a monumental diplomatic challenge. We should be equally realistic about bringing the dysfunctional status quo of repressive regimes and political systems engaged in cosmetic liberalization to an end. The agenda of political change outlined above— starting with "Mediterranean Governance Reform" leading to the "Mediterranean Union" project—rejects the big push for democratization. Instead it favors a more patient and incremental political, diplomatic, and economic agenda aimed at conditional assistance for a transition to constitutional liberalism. Such patience and realism should be premised on a clear understanding of a region where entrenched autocracies are not willing to engage in the kind of political and economic reforms that will end up undermining their power.

When regime survival is at stake, no regional leader will be willing to embrace the kind of reforms that will ensure his demise. As Robert Kagan realistically argues:

> The "liberalizing autocrat" turns out to be a rare creature. Autocrats, as it happens, are disinclined to lay the foundations for their own demise. They do not create independent political institutions, foster the rule of law or permit a vibrant civil society precisely because these would threaten their hold on power. Instead, they seek to destroy institutions and opposition forces that might someday pose a challenge to their dictatorial rule.[7]

Kagan is right. Yet, successful autocrats also often have a basic understanding of the economic challenges they are facing. They know their autocratic legitimacy is tenuous in the absence of capacity, particularly in terms of providing employment, services, and upward mobility for their citizens. They are therefore more willing to embrace development and modernization projects than political reforms aimed at constitutional liberalism and the rule of law. What they often fail to realize is that one seldom comes without the other: economic development is hardly sustainable without good governance and stronger, more inclusive institutions. Therefore, the challenge for external actors pushing for incremental constitutional reforms in the Middle East is to convince autocratic regimes to see economic development in the context of inclusive governance. Admittedly, this is an uphill struggle that stands a chance only if presented in the framework of long-term gradualism with strong conditionality linking economic assistance to political reforms.

The nature of conditionality and the nature of our expectations will make or break the MGR.[8] Ambitious conditionality will surely backfire if not tempered by realism. This is why the MGR needs to be based on long-term "realistic conditionality" and "patient gradualism." The pooling of all Western foreign assistance thanks to coordination between the World Bank and the trio behind MGR can hopefully create not only unity of effort but also unprecedented leverage in terms of political pressure for incremental reforms. The MGR, in that sense, will have significant political power to incentivize genuine change. The strategy aimed at slow but real constitutional change, without a big push for elections, will be the main focus. Free and fair elections should be seen as the culmination of a long-term process of reforms, not the inauguration of sudden change. Constitutional reforms aimed at establishing the rule of law under a genuinely liberal system will have to be prioritized. Autocratic regimes will have financial as well as political incentives thanks to such gradualism and conditionality.

Defining what gradualist conditionality will try to achieve with inclusive governance is also critical for any realistic chance of success. Inclusive governance can only come if political reforms from above are matched with societal change from below. Inclusive governance should be a wholistic effort. It should be aimed at not only incentivizing constitutional reforms assuring freedom of speech, association, religion, and the independence of the judiciary but also assistance for civil society and socioeconomic upward mobility. Institutional reforms for better governance can and should include almost all social, economic, and political dynamics in the country ranging from the judicial to the education system. For instance, addressing the mismatch between the education and labor market in targeting youth employment—with more technical schools leading to jobs and more gender focus with microfinance programs—should be integral to inclusive governance reforms.

Change from above will have to be synchronized with such grassroots-level civic, social, and economic engagement. Constitutional liberties ensuring rights and liberties will gain traction only if political reforms from above are accompanied with such socioeconomic mobilization for human development at the bottom. Synchronizing and harmonizing the reform agenda is critical because civic engagement from below creates much-needed organic pressure for political liberalization. Such pressure will prove absolutely critical in legitimizing MGR conditional assistance programs aimed at incremental change.

Why prioritize such a process of gradual, and ideally organic, institutional change? The short answer is to prepare the system for democratic elections. In that sense, the incremental opening and liberalization of the political system with constitutional reforms is a prerequisite for the next step of inclusive governance: free and fair elections. Rushing to elections without building the infrastructure of a democratic system is a recipe for a populist disaster. This is why constitutional liberalism with the rule of law needs to precede electoral democracy. Gradualism, with liberal reforms first, will prove absolutely crucial if we want to avoid rushed elections that will end up with the tyranny of the majority. The inclusion–moderation model for political Islam discussed in the context of the Muslim Brotherhood in Egypt should be analyzed in this framework. Inclusion of Islamist parties to the system will have a chance of success only if we are talking about inclusion to a system where effective checks and balances are in place. In practice, this means liberalism with constitutional reforms first, democratic elections later.

In case waiting for democratic elections will not prove politically feasible, the choice should be in favor of experiments at the local level. Elections in large urban areas such as the municipalities of Cairo, Alexandria, Amman, Rabat, and Casablanca before a national experiment at the center of state power will prove relatively preferable for autocratic regimes willing to experiment with incremental steps toward democratization. Once again, the key for MGR will be to make external assistance conditional on gradual, yet tangible, progress toward inclusive governance and rule of law. In seeking the right balance between liberalism and democracy in the Arab world, we should not forget that it took centuries for constitutional liberties and the rule of law to emerge in the West before electoral democracy became the norm.[9]

Our ambition for inclusive governance in the Middle East should therefore come with a sense of humility. The Western journey to universal suffrage and constitutional liberalism was very bumpy. Constitutions and parliaments restricted both monarchic and popular political power with clear rules, rights, freedoms, and responsibilities. European political systems evolved very slowly from liberalism toward democracy. Popular elections with the extension of the right to vote to all citizens from only white male property owners represented the culmination of a nonlinear path. It was often a chaotic process of political, social, economic, and cultural evolution rather than a big bang of democracy. In that sense, it is always essential to keep in mind that the path from the reformation, enlightenment, and the industrial revolution in Europe to what is known as liberal democracy today witnessed world wars, systemic collapse, economic depression, fascism, totalitarianism, and the Holocaust.

A balanced approach to this question of sequencing between democracy and liberalism will therefore have to recognize the imperative of gradualism. Yet, gradualism should not turn into an excuse for business as usual. For instance, a repressive regime in Cairo should not be allowed to declare the most popular political party in the country—the Muslim Brotherhood—a terrorist organization. The MGR incentives should discourage such repression that will turn a relatively moderate Islamist political party into a terrorist organization converging with the likes of

Al Qaeda. There is no point in uniting moderate Islamists with radical jihadists. When it comes to dealing with political Islam, the Western strategic objective should be to divide the radicals and to empower the moderates, not to unite moderates with extremists.

To recap, the trajectory proposed with the Mediterranean Governance Project will be based on the following steps and principles: coordination between the United States, the EU, and Japan to pool resources and set the agenda; empower the World Bank for the project; engage in long-term planning for "the Mediterranean Union"; establish conditionality in assistance for inclusive governance; incremental opening of regimes; liberalization before democratization; and local elections before national ones.

A parallel effort based on a division of labor between the United States and the European Union will also need to prioritize the more urgent imperative of ending the civil wars. This will require launching a major diplomatic effort by inviting all regional and international actors involved in Syria, Libya, and Yemen to a series of United Nations-sponsored summits. This is a highly ambitious and comprehensive agenda. It will have to be implemented with realistic patience and determination. Nothing short of a new social contract between state and society will change the Middle East.

Conclusion: Time for Hard Choices

The West is facing a clear choice. The first alternative is to continue with the current path: maintain assistance to friendly autocracies with the hope they will contain the terrorist threat and provide stability against the tide of economic and political refugees desperate to reach Western shores. This is a risky bet and ultimately an unsustainable strategy for a simple reason: repression exacerbates the threat of terrorism and the problem of underdevelopment. Neither terrorism nor refugees are problems autocratic regimes are well-equipped to address in the long run. They can only provide short-term solutions focused on symptoms. The second alternative for the West is to start building a new strategy—one that goes beyond the fear of Islam, terrorism, and refugees—in order to tackle the root causes of problems. The road less traveled will require thinking about security in the framework of incremental reforms toward political liberalization and inclusive governance.

Unfortunately, the current state of affairs in the West is moving in the opposite direction. Rampant identity politics is fueling the tendency to focus on the Islamist threat. The West is still coming to terms with two major traumas that have so far defined the twenty-first century: the 9/11 terrorist attacks and the 2008 global financial crisis. The clash of civilizations, Islamophobia, the fear of immigrants, the rise of populist nativism, the surge of antiglobalism, and mercantilist protectionism are all combined products of these two traumas of the last two decades. The crisis of Western capitalism in 2008 coupled with the fear of jihadist terrorism exacerbated political polarization and paved the road for an even more poisonous kind of identity politics. The clash of civilizations gained new momentum with rising income disparities, recession, and the populist frustration with political elites. These are the dynamics that have produced the presidency of Donald Trump, Brexit, and political victories for right-wing extremism across continental Europe. Today, the rise of these reactionary and nativist forces presents a major challenge to a rules-based liberal world order. Far from an enlightened and progressive vision, we are faced with proto-fascist political movements at a global scale. More than liberalism they are embracing the discourse of nationalist sovereignty.

In a West, where the liberal order is under assault and identity politics is on the rise, Islamophobia is naturally rampant. To shift the focus from Islam to the need for democratic governance in the Middle East in such a populist political environment is a monumental challenge. Yet, it is precisely because the current trends are so alarming that the need for change is so urgent. The polarized identity politics fueled by the clash of civilizations and the aftershocks of a systemic crisis of capitalism are now presenting a major threat for the future of Western democracy itself. With the rise of xenophobic political parties in Europe and a nationalist–populist discourse already in power in the United States, nothing less than Western liberalism and the future of a rules-based international order is at stake.

We, in the West, are therefore at a crossroads. In today's political environment, business as usual means something much more ominous than mere continuity in the Western overstatement of Islam as a security and political threat. Given the dangerous rise of identity politics, angry nationalism, and the extreme right in Europe and the United States, overstating Islam has now gained an additional dimension: a threat to Western democracy and to the liberal international system. Populism, reactionary nationalism, and illiberalism now fuel more than just Islamophobia. They also lay the ground for the end of liberalism in the West.

We also should not forget that rising Islamophobia in the West and rising hatred of the West in the Muslim world are parallel, toxic dynamics that reinforce each other. Radicalism and extremist violence are the main beneficiaries of this vicious cycle. More hatred of the West in the Islamic world will produce more jihadist terrorism targeting the West. And more jihadist terrorism will only create more Western reliance on friendly autocrats in the Middle East. In short, the current trend is highly alarming. Today, the West has a rapidly narrowing window of opportunity to address the real causes behind radicalization, state collapse, autocracy, and stagnation in the Middle East. It will tragically be too late for any change of course when another catastrophic terrorist attack at the scale of 9/11 causes irreparable damage to Western democracy.

This sense of urgency should force all progressive forces in the West to unite against identity politics based on fear. Only such a concerted effort will forge a positive engagement with the Middle East based on the imperative of governance reforms. New ways of thinking about security and new initiatives about the Middle East should go beyond counterterrorism and refugees. Underlying causes of the problems rather than their symptoms need to be addressed. For a new beginning, instead of Islam, the real regional challenges—civil wars, failed or failing states, authoritarianism and geostrategic rivalries—should guide Western diagnosis and prescriptions.

What I offered in this book is a modest contribution in this new direction. Wherever we see Islamism, sectarianism, and even jihadist violence, we can scratch the surface and find a nationalist narrative of victimhood that resonates with masses suffering under failed institutions. Nationalism fueled by bad governance is an analytical and conceptual tool that provides a political alternative to religion and civilization as the drivers of conflicts. My hope is that understanding the political, economic, and social dimensions of problems, instead of their supposedly religious essence, will better equip us to counter gloomy predictions of a civilizational clash with immutable ancient roots. Who knows, with some luck, maybe even some of my students will no longer feel like they need to read the Koran to better understand the Middle East.

NOTES

INTRODUCTION

1 Samuel Huntington, *The Clash of Civilizations and the Remaking of the World Order* (London: Touchstone Books, 1998).

2 For a sophisticated critique of the essentialist fallacy, see Olivier Roy, *Holy Ignorance* (New York: Columbia University Press, 2010).

3 Governance has become a widely used concept and a difficult one to capture in a single definition. My approach is a straightforward one that emphasizes the art of governing and the primacy of political institutions. It is centered on the exercise of power with the goal of improving the security, prosperity, and capacity of citizens in any given state. The World Bank popularized the concept and provides a good source for its multidimensional nature. See https://www.worldbank.org/en/topic/governance/overview.

4 For the importance of inclusive institutions, see Daron Acemoglu and James A. Robinson, *Why Nations Fail: The Origins of Power, Prosperity and Poverty* (London; New York: Profile; Crown, 2013).

5 For a pioneering study on state power and misperceptions of strength, see Joel Migdal, *Strong Societies and Weak States: State-Society Relations and State Capabilities in the Third World* (Princeton, NJ: Princeton University Press, 1988), pp. 3–41.

Chapter 1

1 Theodore Schleifer, "Donald Trump: 'I Think Islam Hates Us.'" *Cable News Network*, website (March 10, 2016).

2 "Ipsos Perils of Perception 2016," p. 5 (website). The gross overestimation of the Muslim population by Europeans is indicative of the perception of Muslims as a demographic threat and the widespread paranoia and fear toward this minority. This perception of Muslims as a security and demographic threat is accompanied by a fear of Muslims as a fundamental menace to Western liberal culture and social cohesion.

3   The publication of Edward Said's "Orientalism" in the late 1970s had
    a major impact on Middle East and postcolonial studies. Said's work
    described how the West formed its own image of the "East" during
    colonialism and after. See Edward Said, *Orientalism* (New York: Vintage
    Books, 1979), pp. 3–5.

4   For a vivid account, see Yaroslav Trofimov, "The Siege of Mecca: The
    Forgotten Uprising in Islam's Holiest Shrine and the Birth of Al Qaeda"
    (New York: Doubleday, 2007).

5   Thomas Friedman, "For the Mideast, It's Still 1979." *New York Times*,
    website (July 29, 2015).

6   Samuel P. Huntington, "The Clash of Civilizations?" *Foreign Affairs* 72, no.
    3 (1993): 22 (website).

7   For a rebuttal in the same journal of international foreign relations, see
    Fouad Ajami, "The Summoning." *Foreign Affairs*, 73, no. 4 (website).

8   A survey of ten European countries revealed that 55 percent of the
    population supports a halt to migration from Muslim majority nations.
    See Matthew Goodwin, Thomas Raines, and David Cutts, "What Do
    Europeans Think about Muslim Immigration?" Chatham House, website
    (December 7, 2017).

9   Liam Stack, "College Student Is Removed from Flight after Speaking Arabic
    on Plane." *New York Times*, website (April 17, 2016).

10 For a balanced analysis of this alarmist discourse, see Doug Sanders, *The
    Myth of the Muslim Tide* (New York: Vintage Books), 2012.

11 Most citizens of Muslim majority countries hold unfavorable views of
    Westerners, categorizing them as violent, greedy, immoral, and fanatical.
    See "Chapter 2. How Muslims and Westerners View Each Other." Pew
    Research Center's Global Attitudes Project, website (June 1, 2011).

12 Francis Fukuyama, "The End of History." *The National Interest* 16 (Summer
    1998): 3–18.

13 Samuel Huntington, *The Clash of Civilizations and the Remaking of the
    World Order* (New York: Simon & Schuster, 1996), pp. 217–18.

14 Glenn Thrush and Julie Hirschfeld Davis. "Trump, in Poland, Asks If West
    Has the 'Will to Survive.'" *New York Times*, website (July 6, 2017).

15 Piyasree Dasgupta, "Islamic Terrorism Is a Form of Islam and We Can't
    Deny It, Says Salman Rushdie." *HuffPost India*, website (July 15, 2016).

16 Diego Gambetta and Steffen Hertog, *The Engineers of Jihad: The Curious
    Connection between Violent Extremism and Education* (Princeton,
    NJ: Princeton University Press, 2015), pp. 34–83. See also Carol Graham
    and Stefano Pettinato, "Frustrated Achievers: Winners, Losers, and
    Subjective Well-Being in New Market Economies." *Journal of Development
    Studies* 38, no. 4 (2002): 100–40.

17 See Shadi Hamid's "Islamic Exceptionalism" for a sophisticated account. Shadi Hamid, *Islamic Exceptionalism: How the Struggle over Islam Is Reshaping the World* (New York: St. Martin's Press), 2016.

18 Yahya Sadowski, "The New Orientalism and the Democracy Debate." *Middle East Report*, no. 183 (1993): 14 (website).

19 For a balanced criticism of culturalism see Francis Fukuyama, "The Calvinist Manifesto." *New York Times*, website (March 13, 2005).

20 Eva Bellin, "The Robustness of Authoritarianism in the Middle East: Exceptionalism in Comparative Perspective." *Comparative Politics* 36, no. 2 (2004): 139–57 (website).

21 Yahya Sadowski, "The New Orientalism and the Democracy Debate." *Middle East Report*, no. 183 (1993) (website).

22 Max Weber, "Politics as a Vocation," in Patrick H. O'Neil and Ronald Rogowski (eds.), *Essential Readings in Comparative Politics* (New York: W.W. Norton, 2013), pp. 39–45.

23 For different definitions of rule of law and various challenges in its implementation, see Thomas Carothers (ed.), *Promoting the Rule of Law Abroad: In Search of Knowledge* (Washington, DC: Carnegie Endowment for International Peace, 2016).

24 Daron Acemoglu and James A. Robinson. "The Path to Inclusive Institutions." *The Pearson Institute*, , January 19, 2016. Working Paper 39 (website).

25 For an excellent study of the Western political journey to liberalism, see Fareed Zakaria, *The Future of Freedom: Illiberal Democracy at Home and Abroad* (New York: W.W. Norton, 2004), pp. 29–87.

26 It is impossible to have a definitive number. As a compilation, 80 million is a total, civilian and military, figure of casualties. According to most estimates, the total figure for the Second World War is between 55 and 75 million, while the number for the First World War is around 20 million, website (March 20, 2020).

27 These figures are from Larry Diamond, "Why Are There No Arab Democracies?" *Journal of Democracy* 21, no. 1 (2009): 93–112, p. 93 (website).

28 Eva Bellin, "The Robustness of Authoritarianism in the Middle East: Exceptionalism in Comparative Perspective." *Comparative Politics* 36, no. 2 (2004): 139–57 (website).

29 Bellin, "The Robustness of Authoritarianism in the Middle East."

30 Larry Diamond, "Why Are There No Arab Democracies?" *Journal of Democracy* 21, no. 1 (2009): 93–112 (website).

31 Hazem Beblawi, "The Rentier State in the Arab World." In *The Arab State*, ed. Giacomo Luciani (Berkeley: University of California Press, 1990).

32 Samuel Huntington, *The Third Wave: Democratization in the Late Twentieth Century* (Norman: University of Oklahoma Press, 1991), p. 65.

33 Daniel Brumberg, "The Trap of Liberalized Autocracy." *Journal of Democracy* 13, no. 4 (2002): 56–68 (website).

34 For an insightful study of metrics that preclude democratization in autocracies, see Raj M. Desai, Anders Olofsgård, and Tarik M. Yousef, "The Logic of Authoritarian Bargains." *Economics & Politics* 21, no. 1 (March 2009): 93–125 (website).

35 Yahya Sadowski, "The New Orientalism and the Democracy Debate." *Middle East Report*, no. 183 (1993) (website).

Chapter 2

1 For the patriarchal nature of Turkish politics, see Jenny White, "The Turkish Complex." *The American Interest*, website (February 2, 2015).

2 Samuel Huntington, *The Clash of Civilizations and the Remaking of the World Order* (New York: Simon & Schuster, 1996), p. 74.

3 Feroz Ahmad, *Turkey: The Quest for Identity* (Oxford: One world, UK, 2003), p. 24.

4 Xavier Jacob, *L'Enseignement Religieux dans la Turquie Moderne* (Berlin: Klaus Schwarz Verlag, 1982), pp. 18–19.

5 Bahattin Aksit, "Islamic Education in Turkey: Medrese Reform in Late Ottoman Times and Imam-Hatip Schools in the Republic," in Richard Tapper (ed.), *Islam in Modern Turkey* (London: I.B. Tauris, 1991), pp. 160–2.

6 Sadi Albayrak, *Seriattan Laiklige* (Istanbul: Sebil Yayinlari, 1977), pp. 333–7.

7 For the report itself, see Osman Ergin, *Turkiye Maarif Tarihi Vol. V* (Istanbul: Eser Matbaasi, 1977), pp. 1639–41.

8 In the eighteenth century, however, the institutionalization of tax-farming led to an increasing control of the land by the local notables. See Halil Inalcik, "Centralization and Decentralization in Ottoman Administration," in T. Naff and R. Owen (eds.), *Studies in Eighteenth Century Islamic History* (Chicago: Southern Illinois Press, 1977), pp. 107–20.

9 At the tribal stage, Shamanism constituted a bridge between the secular and the sacred, between this world and the world beyond, a distance that was traveled under the guidance of esoteric Shamans clicking their bones. Needless to say, these mystical Shamans were not state-authorized interpreters but free agents who kept access to the gods through their gift of charisma. For a detailed study on Shamanism in Central Asia and the

Turkic tribes' conversion to Islam, see Umit Hassan, *Eski Turk Toplumu Uzerine Incelemeler* (Ankara: V yayinlari, 1985), pp. 51–107.

10 One of the first clashes between the state and religious functionaries occurred when the *Ulema* family the Candarli, which had provided a number of statesmen to the Ottoman government, fell out of favor with the ruling dynasty. See Stanford J. Shaw, *History of the Ottoman Empire and Modern Turkey Vol. I* (London: Cambridge University Press, 1977), pp. 41–2.

11 Serif Mardin, "Freedom in an Ottoman Perspective," in Metin Heper and Ahmet Evin (eds.), *State, Democracy and the Military: Turkey in the 1980s* (Berlin: Walter de Gruyter, 1988), pp. 26–30.

12 According to the Sunni juridical statements on the institution of the sovereignty, the ruler did not derive his authority from descent, and even God was not the immediate source of his authority. The principal obligation assumed by the Sultan under the Sunni juridical statement was to maintain the Sacred Law (Sheriat), which he could not change and by which he was bound no less than the humblest of his subjects. See Serif Mardin, "Religion and Secularism in Turkey," in Albert Hourani, Philip S. Khoury, and Mary C. Wilson (eds.), *The Modern Middle East* (Berkeley: University of California Press, 1993), pp. 350–2.

13 Cetin Ozek, *Turkiye'de Laiklik* (Istanbul: Baha Matbaasi, 1962), p. 42.

14 For an excellent study of Ottoman management of religious diversity, see Karen Barkey, *Empire of Difference: The Ottomans in Comparative Perspective* (Cambridge: Cambridge University Press, 2008).

15 Tim Arango, "Turkey's Suspicious Mind-Set Has Been a Century in the Making." *New York Times*, website (September 12, 2016).

16 Bernard Lewis, "Turkey: Westernization," in G. E. von Grunebaum (ed.), *Unity and Variety in Muslim Civilization* (Chicago: University of Chicago Press, 1955), p. 326.

17 According to the agreement all Christian Orthodox communities, including the ones defining themselves as "Christian Turks" and did not speak Greek such as the Karamans, were also deported to Greece. See Baskin Oran, *Ataturk Milliyetciligi: Resmi İdeoloji Dışı bir İnceleme* (Ankara: Bilgi Yayinevi, 1988), pp. 174–5.

18 Ibid., p. 159.

19 Ayhan Aktar, "Cumhuriyetin Ilk Yillarinda Uygulanan Turklestirme Politikalari." *Tarih ve Toplum*, no. 156 (1996): 23.

20 Oran, *Ataturk Milliyetciligi*, p. 181.

21 See David Brown in Foreword to Faik Okte, *The Tragedy of the Turkish Capital Tax* (London: Croom Helm, 1964).

22 Established by Kurdish nationalists, ex-officers of the Ottoman army, and estranged Kurdish heads of tribes, the Azadi movement also included

one-time Kurdish members of the Grand National Assembly who failed to be elected in the 1923 elections since they were denied the right to return to their constituencies, McDowall, *A Modern History of the Kurds*, p. 191.

23 Mete Tuncay, *Türkiye Cumhuriyetinde Tek-Parti Yönetiminin Kurulmasi (1923-1931)* (Ankara: Tarih Vakfı Yurt Yayınları, 1981), p. 136.

24 Chris Kutschera, *Le Mouvement National Kurde* (Paris: Flammarion, 1979), p. 20.

25 Robert W. Olson, *The Emergence of Kurdish Nationalism (1880-1925)* (Austin: University of Texas Press, 1991), pp. 75-6.

26 Nurhan Tezcan, *Ataturk'un Yazdigi Yurttaslik bilgileri* (Istanbul: Yurt Yayinlari, 1989), p. 20.

27 Ismail Besikci, *Zorunlu Gocler Uzerine* (Istanbul: Dicle Yayinlari, 1976), pp. 5-9.

28 Fırat Bilgel and Burhan Can Karahasan, "The Economic Costs of Separatist Terrorism in Turkey." *Journal of Conflict Resolution* 61, no. 2 (2017): 457-79.

29 Murat Ucer, "Turkey's Economy: Now for the Hard Part." *Foreign Policy*, website (August 12, 2014).

30 Josh Rogin, "Obama Names His World Leader Best Buddies!" *Foreign Policy*, website (January 19, 2012).

31 Dexter Filkins, "The Deep State." *New Yorker*, website (March 4, 2012).

32 Filkins, "The Deep State."

33 Asli Aydintasbas, "The Good, the Bad, and the Gulenists: The Role of the Gulen Movement in Turkey's Coup Attempt," website (September 23, 2016).

34 For an objective account of the failed coup attempt, see Dexter Filkins, "The Thirty-Year Coup." *New Yorker*, website (October 17, 2016).

35 For the deterioration of Turkish–American relations as a result of Turkey's pivot to Russia, see "Beyond the Myth of Partnership: Rethinking U.S. Policy Toward Turkey." Bipartisan Policy Center, website (December 5, 2016).

36 For Turkish nationalism with a religious and conservative tilt, see Jenny White, *Muslim Nationalism and the New Turks* (Princeton, NJ: Princeton University Press, 2013).

Chapter 3

1 For an insightful exception, see F. Gregory Gause, *Beyond Sectarianism: The New Middle East Cold War*, Brookings Doha Center Analysis Paper, website (July 11, 2014).

2 See Karla Adam, "Obama Ridiculed for Saying Conflicts in the Middle East 'Date Back Millennia' (Some Don't Date Back a Decade)." *Washington Post*, website (January 13, 2016); James Arkin, "Palin: Let Allah Sort It Out." *Politico*, website (August 31, 2013).

3 For a good introduction to the history of Islam, see Malise Ruthven, *Islam: A Very Short Introduction* (New York: Oxford University Press, 2012).

4 Vali Nasr, *The Shia Revival: How Conflicts within Islam Will Shape the Future* (New York: W.W. Norton, 2006), p. 20.

5 For a series of insightful essays on the process of how sectarian identity is mobilized in the Middle East, see Nader Hashemi and Danny Postel (eds.), *Sectarianization: Mapping the New Politics of the Middle East* (Oxford: Oxford University Press, 2017).

6 Hashemi and Postel, *Sectarianization*, pp. 2–3.

7 Ibid., p. 2.

8 Ibid., p. 3.

9 Michael T. Kaufman, "The Dangers of Letting a President Read." *New York Times*, website (May 22, 1999).

10 "Remarks by the President in Address to the Nation on Syria." The White House Office of the Press Secretary, website (September 10, 2013).

11 Stephen Schwartz, "Beyond 'Ancient Hatreds.'" *Policy Review*, Hoover Institute, website (October 1, 1999).

12 For an overly romanticized view of Convivencia in Medieval Spain, see Maria Rosa Menocal, *The Ornament of the World: How Muslims, Jews and Christians Created a Culture of Tolerance in Medieval Spain* (New York: Little, Brown, 2002).

13 For a collection of essays on state weakness in the Middle East, see Mehran Kamrava (ed.), *Fragile Politics: Weak States in the Greater Middle East* (London: C. Hurst, 2016).

14 Barry R. Posen, "The Security Dilemma and Ethnic Conflict." *Survival* 35, no. 1 (Spring 1993): 27–47.

15 For the importance of urban context, economic conditions, and educational attainment as accurate predictors explaining intermarriage between different sects in Iraq, see Fanar Haddad, *Sectarianism in Iraq: Antagonistic Visions of Unity* (London: Oxford University Press, 2011), pp. 58–60.

16 For an objective and sophisticated analysis that goes beyond the Islamic façade of the Saudi–Iranian rivalry, see Simon Mabon, *Saudi Arabia and Iran: Soft Power Rivalry in the Middle East* (New York: I.B. Tauris, 2013).

17 Ibid., pp. 12–13.

18 Kim Ghattas, *The Black Wave* (New York: Henry Holt, 2020) p. 82.

19 Frederic Wehrey (ed.), *Beyond Sunni and Shia: The Roots of Sectarianism in the Middle East* (New York: Oxford University Press, 2017), p. 3.

20 See King Abdullah's comments to the *Washington Post*, website (December 8, 2004).

21 Daniel Byman, "Sectarianism Afflicts the New Middle East." *Survival* 56, no. 1 (February–March 2014): 79–100.

22 Amatzia Baram, "The Iraqi Tribes and the Post-Saddam System." *Brookings Report*, website (July 5, 2003).

23 Nir Rosen, "What Bremer Got Wrong in Iraq." *Washington Post*, website (May 16, 2007).

24 Musa Al Gharbi, "The Myth and Reality of Sectarianism in Iraq." *Al Jazeera Opinion*, website (August 18, 2014).

25 According to an unclassified wartime US intelligence report on Iraq, during the Iran–Iraq war there were "hundreds of thousands of Shias inducted into the Army and many others have risen to senior positions in the officer corps, previously almost exclusively a Sunni preserve. Iraq could not continue without the support of the Shias, who make up 80 percent of the enlisted and noncommissioned officer ranks of Iraq's armed forces." See *Iraq's Shia: Saddam Blunts a Potential Threat*, An Intelligence Assessment, Directorate of Intelligence, November 1984, CIA. (website).

26 Andrew Flibbert, "The Consequences of Forced State Failure in Iraq." *Political Science Quarterly* 128, no. 1 (2013): 67–95.

27 Alissa Rubin, "Iraq Tries to Prove Autonomy and Makes Inroads." *New York Times*, website (April 14, 2009).

28 International Crisis Group Report 186, "Saudi Arabia: Back to Baghdad." website (May 22, 2018).

29 Patrick Seal, *Asad: The Struggle for the Middle East* (Los Angeles: University of California Press, 1988).

30 Susan Pedersen, "*The Meaning of the Mandates System: An Argument.*" *Geschichte und Gesellschaft* 32, no. 4 (October–December 2006): 561–2.

31 See Frederic Wehrey and Karim Sadjadpour, "Elusive Equilibrium: America, Iran and Saudi Arabia in a Changing Middle East." Carnegie Endowment for International Peace, website (May 22, 2014).

32 For an excellent analysis of the Syrian Civil War, see Nikolaos Van Dam, *Destroying a Nation: The Civil War in Syria* (London: I.B. Tauris, 2018).

33 Paul Dresch, *A History of Modern Yemen* (Cambridge: Cambridge University Press, 2000), p. 48.

34 Bruce Riedel, "*Who Are the Houthis and Why Are We at War with Them?*" *Brookings, Markaz Report*, website (December 18, 2017).

35 Marc Lynch, "Why Saudi Arabia Escalated the Middle East's Sectarian Conflict." *The Monkey Cage (Washington Post blog)*, website (January 4, 2016).

36 Max Weiss, *In the Shadow of Sectarianism: Law, Shi'ism and the Making of Modern Lebanon* (Cambridge, MA: Harvard University Press, 2010).

37 Michael Young, "The Lebanon Exception?" Carnegie Middle East Center, website (July 19, 2017).

38 Hannes Baumon, "Lebanon's Economic Dependence on Saudi Arabia Is Dangerous." *Washington Post*, website (December 7, 2017).

Chapter 4

1 For a sophisticated bestseller of this genre, see Will McCants, *The ISIS Apocalypse: The History, Strategy, and Doomsday Vision of the Islamic State* (New York: St Martin's Press, 2015).

2 Fawaz A. Gerges, "ISIS and the Third Wave of Jihadism." *Current History*, website (December 2014).

3 Juan Cole, "How Islamic Is the Islamic State?" *The Nation*, website (February 24, 2015).

4 Nir Rosen, "What Bremer Got Wrong in Iraq." *Washington Post*, website (May 16, 2007).

5 Fawaz A. Gerges, "ISIS and the Third Wave of Jihadism." *Current History*, December 2014.

6 Isabel Coles and Ned Parker, "How Saddam's Men Help Islamic State Rule." Reuter, website (December 11, 2015).

7 Amatzia Baram, *Saddam Husayn and Islam, 1968–2003: Ba'thi Iraq from Secularism to Faith* (Baltimore: Johns Hopkins University Press, 2014), p. 176.

8 Cited in Liz Sly, "The Hidden Hand behind the Islamic State's Militants?: Saddam Hussein's." *Washington Post*, April 4, 2015. According to Sly many within ISIS expressed resentment toward former Baathists "emirs" on the grounds that they followed Islamic tenets in pursuit of power. "They pray and they fast and you can't be an emir without praying, but inside I don't think they believe it much," he said. "The Baathists are using Daesh. They don't care about Baathism or even Saddam. "They just want power. They are used to being in power, and they want it back. A lot of these Baathists are not interested in ISIS running Iraq. They want to run Iraq. A lot of them view the jihadists with this Leninist mind-set that they're useful idiots who we can use to rise to power" (website).

9 Ibid.

10   Fawaz A. Gerges, "ISIS and the Third Wave of Jihadism." *Current History*, website (December 2014).

11   Liz Sly, "The Hidden Hand behind the Islamic State's Militants?: Saddam Hussein's." *Washington Post*, April 4, 2015.

12   Olivier Roy, *Jihad and Death* (New York: Oxford University Press, 2017), p. 41.

13   This hypothesis is based mostly on the relative deprivation theory as proposed by Ted Robert Gurr, an expert on violent behaviors and movements, and reformulated by J. C. Davies and Joseph Margolin. See Ted Robert Gurr. *Why Men Rebel* (Princeton, NJ: Princeton University Press, 1970); J. C. Davies "Aggression, Violence, Revolution and War," in Jeanne N. Knutson (ed.), *Handbook of Political Psychology* (San Francisco: Jossey-Bass, 1973), pp. 234–60; Joseph Margolin, "Psychological Perspectives in Terrorism," in Yonah Alexander and Seymour Maxwell Finger (eds.), *Terrorism: Interdisciplinary Perspectives* (New York: John Jay, 1977), pp. 273–4.

14   Carol Graham and Stefano Pettinato, "Frustrated Achievers: Winners, Losers, and Subjective Well-Being in New Market Economies." *Journal of Development Studies* 38, no. 4 (2002): 100–40.

15   Cited in Katy Gilsinan, "Could ISIS Exist without Islam?" *The Atlantic*, website (July 3, 2015).

16   Roy, "Jihad and Death," p. 42.

17   An Associated Press (AP) analysis of thousands of leaked Islamic State documents reveals most of its recruits from its earliest days came with only the most basic knowledge of Islam. A little more than three thousand of these documents included the recruits' knowledge of Shariah, the system that interprets into law verses from the Quran and "hadith"—the sayings and actions of the Prophet Muhammad. According to the documents, which were acquired by the Syrian opposition site Zaman al-Wasl and shared with the AP, 70 percent of recruits were listed as having just "basic" knowledge of Shariah—the lowest possible choice. Around 24 percent were categorized as having an "intermediate" knowledge, with just 5 percent considered advanced students of Islam. Five recruits were listed as having memorized the Quran. See Aya Batrawi, "Leaked ISIS Documents Reveal Recruits Have Poor Grasp of Islamic Faith." *Independent*, website (August 16, 2016).

18   Ibid.

19   Colleen McCue, Joseph T. Massengill, Dorothy Milbrandt, John Gaughan, and Meghan Cumpston, "The Islamic State Long Game: A Tripartite Analysis of Youth Radicalization and Indoctrination." *CTC Sentinel* 10, no. 8 (September 2017): 24 (website).

20   Mara Yevkin, "ISIS's Social Contract: What the Islamic State Offers Civilians." *Foreign Affairs*, website (January 10, 2016).

21 Mara Yevkin and Will McCants, "Is ISIS Good at Governing?" Brookings Markaz, website (November 20, 2015).

22 Rukmini Callimachi, "The ISIS Files." *New York Times*, website (April 4, 2018).

23 Mara Yevkin, "ISIS's Social Contract: What the Islamic State Offers Civilians." *Foreign Affairs*, website (January 10, 2016).

24 Graeme Wood, "What ISIS Really Wants." *The Atlantic*, website (March 2015).

Chapter 5

1 For a balanced discussion of the issue, see Jeffrey Goldberg, "What Obama Actually Thinks of Radical Islam." *The Atlantic*, website (June 15, 2016).

2 Francis Fukuyama, "Against Identity Politics: The New Tribalism and the Crisis of Democracy." *Foreign Affairs*, website (September/October 2018).

3 Dani Rodrik, *The Globalization Paradox: Democracy and the Future of the World Economy* (New York: W.W. Norton, 2011).

4 Martin Wolf, "The Economic Origins of the Populist Surge." *Financial Times*, website (June 27, 2017).

5 Glenn Thrush and Julie Hirschfeld Davis, "Trump, in Poland, Asks If West Has the 'Will to Survive.'" *New York Times*, website (July 6, 2017).

6 For an exception, see Shadi Hamid and Peter Mandaville, "Islam as Statecraft: How Governments Use Religion in Foreign Policy." *Brookings Report*, website (November 2018).

7 Peter Mandaville, "Islam and International Relations of the Middle East," in L. Fawcett (ed.), *International Relations of the Middle East*, 3rd ed. (Oxford: Oxford University Press, 2012), pp. 167–84.

8 Mohammed Ayoob, *The Many Faces of Political Islam: Religion and Politics in the Muslim World* (Ann Arbor: University of Michigan Press, 2008).

9 For an excellent analysis of how nationalism and religion are intertwined, see Nathanael Chouraki, "Are Arab Nationalism and Islamism Two Sides of the Same Coin?" *E-International Relations, (E-IR) Views*, website (September 2, 2016).

10 The inability of the Islamists to offer solutions for modern governance is aptly analyzed in Olivier Roy, *The Failure of Political Islam* (Cambridge, MA: Harvard University Press, 1994).

11 Rogers Brubaker, "Religion and Nationalism: Four Approaches." *Nations and Nationalism* 18 (2012): 2–20.

12 For the symbiotic nature of Islam and Arabism, see Sami Zubaida, "Islam and Nationalism: Continuities and Contradictions." *Nations and Nationalism* 10, no. 4 (2004): 407–20.

13 Jocelyne Cesari, *What Is Political Islam* (Boulder: Lynne Rienner, 2018), p. 6.

14 Graham Fuller, "America's Uncomfortable Relationship with Nationalism." *The Stanley Foundation, Policy Analysis Brief*, website (July 2006).

15 Max Weber, *The Protestant Ethic and the "Spirit" of Capitalism* (London: Unwin Hyman, 1930).

16 "Render therefore unto Caesar the things that are Caesar's, and unto God the things that are God's" (Matthew 22: 1–22). website.

17 Jonathan Evans, "U.S. Adults Are More Religious Than Western Europeans." Pew Research Center, website (September 5, 2018).

18 Daniel Benjamin and Jason Blazakis, "The Muslim Brotherhood Is Not a Terrorist Organization: How Designating It Would Undermine the United States." *Foreign Affairs*, website (May 17, 2019).

19 For instance, in a 2012 Pew survey conducted in Egypt, 60 percent of respondents favored laws strictly adhering to the Quran's teachings. An April 2011 survey found that only 18 percent of Egyptians would "support a woman president." In a 2011 poll, 80 percent said that adulterers should be stoned, 70 percent favored severing the hands of thieves, and 88 percent endorsed death as the penalty for apostasy. The same percentages in Jordan were 65, 54, and 83, respectively. As former Muslim Brotherhood member and one-time Egyptian presidential candidate Abdel Moneim Aboul Fotouh once remarked in an interview with Hamid, "Whether you are a communist, socialist, or whatever, you can't go against the prevailing culture. There is already a built-in respect for sharia." For his work on the Muslim Brotherhood and illiberalism, see Shadi Hamid, *Temptations of Power: Islamists and Illiberal Democracy in a New Middle East* (New York: Oxford University Press, 2014), p. 16.

20 Ibid., p. 17.

21 George W. Bush, Press Conference, website (March 16, 2005).

22 Max Weber, *The Protestant Ethic and the Spirit of Capitalism* (London: Unwin Hyman, 1930).

23 Timur Kuran, *The Long Divergence: How Islamic Law Held Back the Middle East* (Princeton, NJ: Princeton University Press, 2011).

24 For an interesting discussion on the relevance of law, see Guy Sorman, "Is Islam Compatible with Capitalism: The Middle East's Future Depends on the Answer." *City Journal*, website (Summer 2011).

25 Giacomo Luciani and Hazem Al Beblawi, "The Rentier State in the Arab World," in Giacomo Luciani (ed.), *The Arab State* (London: Routledge), pp. 87–8.

26   For insightful studies on youth unemployment and its social ramification,
     see Navtej Dhillon and Tarik Yousef (eds.), "Generation in Waiting: The
     Unfulfilled Promise of Young People in the Middle East." The Brookings
     Institution Press, 2009 (website); and United Nations Development
     Program (UNDP), *Arab Human Development Report 2016. Youth and the
     Prospects for Human Development in a Changing Reality* (New York: UNDP,
     2016), p. 78 (website).

27   According to EU figures in 2017, Egypt received a total amount of 1.3
     billion euros in EU grants, see https://eeas.europa.eu/delegations/egypt_
     en/1157/EU%20Projects%20with%20Egypt. For a critical perspective,
     see Richards Youngs and Ken Godfrey, "Towards a New EU Democracy
     Strategy." Carnegie Europe Paper, website (September 17, 2019).

28   Egypt is the second largest recipient of foreign assistance from the United
     States after Israel and received nearly USD 79 billion in bilateral foreign aid
     between 1946 and 2017. See "US Foreign Assistance to Egypt." AmCham
     (website).

29   Gideon Rachman, "Islamophobia and the New Clash of Civilizations."
     Financial Times, website (February 18, 2019).

Chapter 6

1   For a collection of essays that promote a redefinition of security, see
    Lael Brainard (ed.), *Security by Other Means: Foreign Assistance, Global
    Poverty, and American Leadership* (Washington, DC: Brookings Institution
    Press, 2007).

2   Daniel Byman and Tamarra Coffman Wittes, "Now That the Muslim
    Brotherhood Is Declared a Terrorist Group, It Just May Become One."
    Washington Post, website (January 10, 2014).

3   For the term "rational security," I owe my inspiration to Brookings
    colleagues who have weekly roundtable podcast with the same name
    (website).

4   A series of UNDP Arab Human Development reports published since
    2002 by leading Arab scholars in their fields have abundantly illustrated
    these deficits with respect to freedom, knowledge, gender, human security,
    youth, and citizenship. For UNDP Arab Human Development reports, see
    http://www.arab-hdr.org.

5   For the case of incrementalism in promoting political reforms, see
    Catharin E. Dalpino, *Deferring Democracy: Promoting Openness
    in Authoritarian Regimes* (Washington, DC: Brookings Institution
    Press, 2000).

6   For a good policy example of a comprehensive analysis and agenda based
    on a prioritized action plan, see the following report convened by Tamarra

Coffman Wittes, *Politics, Governance and State-Society Relations; Real Security: The Interdependence of Governance and Stability in the Arab World* (Atlantic Council, A Working Group Report of the Middle East Strategy Task Force, 2016), website.

7   Robert Kagan, "The Myth of the Modernizing Dictator." *Washington Post*, website (October 21, 2018).

8   For a comprehensive study on conditionality in economic assistance sponsored by the European Commission and the OECD, see Anwar Shah, "Development Assistance and Conditionality: Challenges in Design and Options for More Effective Assistance." *OECD*, 2018 (website).

9   Fareed Zakaria, *The Future of Freedom: Illiberal Democracy at Home and Abroad* (New York: W.W. Norton, 2004), p. 254.

BIBLIOGRAPHY

Acemoglu, Daron, and James A. Robinson. "The Path to Inclusive Institutions." The Pearson Institute, Working Paper 39, 2016, pp. 15–24.

Acemoglu, Daron, and James A. Robinson. *Why Nations Fail the Origins of Power, Prosperity, and Poverty.* London: Profile, 2013.

Adam, Karla. "Obama Ridiculed for Saying Conflicts in the Middle East 'Date Back Millennia' (Some Don't Date Back a Decade)." *Washington Post*, website (January 13, 2016).

Ahmad, Feroz, *Turkey: The Quest for Identity.* Oxford: One world, UK, 2003.

Ajami, Fouad. "The Summoning." *Foreign Affairs*, website (August 31, 2017).

Aksit, Bahattin. "Islamic Education in Turkey: Medrese Reform in Late Ottoman Times and Imam-Hatip Schools in the Republic." In Richard Tapper (ed.), *Islam in Modern Turkey: Religion, Politics and Literature in a Secular State.* London: I.B. Tauris, 1991, p. 145.

Aktar, Ayhan. "Cumhuriyetin Ilk Yillarinda Uygulanan Turklestirme Politikalari." *Tarih ve Toplum* no. 156 (1996): 4–17.

Albayrak, Sadi. *Seriattan Laikliğe.* Istanbul: Sebil Yayinlari, 1977.

Arango, Tim. "Turkey's Suspicious Mind-Set Has Been a Century in the Making." *New York Times*, website (September 12, 2016).

Arkin, James. "Palin: Let Allah Sort It Out." *Politico*, website (August 31, 2013).

Aydintasbas, Asli. "The Good, The Bad, and the Gulenists: The Role of the Gulen Movement in Turkey's Coup Attempt." European Council on Foreign Relations 188, September 23, 2016.

Ayoob, Mohammed. *The Many Faces of Political Islam: Religion and Politics in the Muslim World.* Ann Arbor: University of Michigan Press, 2008.

Baram, Amatzia. "The Iraqi Tribes and the Post-Saddam System." Brookings Report, July 5, 2003.

Baram, Amatzia. *Saddam Husayn and Islam, 1968–2003: Ba'thi Iraq from Secularism to Faith.* Baltimore: Johns Hopkins University Press, 2014.

Barkey, Karen. *Empire of Difference: The Ottomans in Comparative Perspective.* Cambridge: Cambridge University Press, 2008.

Batrawi, Aya. "Leaked ISIS Documents Reveal Recruits Have Poor Grasp of Islamic Faith." *Independent*, website (August 16, 2016).

Baumon, Hannes. "Lebanon's Economic Dependence on Saudi Arabia Is Dangerous." *Washington Post*, December 7, 2017.

Bellin, Eva. "The Robustness of Authoritarianism in the Middle East: Exceptionalism in Comparative Perspective." *Comparative Politics* 36, no. 2 (2004): 139–57 (website).

Benjamin, Daniel, and Blazakis, Jason. "The Muslim Brotherhood Is Not a Terrorist Organization: How Designating It Would Undermine the United States." *Foreign Affairs*, May 17, 2019.

Besikci Ismail. *Zorunlu Göçler Üzerine*. Istanbul: Dicle Yayinlari, 1976.

"Beyond the Myth of Partnership: Rethinking U.S. Policy Toward Turkey." Bipartisan Policy Center, website (December 5, 2016).

Bilgel, Fırat, and Burhan Can Karahasan, "The Economic Costs of Separatist Terrorism in Turkey." *Journal of Conflict Resolution* 61, no. 2 (2017): 457–79.

Brainard, Lael, ed., *Security by Other Means: Foreign Assistance, Global Poverty, and American Leadership*. Washington, DC: Brookings Institution Press, 2007.

Brubaker, Rogers. "Religion and Nationalism: Four Approaches." *Nations and Nationalism* 18, no. 1 (2012): 2–20.

Brumberg, Daniel. "The Trap of Liberalized Autocracy." *Journal of Democracy* 13, no. 4 (2002): 56–68 (website).

Bush, George W. "President's Press Conference." National Archives and Records Administration, website (March 16, 2005).

Byman, Daniel. "Sectarianism Afflicts the New Middle East." *Survival* 56, no. 1 (February–March 2014): 79–100.

Byman, Daniel, and Tamarra Coffman Wittes. "Now That the Muslim Brotherhood Is Declared a Terrorist Group, It Just May Become One." *Washington Post*, January 10, 2014.

Callimachi, Rukmini. "The ISIS Files." *New York Times*, April 4, 2018.

Carothers, Thomas (ed.), *Promoting the Rule of Law Abroad: In Search of Knowledge*. Washington, DC: Carnegie Endowment For International Peace, 2016.

Cesari, Jocelyne. *What Is Political Islam*. Boulder: Lynne Rienner, 2018.

"Chapter 2. How Muslims and Westerners View Each Other." Pew Research Center's Global Attitudes Project, website (June 1, 2015).

Chouraki, Nathanael. "Are Arab Nationalism and Islamism Two Sides of the Same Coin?" E-International Relations, (E-IR) Views, September 2, 2016.

Cole, Juan. "How Islamic Is the Islamic State?" The Nation, February 24, 2015.

Coles, Isabel and Ned Parker "How Saddam's Men Help Islamic State Rule." Reuter, December 11, 2015.

Dalpino, Catharin E. *Deferring Democracy: Promoting Openness in Authoritarian Regimes*. Washington, DC: Brookings Institution Press, 2000.

Dasgupta, Piyasree. "Islamic Terrorism Is a Form of Islam and We Can't Deny It, Says Salman Rushdie." *HuffPost India*, website (July 15, 2016).

Davies, J. C. "Aggression, Violence, Revolution and War." In Jeanne N. Knutson (ed.), *Handbook of Political Psychology*. San Francisco: Jossey-Bass, 1973, pp. 234–60.

Desai, Raj M., Anders Olofsgård, and Tarik M. Yousef. "The Logic of Authoritarian Bargains," *Economics & Politics* 21, no. 1 (March 2009): 93–125 (website).

Dhillon, Navtej, and Tarik Yousef (eds.). *Generation in Waiting: The Unfulfilled Promise of Young People in the Middle East*. Washington, DC: Brookings Institution Press, 2009.

Diamond, Larry. "Why Are There No Arab Democracies?" *Journal of Democracy* 21, no. 1 (2009): 93–112 (website).

Dresch, Paul. *A History of Modern Yemen*. Cambridge: Cambridge University Press, 2000.

Ergin, Osman. *Türkiye Maarif Tarihi Vol. V*. Istanbul: Osmanbey Maatbasi, 1943.

Evans, Jonathan. "U.S Adults Are More Religious Than Western Europeans." Pew Research Center, September, 5, 2018.

Filkins, Dexter. "The Deep State." *New Yorker*, website (March 4, 2012).

Filkins, Dexter. "Turkey's Thirty-Year Coup." *New Yorker*, website (July 9, 2019).

Flibbert, Andrew. "The Consequences of Forced State Failure in Iraq." *Political Science Quarterly* 128, no. 1 (2013): 67–95.

Friedman, Thomas L. "For the Mideast, It's Still 1979." *New York Times*, website (July 29, 2015).

Fukuyama, Francis. "Against Identity Politics: The New Tribalism and the Crisis of Democracy." *Foreign Affairs*, September/October 2018.

Fukuyama, Francis. "The Calvinist Manifesto." *New York Times*, website (March 13, 2005).

Fukuyama, Francis. "The End of History." *The National Interest* 16 (Summer 1998): 3–18.

Fuller, Graham. "America's Uncomfortable Relationship with Nationalism." The Stanley Foundation, Policy Analysis Brief, July 2006.

Gambetta, Diego, and Steffen Hertog. *Engineers of Jihad: The Curious Connection between Violent Extremism and Education*. Princeton, NJ: Princeton University Press, 2018.

Gause, F. Gregory. *Beyond Sectarianism: The New Middle East Cold War*, Brookings Doha Center Analysis Paper, website (July 11, 2014).

Gerges, Fawaz. "ISIS and the Third Wave of Jihadism." *Current History*, December 2014.

Gharbi, Musa Al. "The Myth and Reality of Sectarianism in Iraq." Al Jazeera Opinion, August 18, 2014.

Gilsinan, Katy. "Could ISIS Exist without Islam?" *The Atlantic*, July 3, 2015.

Goldberg, Jeffrey. "What Obama Actually Thinks of Radical Islam." *The Atlantic*, June 15, 2016.

Goodwin, Matthew, Thomas Raines, and David Cutts. "What Do Europeans Think about Muslim Immigration?" Chatham House, website (December 7, 2018).

Graham, Carol, and Stefano Pettinato. *Frustrated Achievers: Winners, Losers, and Subjective Well Being in New Market Economies*. Washington, DC: Center on Social and Economic Dynamics, 2001.

Gurr, Ted Robert. *Why Men Rebel*. Princeton, NJ: Princeton University Press, 1970.

Haddad, Fanar. *Sectarianism in Iraq: Antagonistic Visions of Unity*. London: Hurst/ Oxford University Press, 2011.

Hamid, Shadi. *Islamic Exceptionalism: How the Struggle over Islam Is Reshaping the World*. New York: St. Martins Press, 2016.

Hamid, Shadi. *Temptations of Power: Islamists and Illiberal Democracy in a New Middle East*. New York: Oxford University Press, 2014.

Hamid, Shadi, and Peter Mandaville. "Islam as Statecraft: How Governments Use Religion in Foreign Policy." Brookings Report, November 2018.

Hashemi, Nader, and Danny Postel. *Sectarianization: Mapping the New Politics of the Middle East*. New York: Oxford University Press, 2017.

Hassan, Ümit. *Eski Turk Toplumu Uzerine Incelemeler*. Ankara: V yayinlari, 1985.

Huntington, Samuel P. "The Clash of Civilizations?" *Foreign Affairs* 72, no. 3 (1993): 22 (website).

Huntington, Samuel P. *The Clash of Civilizations and Remaking of World Order*. New York: Simon & Schuster, 1996.

Huntington, Samuel P. *The Third Wave: Democratization in the Late Twentieth Century*. Norman: University of Oklahoma Press, 1991.

Inalcik, Halil. "Centralization and Decentralization in Ottoman Administration." In T. Naff and R. Owen (eds.), *Studies in Eighteenth Century Islamic History*. Chicago: Southern Illinois Press, 1977.

International Crisis Group Report 186, "Saudi Arabia: Back to Baghdad," website (May 22, 2018).

"Ipsos Perils of Perception 2016." website (accessed September 18, 2019).

"Iraq's Shia: Saddam Blunts a Potential Threat." An Intelligence Assessment, Directorate of Intelligence, November 1984, CIA.

Jacob, Xavier. *L'Enseignement Religieux Dans La Turquie Moderne*. Berlin: Klaus Schwarz Verlag, 1982.

Kagan, Robert. "The Myth of the Modernizing Dictator." *Washington Post*, October 21, 2018.

Kamrava, Mehran (ed.). *Fragile Politics: Weak States in the Greater Middle East*. London: C. Hurst, 2016.

Kaufman, Michael T. "The Dangers of Letting a President Read." *New York Times*, website (May 22, 1999).

Kuran, Timur. *The Long Divergence: How Islamic Law Held Back the Middle East*. Princeton, NJ: Princeton University Press, 2011.

Kutschera, Chris. *Le Mouvement National Kurde*. Paris: Flammorion, 1979.

Lewis, Bernard. "Turkey: Westernization." In G. E. von Grunebaum (ed.), *Unity and Variety in Muslim Civilization*. Chicago: University of Chicago Press, 1955, p. 312.

Luciani Giacomo, and Hazem Al Beblawi. "The Rentier State in the Arab World." In Giacomo Luciani (ed.), *The Arab State*. London: Routledge, pp. 85–98.

Lynch, Marc. "Why Saudi Arabia Escalated the Middle East's Sectarian Conflict," Monkey Cage (Washington Post blog), January 4, 2016.

Mabon, Simon. *Saudi Arabia and Iran: Soft Power Rivalry in the Middle East*. New York: I.B. Tauris, 2013.

Mandaville, Peter. "Islam and International Relations of the Middle East." In L. Fawcett (ed.), *International Relations of the Middle East*, 3rd ed. Oxford: Oxford University Press, 2012, pp. 176–93.

Mardin, Serif. "Freedom in an Ottoman Perspective." In Metin l and Ahmet Evin (eds.), *State, Democracy and the Military: Turkey in the 1980s*. Berlin: Walter de Gruyter, 1988, pp. 23–35.

Mardin, Serif. "Religion and Secularism in Turkey." In Albert Hourani, Philip S. Khoury and Mary C.Wilson (eds.), *The Modern Middle East*. Los Angeles: University of California Press, 1993, pp. 347–74.

Margolin, Joseph. "Psychological Perspectives in Terrorism." In Yonah Alexander and Seymour Maxwell Finger (eds.), *Terrorism: Interdisciplinary Perspectives*. New York: John Jay, 1977, pp. 270–82.

McCants, Will. *The ISIS Apocalypse: The History, Strategy, and Doomsday Vision of the Islamic State*. New York: St Martin's Press, 2015.

McCue, Colleen, Joseph T. Massengill, Dorothy Milbrandt, John Gaughan, and Meghan Cumpston "The Islamic State Long Game: A Tripartite Analysis of Youth Radicalization and Indoctrination." *CTC Sentinel* 10, no. 8 (2017): 24 (website).

McDowall, David. *A Modern History of the Kurds*. London: I.B. Tauris, 2017.

Menocal, Maria Rosa. *The Ornament of the World: How Muslims, Jews and Christians Created a Culture of Tolerance in Medieval Spain*. New York: Little, Brown, 2002.

Migdal, Joel. *Strong Societies and Weak States: State-society Relations and State Capabilities in the Third World*. Princeton, NJ: Princeton University Press, 1988, pp. 3–41.

Nasr, Vali. *The Shia Revival: How Conflicts within Islam Will Shape the Future*. New York: W.W. Norton, 2006.

Okte, Faik. *The Tragedy of the Turkish Capital Tax*. London: Croom Helm, 1964.

Olson, Robert W. *The Emergence of Kurdish Nationalism (1880–1925)*. Austin: University of Texas Press, 1991.

Oran, Baskın. *Atatürk Milliyetçiliği: Resmi İdeoloji Dışı Bir İnceleme*. Ankara: Yurt Yayınlari, 1981.

Ozek, Cetin. *Turkiye'de Laiklik*. Istanbul: Baha Matbaasi, 1962.

Pedersen, Susan. "The Meaning of the Mandates System: An Argument." *Geschichte und Gesellschaft* 32, no. 4 (October–December 2006): 560–82.

Posen, Barry R. "The Security Dilemma and Ethnic Conflict." *Survival* 35, no. 1 (Spring 1993): 27–47.

Rachman, Gideon. "Islamophobia and the New Clash of Civilizations." *Financial Times*, February 18, 2019.

"Remarks by the President in Address to the Nation on Syria." The White House Office of the Press Secretary, website (September 10, 2013).

"Render Unto Caesar: An Exposition of Matthew 22:15–22." Institute for Principle Studies (IPS), website (April 21, 2018).

Riedel, Bruce. "Who Are the Houthis and Why Are We at War with Them?" *Brookings, Markaz Report*, December 18, 2017.

Rodrik, Dani. *The Globalization Paradox: Democracy and the Future of the World Economy*. New York: W.W. Norton, 2011.

Rogin, Josh. "Obama Names His World Leader Best Buddies!" *Foreign Policy*, website (January 19, 2012).

Rosen, Nir. "What Bremer Got Wrong in Iraq." *Washington Post*, May 16, 2007.

Roy, Olivier. *The Failure of Political Islam*. Cambridge, MA: Harvard University Press, 1994.

Roy, Olivier. *Jihad and Death*. New York: Oxford University Press, 2017.

Roy, Olivier. *Holy Ignorance*. New York: Columbia University Press, 2010.

Rubin, Alissa. "Iraq Tries to Prove Autonomy and Makes Inroads." *New York Times*, website (April 14, 2009).

Ruthven, Malise. *Islam: A Very Short Introduction*. New York: Oxford University Press, 2012.

Sadowski, Yahya. "The New Orientalism and the Democracy Debate." *Middle East Report*, no. 183 (1993): 14 (website).

Said, Edward. *Orientalism*. New York: Vintage Books, 1979.

Sanders, Doug. *The Myth of the Muslim Tide*. New York: Vintage Books, 2012.

Schleifer, Theodore. "Donald Trump: 'I Think Islam Hates Us.'" *Cable News Network*, website (March 10, 2016).

Schwartz, Stephen. "Beyond "Ancient Hatreds." *Policy Review*, Hoover Institution, October 1, 1999.

Seal, Patrick. *Asad: The Struggle for the Middle East*. Los Angeles: University of California Press, 1988.

Shah, Anwar. "Development Assistance and Conditionality: Challenges in Design and Options for More Effective Assistance." *OECD*, 2018.

Shaw, Stanford, and Ezel Kural Shaw. *History of the Ottoman Empire and Modern Turkey Vol I*. London: Cambridge University Press, 1977.

Sly, Liz. "The Hidden Hand behind the Islamic State Militants?: Saddam Hussein's." *Washington Post*, April 4, 2015.

Sorman, Guy. "Is Islam Compatible with Capitalism: The Middle East's Future Depends on the Answer." *City Journal*, Summer 2011.

Stack, Liam. "College Student Is Removed from Flight after Speaking Arabic on Plane." *New York Times*, website (April 17, 2016).

Tezcan, Nurhan. *Ataturk'un Yazdigi Yurttaslik bilgileri*. Istanbul: Yurt Yayinlari, 1989.

"The Hidden Hand behind the Islamic State's Militants?: Saddam Hussein's." *Washington Post*, April 4, 2015.

Thrush, Glenn, and Julie Hirschfeld Davis. "Trump, in Poland, Asks If West Has the 'Will to Survive.'" *New York Times*, website (July 6, 2017).

Tuncay, Mete. *Türkiye Cumhuriyetinde Tek-Parti Yönetiminin Kurulması: (1923–1931)*. Ankara: Tarih Vakfı Yurt Yayınları, 1981.

United Nations Development Program (UNDP). *Arab Human Development Report 2016. Youth and the Prospects for Human Development in a Changing Reality*. New York: UNDP, 2016.

"US Foreign Assistance To Egypt." AmCham (website).

Yevkin, Mara. "ISIS's Social Contract." *Foreign Affairs*, January 10, 2016.

Yevkin, Mara, and Will McCants. "Is ISIS Good at Governing?" Brookings Markaz, November 20, 2015.

Young, Michael. "The Lebanon Exception?" Carnegie Middle East Center, July 19, 2017.

Youngs, Richards, and Ken Godfrey. "Towards a New EU Democracy Strategy." Carnegie Europe Paper, September 17, 2019.

Van Dam, Nikolaos. *Destroying a Nation: The Civil War in Syria*. London: I.B. Tauris, 2018.

Weber, Max. "Politics as a Vocation." In Patrick H. O'neil and Ronald Rogowski (eds.), *Essential Readings in Comparative Politics*. New York: W.W. Norton, 2013, pp. 39–45.

Weber, Max. *The Protestant Ethic and the "Spirit" of Capitalism*. London: Unwin Hyman, 1930.

Weddington, Derika. *Rivalry in the Middle East: The History of Saudi-Iranian Relations*. Unpublished MA thesis, Missouri State University, 2017.

Wehrey, Frederic (ed.). *Beyond Sunni and Shia: The Roots of Sectarianism in the Middle East*. New York: Oxford University Press, 2017.

Wehrey, Frederic, and Karim Sadjadpour. "Elusive Equilibrium: America, Iran and Saudi Arabia in a Changing Middle East." Carnegie Endowment For International Peace, May 22, 2014.

Weiss, Max. *In the Shadow of Sectarianism: Law, Shi'ism and the Making of Modern Lebanon*. Cambridge, MA: Harvard University Press, 2010.

White, Jenny. *Muslim Nationalism and the New Turks*. Princeton, NJ: Princeton University Press, 2013.

White, Jenny. "The Turkish Complex." *The American Interest*, website (February 2, 2015).

Wittes, Tamarra Coffman. "Politics, Governance and State-Society Relations; Real Security: The Interdependence of Governance and Stability in the Arab World." *Atlantic Council*, A Working Group Report of the Middle East Strategy Task Force, 2016.

Wolf, Martin. "The Economic Origins of the Populist Surge." *Financial Times*, June 27, 2017.

Wood, Graeme. "What ISIS Really Wants." *The Atlantic*, March 2015.

Zakaria, Fareed. *The Future of Freedom: Illiberal Democracy at Home and Abroad*. New York: W.W. Norton, 2004.

Zubaida, Sami. "Islam and Nationalism: Continuities and Contradictions." *Nations and Nationalism* 10, no. 4 (2004): 407–20.

INDEX

Abdullah, King of Jordan 126
absolute deprivation 33
absolutism, Ottoman 68
accountability 8, 114, 119, 120, 211,
    213, 227
    overstating Islam and 43–5, 52–3
Acemoglu Daron 237 n.4
Afghanistan 125, 167
Ahmadinejad, Mahmoud 126
Ajami, Fouad 238 n.7
Akseki, Ahmet Hamdi 64
al-Assad, Hafez 135, 137, 154
Alawite regime, in Syria 127, 128,
    135–7, 150, 153
al-Baghdadi, Abu Bakr 156
al-Banna, Hassan 99
Algeria 53, 54, 213, 218
al Houthi, Hussein 141
alienation 17, 34, 153, 164
al-Maliki, Nouri 133, 134, 158
Al Qaeda 150, 222
    and America, in Iraq 151–4
    and ISIS compared 155–6
al-Sisi, Abdel Fattah 220, 222
al-Turkmani, Abu Muslim 158
al-Zarqawi, Abu Musab 126, 152,
    153, 155
Anatolia 75, 77
    Azad (Freedom) in 79
"Anatolian tigers" 87, 92
ancient hatred, idea of 116–17, 121
Arab–Israeli conflict 53–4
Arab Spring (2011) 21, 39, 48, 50,
    126–7, 141, 144, 202, 206
Armenia 195
    nationalism and separatism
        threat in 78

Assad, Bashar 127, 135–6, 139, 145,
    153, 230
assimilation 25, 75, 76, 78–81
Associated Press (AP) 246 n.17
Astana Process 230
Atatürk, Mustafa Kemal 57, 61, 63, 73,
    75, 79–81
Atlantic Magazine, The 175
Austria 215
authoritarianism 49, 52, 59, 81, 96–9,
    107, 229
autocracy 2, 8–13, 217, 218, 223–5,
    228, 230–4, 236, 240 n.34
    fiscal power and 51–4
    friendly regimes of 219–22
    liberal 52–3
    secularism and 203
    successful 231
    Sunnis versus Shiites and 119,
        126, 137
    Turkey and 47–50, 56–8, 60, 63,
        67, 68, 84, 85, 91, 95–7,
        102–4, 106
    Western disconnect and 191,
        202–6, 213–15
Azadi movement 241–2 n.22
Azerbaijan 195

Baathism 245 n.8
    and ISIS, common traits
        with 159–61
    paradox and 156–9
Baath Party (Syria) 136
Bahçeli, Devlet 104
Bahrain 126, 133, 174, 218
balance and context, need for 20–3
Balkan Ghosts (Kaplan) 116

Bangladesh 47, 49
Barkey, Karen 241 n.14
Batrawi, Aya 246 n.17
Belgium 164
Bellin, Eva 41, 48
bin Laden, Osama 18, 132, 155, 178
bin Salman, Mohammed 144, 222
Brainard, Lael 249 n.1
Bremer, L. Paul 152
Brumberg, Daniel 53
Bush, George W. 152, 205

capacity 8, 9, 12, 59, 219, 224, 227–9, 237 n.3
    ISIS and 151, 153, 170–3
    overstating Islam and 41–4, 47, 48, 52, 55, 56
    Sunnis versus Shiites and 111, 113, 118–20, 130, 145
capitalism 28, 185, 195–8, 208–9
Capital Tax law (1942) 77
Carothers, Thomas 239 n.23
Cesari, Jocelyne 194
China 184, 209, 225
Chouraki, Nathanael 247 n.9
civic consciousness 52, 114
civilizational identity 29
civil society 84, 100, 232
    and liberal democracy 45
    strong 58, 207
    weak 49, 97
civil war x, 13, 97, 217, 218, 223, 229–30, 234
    ISIS and 149, 150, 152–4, 167, 170
    overstating Islam and 21, 39, 42, 49, 50
    Sunnis versus Shiites and 109, 110, 113, 115–17, 126, 127, 131, 132, 134, 137–43, 145
clash of civilization ix, 2, 6, 13, 90, 118, 217, 235
    overstating Islam and 17, 19, 26, 28, 32, 55
    Western disconnect and 178, 179, 181, 185–7, 194, 196, 197, 215

"Clash of Civilizations and the Remaking of the World Order, The" (Huntington) 2, 19, 28–9
Clinton, Bill 116
Coalition Provisional Authority (CPA) 131
coercion 50, 114, 129, 175, 213, 223
    arbitrary and abusive 120
    monopolization of 170
Cold War 17, 27, 52, 80, 82–3, 195–7, 213
    end of 19, 48, 86, 88, 90
Cole, Juan 151
Combating Terrorism Center, US military 169
communism 17, 18, 27–8, 85, 186, 195–6
    co-optation of religion against 88
    and political Islam, comparison of 195
conditionality 13, 104, 224–33, 250 n.8
confessionalism, significance of 142
conservative populism 84
constitutional liberalism/liberties 45–6, 55, 205, 207, 224–8, 230–3
cosmetic liberalism 52, 203, 230
    alternative of 204
cronyism, significance of 213
Crusades versus Convivencia arguments 118
Cruz, Ted 115
cultural determinism x, 2, 34, 37, 38, 47
    problem with 30–2
    Western disconnect and 182, 183, 198, 208, 215
culturalism 3, 182, 239 n.19. See also multiculturalism
    empty 13
    fallacy of 31, 39
    Islam and 36–8, 47, 177

religious identity and
conflicts and 30
significance of xi, 3
socioeconomic deprivation and
radicalism and 162
and structuralism compared xi, 30,
39–41, 209
Cutts, David 238 n.8
Cyprus 91

Dalpino, Catharin E. 249 n.5
Davies, J. C. 246 n.13
de-Baathification 158
law 152
"deep state" 101
Demirtaş, Selahattin 104, 105
democracy 27, 152
Arab Spring and 48, 50
culturalism and 30, 38
electoral 45–8, 83, 84, 177–8, 205,
232, 233
illiberal 58, 60, 82–4, 205, 218
and Islam 2, 11, 31, 36–41,
47–8, 54–5, 96, 180, 181, 202,
204, 207
and liberalism ix, 28, 38, 89, 91,
182, 183, 207–8, 233
compared 44–7
social 28
transition to 49, 204–5
Turkish (see Turkey)
democratization 89, 91, 222–5, 230,
233, 234
Arab deficit in 47–51
overstating Islam and 37–41, 44,
52–4, 56
Western disconnect and 201–3,
206, 211, 213
Democrat Party (DP) (Turkey) 84
Denmark 186
Desai, Raj M. 240 n.34
Dhillon, Navtej 249 n.26
Diamond, Larry 50, 239 n.27
Directorate of Religious Affairs
(DRA) 64, 88
Dulaimi, Hassan 158

Egypt 49, 53, 54, 140, 141, 154, 189,
195, 196, 213, 225, 248 n.19,
249 nn.27–8
friendly autocratic regime
and 220–1
on Muslim Brotherhood 202
political Islam and 203, 204–5
poor economic performance of 212
electoral democracy 45–8, 83, 84,
177–8, 205, 232, 233
End of History (Fukuyama) 28
Erbakan, Necmettin 88, 94
Erdoğan, Recep Tayyip 11, 58, 59,
87–90, 96–7, 106–8, 214, 222
during AKP era 91–5
authoritarianism of 98–9
clash within Islamic Bloc
and 97–103
Kemalism, and Kurdish
problem 103–6
Ergenekon investigation 101, 102
Ergin, Osman 240 n.7
essentialism 29
bias and overstating Islam 179–80
fallacy of 6–7, 237 n.2
orientalism and 36, 180
reverse 20, 148, 182
view, of Islam 20, 37, 72, 180
ethnic diversity, possibility of 121
ethnic nationalism 73, 192, 195
European Union 54, 90, 212, 218, 225,
226, 230

failed/failing states 10, 12, 215, 219,
223, 229, 230, 236. See also
weak states
ISIS and 148–9, 155, 167, 176
overstating Islam and 42, 50
sectarianized proxy war in 139–42
Turkey and 110, 111, 113–14, 119,
121, 128
Faith Campaign (1994) 157
Filkins, Dexter 242 n.34
"foot soldiers" 167
foreign direct investment (FDI),
importance of 227–8

Fotouh, Abdel Moneim Aboul
      248 n.19
France 25, 117, 136, 186, 215
fratricide 60, 98, 107
Free Syrian Army 138
French laicism 200–1
Freud, Sigmund 183
Friedman, Thomas 19, 115
friendly autocrats, problem
      with 218–21
frustration 2, 4, 13, 181, 184, 235
   ISIS and 151, 153, 155, 167–8
   overstating Islam and 32–5, 53
   relative deprivation and 162–6
   Turkey and 59, 88, 106
Fukuyama, Francis 28, 208, 239 n.19

Gagauz Turks 76–7
Gause, F. Gregory 242 n.1
Gerges, Fawaz 160
Germany x, 1, 25–6, 61, 186, 215
   ancient hatred in 117
Gezi Park protests (Turkey) (2013) 96,
      97, 103
Ghali, Boutros Boutros 66
Ghazali 39
globalization x, 16, 17, 19, 35,
      163, 183–5
   identity politics and 184
   losers of 184–5
   nationalist populism 187
   relative deprivation and 33, 164
Godfrey, Ken 249 n.27
Goldberg, Jeffrey 247 n.1
Goodwin, Matthew 238 n.8
governance 7–8, 237 n.3. See also
      capacity; inclusive governance;
      legitimacy; rule of law;
      security
   democracy and 44–5
   good 8–9, 41, 43–4, 55
      absence of 114
   institutional dynamics and 9
   ISIS system of 170–6
Greece 75, 76
Gül, Abdullah 89, 94–5

Gülen, Fethullah 92–4, 96–7, 100, 102
   self-imposed exile of 93, 99
Gülen movement 60, 94, 96, 98–102
   Ergenekon investigation and 101
   failed coup of 2016 and 102–3
   focus on education 100
   influence over Turkish
      judiciary 101
   origin of 99–100
Gulf Cooperation Council (GCC) 133
Gurr, Ted Robert 246 n.13

Haddad, Fanar 243 n.15
Hamas 219
Hamid, Shadi 205, 247 n.6,
      248 n.19
Hamid II, Abdul 74
Hashemi, Nader 115
Hashemi, Nader 243 n.5
Hass, Richard 116
Hassan, Umit 241 n.9
Hezbollah 143, 219
hisba (concern for good and just
      order) 69
Houthis 141
humiliation 34, 74, 134, 141, 164,
      166, 167
Hungary 215
Huntington, Samuel ix, x, 2, 19, 28–9,
      51, 61, 187
Hussein, Saddam 125, 126, 128–30,
      137, 157, 160

identity politics ix–xi, 5, 15–16, 21, 23,
      26, 180, 215, 223
   polarized 235
   political economy of 183–7
   social psychology and 24
identity versus ideology 23–4
illiberal democracy 49, 58, 60,
      205, 218
   under military guardianship
      in 82–4
Inalcik, Halil 240 n.8
inclusion–moderation thesis 232–3
   challenge of 205–6

inclusive governance 8, 13, 43–4, 114,
202, 221, 228–34. *See also*
governance; rule of law
advantage of 55
ambition for 233
Mediterranean Governance Reform
and 227
significance and need for 223–6
incrementalism and political reforms
249 n.5
Independence War (1919–22) 75–6
India 47, 49, 184
Indonesia 39, 47, 49, 184, 208
İnönü, İsmet 81
instrumentalization, of religion
64–5
Interim Governing Council (IGC) 131
Iran 17, 26, 135, 174, 189, 195, 196,
218, 219, 221, 230
and Iraq, post American invasion
133, 134, 153
Israel and 143–4
Saudi Arabia and 121, 122–4, 140,
142, 143, 145, 146
first wave 124–6
second wave 126
third wave 126–7
and Syria, relationship with
137, 143
Iraq 48, 92, 93, 109, 110, 113, 174,
218, 244 n.25
American and Al Qaeda in 151–4
Kurds in 80
Lebanization of 132
relationship post American
invasion
with Iran 133, 134, 153
with Saudi Arabia 133–4
sectarian conflicts and 119,
127, 128–30
American mistakes in 130–4
Islam. *See also* Sunnis versus Shiites,
sectarian conflicts and
and Arabism, symbiotic nature of
248 n.12
bloody borders of 28–9

and Christianity compared
198–200, 209
democracy and 36–41
and economic development 208–15
generalizations on 2
as malleable 7
moderate 92, 94
nationalism and 10
overstating (see also individual
entries) 4, 6, 9, 10, 12, 13,
15–16, 31, 35, 40, 47, 57–60,
63, 96, 106, 107, 109, 111, 113,
118, 146–8, 160, 177, 188
political 83, 87–9, 99, 180, 185, 189
promised land beyond 3–6
radicalization and 169–70
relative deprivation and 165
and roots of fear 16–20
and roots of terror 32–6
under state control 67–70
Turkish, and Ottoman
secularism 70–2
Turkish nationalism as unifier, and
secularism 73–8
Western obsession with 2, 17
Islamic banks 211
Islamic State in Iraq and Syria (ISIS)
12, 109, 134, 138, 139
America and Al Qaeda in Iraq
and 151–4
and Baathism, common traits
with 159–61
Baathist paradox and 156–9
documents of the city" and 173–5
foreign fighters and 161–2
genesis of 154–6
governance and 170–6
Islamization of radicalism
and 168–9
radicalism versus terrorism
and 166–8
relative deprivation and frustrated
achievers and 162–6
religious nationalism among Sunnis
and 149–51
weak governance resulting in 147–9

Islamic State of Iraq (ISI) 132
Islamist Nationalist Salvation Party
    (Turkey) 83
Islamization, of opposition 203
Islamophobia 4, 20, 23, 24, 188,
    215, 235
  in France 25
  in Germany 25–6
  and overstating Islam
    compared 179–82
Israel 53–5, 92, 99, 212, 249 n.28
  Iran and 143–4
  Sunnis versus Shiites and 123, 136,
    137, 140, 142
Italy ix, x, 61, 186, 215

Japan 209, 217, 225, 226
Jihadism 1, 5, 10, 12, 219–22, 234–6,
    245 n.8
  ISIS and 147, 150–4, 156, 157,
    160–2, 167–71, 175
  overstating Islam and 15, 16, 18, 19,
    20, 29, 31, 32, 50, 54
  Sunnis versus Shiites and 103,
    134, 138
  Western disconnect and 178, 180–
    1, 185, 194, 195, 197, 215
Jordan 52, 53, 54, 203, 212, 218, 225,
    248 n.19
Justice and Development Party (AKP)
    (Turkey) 58, 59, 87, 89, 90, 214
  era of 91–5
  Gülen movement and 60, 94,
    96, 98–102

Kagan, Robert 231
Kamrava, Mehran 243 n.13
Kaplan, Robert 116
Kemalism 57, 63, 100
  AKP and 91, 93, 95
  Kurdish problem and 80, 83,
    85, 103–6
  nationalism and 73, 76–7
  secularism and 62–3, 72
  social engineering aspect of 65
  Turkish General Staff (TGS) 83

  for Westernization and
    nationalization 71
Khashoggi, Jamal 222
Khatami, Mohammad 126
Khomeini, Ayatollah 17
Köprülü, Mehmed Fuat 65
Kuran, Timur 210
Kurdish problem 59, 98
  Kemalism and 80, 83, 85, 103–6
  Turkey and 78–82
Kuwait 53, 126, 130, 133, 218

Lebanon 48, 109, 110, 113, 114,
    174, 218
  France and 136
  Iran and 143
  Saudi Arabia and 144
  sectarian conflicts and 119, 126,
    128, 132, 142–5
legitimacy 8, 9, 12, 59, 219, 224,
    227–9
  ISIS and 151, 153, 170–3
  overstating Islam and 41–4, 47, 48,
    52, 55, 56
  political 44–5, 122, 128
  religious 130
  Sunni versus Shiites and 111, 114,
    118–20, 145
Lewis, Bernard 76
liberal autocracy 52–3
Libya 48, 50, 127, 135, 218, 229, 230
Lipset, Seymour Martin 39
"Long Divergence" 210

Mabon, Simon 243 n.16
McCants, Will 245 n.1
McConnell, Mitch 115
McDowall, David 242 n.22
Maher, Bill 116
Malaysia 39, 47, 208
Mandaville, Peter 247 n.6
Mansour Hadi, Abdu Rabbu 141
Mardin, Serif 69, 241 n.12
Margolin, Joseph 246 n.13
Marx, Karl 40
media and liberal democracy 45

Mediterranean Governance Reform (MGR) 226–9, 231, 233–4
Mediterranean Union (MU) 228–9
Menderes, Adnan 84
Menocal Maria Rosa 243 n.12
Migdal, Joel 237 n.5
millet system, of Ottoman domains 73, 75, 77
"Milli Görüş" movement 99
Mitchell, George 115
Mogahed, Dalia 166
monopolizing violence and state 42
Morocco 52, 53, 54, 203, 213, 218, 225
Mosul question, tackling 80
Motherland Party (Turkey) 86
Mubarak, Hosni 221
multiculturalism x, 12, 15, 118, 121, 183, 184, 215, 223. *See also* culturalism
in Europe 25–7
Muslim Brotherhood (Egypt) 9, 49, 52, 99, 144, 154
demonization of 220–1
opposition for 202
reasons for ousting from power 206–7
Western disconnect and 179, 193, 202, 205–6

Nasr, Vali 113
Nasser, Gamal Abdel 123
nationalism x, 4, 7–12, 56, 184–6, 215–16, 235–6. *See also individual countries*
ethnic 73, 192, 195
ISIS and 148, 149–51, 155–7, 160–1, 174–6
and Islam 10, 65–7, 73–8, 190–1
political Islam and 187–9, 191–3
populism and 11, 96, 97, 105, 183, 187–9. *See also* illiberalism
religious 5, 24, 186, 193–8, 203, 247 n.9
among Sunnis and 149–51
violent 155–6
significance of 9–10

Sunnis versus Shiites and 110–11, 114, 122–9, 135–6, 140, 145–6
Turkish (see Turkey)
Nationalist Action Party (MHP) 104, 105
nation-state 9, 28, 37, 119, 150
Turkey and 63–4, 73, 75, 78–81, 99
Western disconnect and 189–95
Neo-Orientalism, critic of 38–9
the Netherlands 25, 186
New York Times 172
9/11 attack, significance of 19
nonstate actors and sectarian conflicts 127
non-Western world, transition from liberalism to democracy in 46–7
Nursî, Said 99–100

O'Reilly, Bill 116
Obama, Barack 92, 111, 178
Öcalan, Abdullah 89, 92
Olofsgård, Anders 240 n.34
Oman 123, 133, 218
Oran, Baskin 241 n.17
orientalism 2, 3, 179, 180, 200, 208
overstating Islam and 36, 39, 40, 54
"Orientalism" (Said) 238 n.3
Ottoman. *See also* Turkey
absolutism 68
Empire 61
management, of religious diversity 241 n.14
Sultans 69–70
Özal, Turgut 86–7, 214

Pakistan 47, 49
Palestine 53
Palin, Sarah 111
Partiya Karkeran (Kurdistan, Kurdish Workers Party (PKK)) 86, 103, 105, 106
Erdoğan's war dynamics with 103–6
patriotism, significance of 194
Peoples' Democracy Party (HDP) 104, 105

Poland 215
political context 7–10
populist nationalism. *See* nationalist
    populism
Postel, Danny 115, 243 n.5
pothole theory 205
primordial identity 16, 23–4, 28, 29,
    42, 111, 116, 117, 121, 183,
    196
prioritization and gradualism, need
    for 229–34
promised land, beyond Islam 3–6
Protestant Reformation and
    secularism 200
proto-fascism 105
proxy war 12, 53, 120, 135, 138, 218
    sectarianized, in Yemen 139–42

Qatar 133, 144, 218
Quran 38
Qutb, Sayyid 99

Rachman, Gideon 215
racism 13, 16, 163. *See also*
        Islamophobia
    overstating Islam and 20, 23,
        25, 26, 34
    Sunnis versus Shiites and 110, 117
    Western disconnect and 179,
        182, 188
radicalism 1, 3, 4, 5, 12, 13,
        219–23, 236
    ISIS and 153, 159–66
    Islamization of 168–9
    overstating Islam and 20, 25,
        31–6, 56
    Sunnis versus Shiites and 127,
        138, 142
    Western disconnect and 177, 178,
        180–1, 201
radicalization 13, 20, 162–3
    causes of 32–3
    friendly autocratic regimes
        and 219–22
    relative deprivation and 165–6
    socioeconomic factors and 33–6

and terrorism compared 166–8
Rafsanjani, Hashemi 126
Raines Thomas 238 n.8
Reidel, Bruce 141
relative deprivation 33–4, 246 n.13
    and frustrated achievers 162–6
    globalization and 33, 164
religious identity and conflicts 27–9.
        See also individual entries
    culturalism and 30
religious nationalism 5, 24, 247 n.9
    among Sunnis and 149–51
    violent 155–6
    Western disconnect and 286, 193–8
rentier states 51, 52, 211–13
repressive regimes, significance
        of 219–20
Republican People's Party's (CHP)
        (Turkey) 62, 81, 84
Revkin, Mara 171, 172
Risale-i Nur (the Light Collection)
        (Nursî) 100
Robinson, James A. 237 n.4
Robustness of Authoritarianism in the
        Middle East, The" (Bellin) 41
Rosen, Nir 129
Roy, Oliver 161, 168, 247 n.10
rule of law 8, 96, 98, 224, 227, 231–3,
        239 n.23. *See also* governance;
        inclusive governance
    overstating Islam and 41,
        44–7, 50, 55
    Sunni versus Shiites and 114, 118,
        120, 128, 129
    Western disconnect and 202, 205,
        207, 208, 213, 214
Rushdie, Salman 31
Russia 225, 230
Ruthven, Malise 243 n.3

Sadowski, Yahya 38, 41, 56
Safavids, significance of 174
Said, Edward 238 n.3
Said, Sheik 80
Salafism 157
    Sunni 124

Wahhabi 125
Saleh, Ali Abdullah 140–1
Salman, King of Saudi Arabia 144
Sanders, Doug 238 n.10
Saudi Arabia 18, 53, 54, 110, 135,
    145, 174, 189, 218, 221,
    225, 230
  Arab Spring and 137–8
  Iran and 121, 122–4, 140, 142, 143,
    145, 146
    first wave 124–6
    second wave 126
    third wave 126–7
  Lebanon and 144
  on Muslim Brotherhood 202
  political Islam and 203
  relationship with Iraq, post
    American invasion 133–4
  Syria and 137–9
  Yemen and 140–2
Schröder, Gerhard 26, 90
sectarianism, 10–13, 189, 243 n.5.
    See also Sunnis versus Shiites,
    sectarian conflicts and
  ISIS and 152–5, 157, 170
sectarianization 10, 11, 53, 152,
    153, 191
  Sunnis versus Shiites and 110,
    113, 118, 119, 121, 122, 126,
    127, 128–45
"Sectarianization: Mapping the New
    Politics of the Middle East"
    (Hashemi and Postel) 115
secularism x, 11, 38, 57–60
  autocracy and 203
  Kemalism and 62–3, 72
  as Muslim nationalism 65–7
  as nation-building 63–5
  Ottoman 70–2
  Protestant Reformation and 200
  Turkish nationalism and 73–8,
    88–9, 106–7
  Western disconnect and 189, 192–
    3, 199, 200–6
secularization 7, 37, 38, 63, 200, 201

security 4, 7–12, 219–29, 234–6, 237
    n.3, 249 n.1
  coercive 129
  collapse 119, 121, 127, 131
  ISIS and 149, 151–6, 162, 166,
    170–3, 175
  overstating Islam and 41–4, 47,
    48, 50–6
  Sunnis versus Shiites and 110, 111,
    113, 118–21, 130–2, 134, 145
  threat 17, 24, 25, 187, 237 n.2
  Turkey and 59, 86, 87, 93, 95, 105
  Western disconnect and 181, 189,
    206, 212
separatism, fear of 80
Settlement Law (1934) 81
Sèvres treaty (1920) 74, 79
Seyhulislam (sheik of Islam) 70
Shah, Anwar 250 n.8
Shamanism 240–1 n.9
Sharia (Islamic religious law) 25,
    69, 155, 169, 211, 246 n.17,
    248 n.19
  and inheritance 210
Shaw, Stanford J. 241 n.10
Sierra Leone 167
Singapore 209
Sly, Liz 245 n.8
social contract, of ISIS 172–3
Somalia 123, 167
Sorman, Guy 248 n.24
South Korea 209
Soviet Union 27, 125, 195
state. *See also individual entries*
  failing and failed (see failed/failing
    states)
  hegemony 63, 67–8, 70
  illiberal (see illiberal democracy)
  Islam under control of 67–70
  legitimacy of 43
  and religious functionaries, clash
    between 241 n.10
  weak (see weak states)
  Weberian definition of 42
Stewart, Jon 116
structuralism 44

and culturalism compared xi, 30, 39–41, 209
Sudan 167, 196
Sunnis versus Shiites, sectarian conflicts and 109–12. *See also* Islamic State in Iraq and Syria (ISIS)
disconnect from contextual reality and 117–18
Iran versus Saudi Arabia and 122–4
first wave 124–6
second wave 126
third wave 126–7
and Iraq
American mistakes 130–4
as epicenter of sectarianized conflict 128–30
Lebanon and 142–5
strong and weak states and 118–22
Syria and 134–9
timeless conflict and eternal animosity and 112–16
Yemen and 139–42
Sweden 186
Switzerland 61
Syria 48, 50, 92, 167, 213, 218, 229, 230
Alawite nature of the regime in 135–7
France and 136
Iran and 137, 143
ISIS and 154
jihadist violence in 138
Saudi Arabia and 137–9
sectarian conflicts and 109, 110, 113, 116, 119, 127, 128, 134–9, 153–4

Taiwan 209
taxation and representation, correlation between 51
tax-farming, institutionalization of 240 n.8
transnationalism 160
tribalization of politics, significance of 183

Trofimov, Yaroslav 238 n.4
Trump, Donald 16, 29, 179, 186
Tunisia 39, 48, 50, 135, 154, 164, 196, 200, 218
Turkey 57–8, 135, 218, 230, 242 n.36
AKP era in 91–5
clash within Islamic bloc in 98–103
Cold War influencing 82, 86
economic recovery of 214
EU candidacy of 90
Eurasian vision of future of 93
as father state 58–60
illiberal democracy under military guardianship in 82–4
illiberalism, authoritarianism, and Kurdish conflict from 2013 in 96–7
Islam under state control in 67–70
Kurdish problem and 78–82
Kurdish unraveling and Kemalism and 103–6
left-wing and right-wing polarization under military tutelage in 85–7
modernization in 61–2
nationalism as unifier of Islam and secularism in 73–8
1980 coup in 85
Ottoman secularism and Islam in 70–2
political Islam and 87–9
politics and identity in, deciphering 60–2
as Muslim nationalism 65–7
as nation-building 63–5
peculiarity of 62–3
soft coups in 85, 89, 93
Western disconnect and 189, 193, 196, 200, 206, 208
Turkification 79
Turkish General Staff (TGS) 83, 85, 94
Turkish Muslim Reformation 77
Turkishness 66, 74, 76, 78, 81

UK 25, 215
ulema (Islamic Law guardians) 69

umma (Muslim community) 190, 191
United Arab Emirates 54, 133,
    202, 218
United States 27, 102–3, 194–5, 212,
    217, 225, 226
universal suffrage 40
upward mobility 32–4, 42, 94,
    100, 184
  ISIS and 157, 163, 165
  Sunnis versus Shiites and 121, 126,
    129, 136

Van Dam, Nikolaos 244 n.32
Venezuela 52
Vietnam 49, 184

Wahhabism 18
waqf (Muslim welfare
    foundation) 210–11
Washington Consensus,
    rejection of 213
weak states ix, xi, 8–10, 12, 42, 221,
    243 n.13. See also failed/
    failing states
  ISIS and 149, 152, 165
  Sunnis versus Shiites and 110, 111,
    113, 114, 118–23, 125, 127–30,
    133, 134, 140–5
  Western disconnect and 187, 203
Wealth Tax (Varlik Vergisi) 77
Weber, Max 40, 119, 198, 209
Welfare Party (WP) (Turkey) 88–9,
    99, 100
Western disconnect 177–9
  Islam and economic development
    and 208–15
  Islamic reformation possibility and
    198–200

Islamophobia versus overstating
    Islam and 179–82
nationalism in Islamic world
    and 190–1
political economy of identity
    politics and 183–7
and political Islam 195, 202–8
  and nationalist populism
    and 187–9
  as nationalist reaction and 191–3
  religious nationalism and 193–8
  secularism and 200–2
Western obsession, with Islam 2
White, Jenny 240 n.1, 242 n.36
'Why there no Arab Democracies?"
    (Diamond) 50–1
Wittes, Tamarra Coffman 249–50 n.6
Wood, Graeme 175

xenophobia 15, 16, 23, 29, 185

Yasa (Central Asian– Turkic
    precept) 70–1
Yemen 48, 50, 109, 110, 113, 114, 115,
    218, 229, 230
  sectarian conflicts in 119, 126, 127,
    128, 139–42
Youngs, Richards 249 n.27
Yousef, Tarik M. 240 n.34, 249 n.26
Yugoslavia 116, 195

Zaire 123
Zakaria, Fareed 239 n.25
Zaydis 140
Zubaida, Sami 248 n.12